The best of

JOHN T. REED'S
Real Estate Investor's Monthly

Volume One

REAL ESTATE INVESTMENT STRATEGY

Selected articles from
The national newsletter

By
John T. Reed

John T. Reed
342 Bryan Drive
Danville, CA 94526
415-820-6292

To my newsletter subscribers

Published by John T. Reed
342 Bryan Drive
Danville, CA 94526
415-820-6292

Manufactured in the United States of America
by Cal-West Printing & Graphics, Concord, CA.
Library of Congress Catalog Card Number: 90-092270
ISBN: 0-939224-23-2

OTHER MATERIAL BY JOHN T. REED

- *Aggressive Tax Avoidance for Real Estate Investors* (book)
- *High Leverage Real Estate Finance* (cassettes)
- *How to Buy Real Estate for at Least 20% Below Market Value* (cassettes)
- *How to Find Deals that Make Sense in Today's Market* (cassettes)
- *How to Increase the Value of Real Estate* (book)
- *How to Manage Residential Property for Maximum Cash Flow and Resale Value* (cassettes or book)
- *How to Save Tens of Thousands of Tax Dollars by Exchanging* (cassettes)
- *How to Use Leverage to Maximize Your Real Estate Investment Return* (book)
- *John T. Reed's Real Estate Investor's Monthly* (newsletter)
- *Office Building Acquisition Handbook*
- *Residential Property Acquisition Handbook*

For more information, see the order forms in the front and back of this book or contact John T. Reed, 342 Bryan Drive, Danville, CA 94526, or call 800-635-5425.

THANKS TO...

The many, many people who contributed to these articles...my wife, Marty Tunnell, for designing and producing this book.

ABOUT THE AUTHOR

John T. Reed is a real estate writer and investor.

His real estate work experience includes home, land, and investment property brokerage and residential and nonresidential property management. As a property manager, he managed apartment complexes, office buildings, industrial space, farms, and single-family rental houses.

He has invested in New Jersey, Texas, and California.

He is the editor and publisher of *John T. Reed's Real Estate Investor's Monthly*, a national newsletter...and the author and publisher of seven books on various real estate investment subjects.

Mr. Reed has been interviewed about real estate by Morley Safer on *60 Minutes*, by David Hartman on *Good Morning America*, and by Larry King on *Larry King Live* as well as other television and radio programs. His analysis of real estate investing has appeared in *The Wall Street Journal*, *Newsweek*, *U.S. News & World Report*, *Changing Times*, *Money*, and various real estate journals.

He holds a Bachelor of Science degree from West Point and a Master of Business Administration degree from Harvard Business School.

REAL ESTATE
INVESTMENT
STRATEGY

CONTENTS

INTRODUCTION

This is Volume One of a series of books containing *Real Estate Investor's Monthly* articles grouped by subject. Many nonsubscribers have bought back issues of the newsletter since it began in February of 1986. They are typically interested in one article title from the issue in question. But they had to buy the entire issue to get it.

This series of books gives them another option. Through this series, real estate investors will be able to buy articles on the subject in which they are most interested.

Readers of this series may note some inconsistencies in the groups of articles. You don't find such inconsistency in most books because they are written as a single project and checked repeatedly for inconsistency during the writing. This series, however, was not written as a single project. Rather, it was written as individual articles month by month over a five-year period.

During those five years, the real estate investment scene changed dramatically. The Tax Reform Act of 1986 became law. Environmental liability became a huge concern. The saving-and-loan industry financed the most massive overbuilding in history. I also got five years older and wiser.

Rather than try to rewrite my articles, I have left them as originally written (with a few minor exceptions, which have been noted). By thus revealing the evolution of my thought, I may help you see why I abandoned notions that you may still believe.

If you find what you read thought provoking and helpful, I hope you will try subscribing to *Real Estate Investor's Monthly*. If so, you will get the latest version of my analysis of real estate as well as my interpretation of the latest developments in the business.

Best wishes,

John T. Reed
Danville, California

PART ONE

DEALS THAT MAKE SENSE— CASE STUDIES

1
One-Bedroom Houses

July 1988

I have never been able to make the cosmetic renovation approach work," said John Beck at one of his recent seminars. "The only time I got close was when I converted a one-bedroom house to a two-bedroom house."

I've had similar experience. I made some clear cut renovation profits when I converted a store room to a second bedroom of an apartment or to an efficiency apartment.

When I was a real estate salesman, I remember one-bedroom houses were shunned by the market. **Now,** whenever I hear of some property type that is shunned, the opportunity light on my mental control panel goes on.

Beck's house

On May 24, 1977, Beck bought a one-bedroom house on Oriente Avenue in Daly City, CA for $32,000. He sold it just two and a half months later netting $39,000 after transaction costs. Beck's house had an eat-in kitchen **and** a formal dining room. Or at least it did when he bought it.

Beck had a carpenter close the original doorway to the dining room, cut another door in a more appropriate spot, and add a closet. Voila! A **two**-bedroom house with an eat-in kitchen but no dining room. The carpenter charged $500 for the whole thing.

No condos

We're talking **fee simple** houses here. Preferably detached. Townhouses might work, too. We are definitely **not** talking about condos. If you look in your local multiple listing book, you'll find that the vast majority of the one-bedroom homes are condos. (That may be another explanation of why condos have done so poorly on appreciation rates. See articles in the last two issues.)

Merle Avenue

I have a copy of my local multiple listing book from December '82. Its prices are obviously out of date. But it's ratios, not prices that count. Here are a pair of listings I found on Merle Avenue in Martinez, California:

1-bedroom	2-bedroom
$60,950	$68,000
40 x 100 lot	40 x 100 lot
1-car att. garage	"single"
"loads of upgrades new carpet, vinyl roof, and more"	"With some TLC could again be cute little cottage"

There was at least a $7,000 discount for the lack of a second bodroom. And apparently a **greater** than $7,000 discount if you believe the narrative descriptions which indicate that the one-bedroom house had new carpet, vinyl, and roof. While the two bedroom needed TLC (tender loving care) to "again" become "cute." That suggests that a one-bedroom house on this street would sell for a **$10,000** discount or more compared to a two-bedroom house of comparable quality.

Now where to put that second bedroom? Heck, none of us has even seen the place but at least one spot is **obvious**...the attached one-car garage. Rough guess, I figure it would cost about $2,000 or $3,000 to convert a garage to a bedroom. That's for wiring, sheetrock, insulation, carpet, a closet, converting the garage door to a wall, and some sort of heat.

If you keep the house, it'll probably **positive cash flow** given that you bought it for a one-bedroom price but rent it for a two-bedroom rent.

Government approval

Adding a second **apartment** to a house raises its value. But approval to add a second **unit** to a house is very hard to get.

I suspect that's **not** true of adding a second bedroom to a one-bedroom house. For starters, you could probably do it without the local government knowing. Secondly, if they **did** know, you probably would't have to get any more approval than a routine building permit. Finally, even if you **did** need formal approval, I suspect both the government and your neighbors would **rather** your property were a 2-bedroom house.

What about converting a 2 to a 3?

Two-bedroom houses are not very well received in many markets. Had Brick, a Southern New Jersey land developer calls two-bedroom houses a "drug on the market." So, yes, there probably are profit opportunities in converting two-bedroom houses to three-bedroom houses.

But clearly one-bedroom to two- will show better numbers in general. As you move up the spectrum to two-to-three or three-to-four or four-to-five, there will be much less of a discount at purchase time...because the number of people willing to buy a two-bedroom house far exceeds the number willing to buy a one-bedroom and the number willing to buy a three-bedroom exceeds the number willing to buy a two-bedroom.

I'd guess 25% of one-bedroom houses can be profitably converted to two-bedrooms. But the percentage of **twos** that can be profitably converted to threes is probably more like 5%.

They are rare

One-bedroom houses are very rare. Of the 1,985 detached houses currently listed in my local MLS, only five are one-bedrooms. 168 are twos. To pursue a strategy of one one-bedroom conversion a month, you'd probably have to work over a dozen MLSs. Add converting twos to threes to your repetoire and you can probably confine yourself to two or three MLSs.

Most multiple listing services now have the ability to do a **computer** search which produces a list of, say, "all one-bedroom houses which were listed in the last week." You could do searches each week. As soon as you found a one-bedroom house, you're out the door to look at it and make an offer if the numbers work.

Better yet, compile a list of all the one-bedroom houses in the areas you are willing to buy and send **quarterly post cards** to their owners. Tell them you want to buy their home and point out that if they sell to you there will be **no commission**. Since most won't be ready to sell when you contact them, suggest that they put your card with your name and address and phone number where they keep their deed and other house papers so they can find it if they later decide to sell.

Avoid additions

You will probably have to avoid houses where you would need to **add on** to the building in order to have a second bedroom. Additions require foundations, exterior walls, framing, roof, etc. That runs up the cost. Better you should just finish off some unfinished or semi-finished space like a fourth room, garage, attic or porch.

If you **do** need to add, the less work required the better. For example, adding dormers to an otherwise too-small attic. If the attic is too **low** for dormers, it might be cost effective to **raise** the roof. That at least lets you avoid foundation and roofing expense.

Where to find them

Look in **older** neighborhoods, as a general rule. Because modern zoning usually prohibits one-bedroom houses. Zoning was approved by the U.S. Supreme Court in the 1926 case of *Euclid v. Ambler* (272 U.S. 365). It became widespread after that decision.

Also look in areas that were **rural** and therefore outside zoning when the house was built. Or in areas which are **still** rural and therefore under very loose zoning. I noticed that many of the one-bedroom houses in my local area have more than an acre of land. You would typically look to play **two** games with those properties: convert to two-bedrooms **and** split off land not needed for the house. (See "How to Make Money by Splitting Off Excess Land" in the July '86 issue, Chapter 22.)

There are probably even some odd ball situations where someone turned a two-bedroom house into a one-bedroom. Perhaps to discourage obnoxious relatives from staying overnight.

Areas which are now extremely high-priced and much sought-after probably will **not** work. In those places, people will buy **anything** and pay top dollar for it. For example, the July 6th *San Francisco Chronicle* reports that a "tired one-bedroom house at 427 42nd Avenue" in San Francisco was recently listed at $235,000 and sold for $267,000. According to Realtor®, Bill Christiansen, "It needed everything. The floors were buckled in the hallway and the toilet leaked." [For the record, a buckled hallway floor can probably be replaced with plywood and carpet for well under $1,000. Leaky toilets can be fixed for less than $100.]

Bigger buildings

The principle in this article applies to bigger buildings, too. In the "load factor" chapters of my books, *How to Manage Residential Property*...and *How to Increase the Value of Real Estate*, I explained how I turned a store room next to a one-bedroom apartment into that apartment's second bedroom.

The main trick is to find opportunities to add rentable space with less effort and cost than the foundation-to-roof construction that's usually required. And in single-family houses...where every newlywed couple thinks the cost of fixing a fixer upper is about a third of what it **really** is...you need the "leprosy" of one-bedroom strangeness to scare off enough bidders to permit an adequate profit margin. JTR

2
One-Bedroom Houses Revisited

January 1989

In the 7/88 issue(See Chapter 1), I recommended converting one-bedroom houses into two-bedroom houses when the structure allows that to be done without adding exterior walls, roof, foundation, etc. The idea was that one-bedroom houses are leper properties which sell cheap. But two-bedroom houses are much more desirable so the conversion would raise the value of the house by far more than the conversion cost.

An investor I met at a Christmas party wondered if one-bedroom houses wouldn't be a good deal without the conversion. I had just explained to him the theory behind my 12/88 article on two-houses-on-one-lot properties. They also sell cheap because they are leper properties...but they rent for normal rents. That enables you to get positive cash flow in a market where single-family rental houses invariably have negative cash flow.

He's right. Even if you can't convert a one-bedroom house to a two-bedroom house, one-bedroom houses will have much higher capitalization rates than two-or more-bedroom houses...and therefore positive cash flow. The reason is that there tend to be more three-bedroom rental houses than there are people who want to rent three bedroom houses. But in the one-bedroom market, one-bedroom houses stand out as more desirable than competing apartments. And there area great many tenants seeking one-bedroom rentals.

The only one-bedroom **house** for rent I could find in my local paper rents for $1,400. In contrast, the one-bedroom **apartments** in that county top out at $1,300.

Since the appreciation rate on one-bedroom houses is the same as on houses with more bedrooms...but the cash flow is better...one-bedroom houses are superior investments. JTR

3
Rental Houses Revisited

I have been anti-rental house for a long time. My complaint was the numbers didn't work.

I was wrong.

In recent months, I have talked to several readers who say they get **positive cash flow** from day one in single family rental houses. But **not** by throwing a dart at the multiple listing service (MLS) book.

Small positive cash flow

The investors I've been talking to say they get about $75 a month positive cash flow on their rental houses. And that cash flow represents a 10% to 20% return on their cash invested.

High leverage

Rental house investors tend to have **higher loan-to-value ratios** than income property investors. That's because they buy from **less sophisticated sellers** who are often willing to take back loans which are protected by only a 5% to 15%

equity buffer. "Worst that can happen is that I get the property back," seems to be the extent of the seller's analysis.

Also, **institutional** lenders make higher loan-to-value ratio loans on single-family properties than they will on income properties...many of which loans are assumable FHA and VA mortgages. In addition, I suspect that **lying** about owner occupancy is widespread. I do not wink as I write that. People who need to lie to succeed in real estate deserve the bad credit and legal problems they may get as a result of lying.

Low interest rates

Single-family rental house investors also get lower interest rates than income property investors. Institutional lenders have lower interest rates on houses ...especially those loans below $133,250, the Federal National Mortgage Association's max.

House sellers can often be talked into low interest loans... even at rates below the "Applicable Federal Rate," which was 7.00% for mid-term loans with monthly payments in November. "Better than my money market."

Low interest loans increase rental house cash flow.

Why renters don't buy

In the February issue of **Real Estate Investor's Monthly**, I said positive cash flow was almost impossible in rental houses because it would mean the renter was paying more to **rent** than he would to **own** the same house...even before taking into account the tax, appreciation, and pride benefits of owning. I said that was illogical.

Not everyone is logical. Many renters who would clearly be better off financially owning, still rent.

And many who **are** logical are better off renting...or **think** they are. For example, a reader who was buying rental houses in Houston said many of his tenants are waiting for that market to hit bottom before they buy a home. He thinks they're waiting too long. But they're good tenants. So he doesn't argue.

Persons who expect to move within a **few years** are probably better off renting because of the high **transaction costs** of buying and selling a home compared to renting one.

Persons who are in the **low tax brackets** get little benefit (11 to 15% in '87) from the deductibility of mortgage interest and property taxes. A married couple filing jointly can have a taxable income of up to $28,000 in '87 and still be in the 15% bracket. Yet a $28,000 annual income would qualify for a $770 a month rental if you allowed 33% of income to go for housing ($28,000 ÷ 12 = $2,333.33 x 33% = $770).

Other house renters can't save the **down payment.** On a $75,000 house, that'd be a minimum of 5% to 10% or $3,750 to $7,500. In contrast, the security deposit and first month's rent on a rental house would typically be only $1,000 to $1,500.

Cheap houses only

I'm saying it's **possible** to earn a satisfactory return on rental houses. I am **not**, however, saying that **any** rental house you buy is a good investment. You have to be selective.

For starters, you must buy homes at the **low end** of the price spectrum. The higher the price, the higher the gross rent multiplier. The guys who have the positive cash flow buy at gross rent multipliers of 90 to 110 times monthly rent. For example, a house that rents for $750 a month and sells for $80,000 has a gross rent multiplier of $80,000 ÷ $750 = 107. In general, the cheaper the house, the lower the gross rent multiplier. And the lower the gross rent multiplier, the higher the capitalization rate (net operating income divided by price).

Today, my local paper offers a 3-bedroom house in El Cerrito for $1,200 a month. A "for sale" ad offers a 3-bedroom El Cerrito house for $139,900. I do not know if the houses are similar. But the indicated gross rent multiplier is $139,900 ÷ $1,200 = 117.

493 times gross?

In contrast, Tiburon has a house for rent for $2,500. But the cheapest for sale house in Tiburon is priced at $929,000...an indicated multiplier of $929,000 ÷ $2,500 = 372 if the houses are comparable. The '82-'83 *Places and Spaces Housing Almanac* said you could **rent** a 4-bedroom house for $625 to $750 on Philadelphia's Main Line. But to **buy** a 4-bedroom house there cost $60,000 to $370,000...indicating multipliers of 96 at the low end of the price spectrum to 493 at the high end. That, in turn, means positive cash flow at the low end and huge negative cash flow at the high end.

The reason the rents are not proportionately higher for higher-priced properties is that there are far fewer renters in those income brackets. High income people get significant (28% to 38.5%) tax deductions from owning. And they are less likely to move in a few years so transaction costs are less of a factor. Many are business people who are acutely aware of the benefits of ownership.

Bargain price and terms

The investors who were getting positive cash flow also claimed to be getting the houses at **wholesale.** Two bought foreclosures. The other said he was getting the properties for 5% to 10% less than market value for one reason or another. So it's not just a matter of throwing a dart at the MLS book...or even at the cheap part of the MLS book. You must get an extraordinary deal to get positive cash flow in rental houses. If real estate investing was easy, everybody'd be doing it.

Political risk

I have always said houses had an advantage as far as political risk was concerned. Houses rarely come under **rent control** laws. Now there's **another** political risk...tax reform. Congress savagely attacked **income property** owners in the Tax Reform Act of 1986...but **home** owners were almost unscathed as far as their property values are concerned. The new, unfavorable depreciation and passive loss rules apply to rental houses, but since the vast majority of home buyers are **not** investors, **resale values** of primary homes were little affected.

Selected rental houses can be good investments

Rental houses at the low end of the price spectrum...purchased at bargain price and terms...can produce both positive cash flow and an attractive overall return. They are also the most liquid form of real estate and the least susceptible to political risks.JTR

4
A Positive Cash Flow Rental House

On February 6th, Marc Goodfriend (708-858-4663) bought a single-family rental house that shows positive cash flow. Thousands of real estate investors can't figure out how to do that. How'd **he** do it?

Romeoville

The main reason for the cash flow is that the property is in Romeoville, Illinois. Romeoville is a lower middle class, blue-collar, community which has largely been bypassed by recent growth. The houses in the neighborhood virtually all have had their garages converted to bedrooms or bigger living rooms. In a 1970 movie called *Joe*, the title character proudly showed off the basement which he had finished himself. Joe would like Romeoville.

Romeoville property sells for less than most other Chicago suburbs. It also **rents** for less than most other Chicago suburbs. But the **prices** are disproportionately low compared to the rents. That means Romeoville property has higher cap rates than most other Chicago suburban properties. And high cap rates mean positive cash flow.

Quick-sale value

In addition to Romeoville property having higher cap rates, Goodfriend got this property for less than market value. He bought it for **quick sale** value. Goodfriend figures the **market** value is about $54,000 to $55,000. He got it for $46,352.56 (the balance of the land contract plus $11,000 cash down).

The seller had agreed to buy another house...and needed to close the sale of the old house in order to produce the down payment money for the new house. The seller of that house had been waiting for some time already and was threatening to find another buyer. So Goodfriend's seller was under time pressure.

Furthermore, a previous deal had just fallen through. So the seller was willing to sell cheap in order to avoid losing the new house he had his heart set on rather than wait another 90 days or more to sell at market value.

The house

The house in question started its life as a three-bedroom tract house with an attached garage. The garage had been converted...in this case...to two bedrooms.

The seller was handy and had done extensive renovation to the property since he bought it, including: replumbing, new cabinets, new appliances, new windows, deck, and built-in barbecue. In short, little renovation is required by Goodfriend.

The financing

The VA had acquired this house by foreclosure, then sold it, taking back a land contract (land contracts are customary in the midwest and northwest). Goodfriend **assumed** (as opposed to buying subject to) that land contract, which, for the purposes of this article, is essentially the same as a mortgage. The terms were 10%, 30 years.

Investors who have positive cash flow rental houses very often use assumptions of FHA and VA loans (see pertinent items in the Developments section of this issue) to minimize finance costs.

The numbers

Here are the monthly figures on Goodfriend's acquisition:

Rent	$625.00
Taxes	-89.85
Insurance	-21.50
Repairs(5% of gross)	-32.50
N.O.I.	$481.15
debt svc.	-$320.33
cash flow	$160.82

That's a **cap rate** of $481.15 x 12 months per year = $5,773.80 ÷ $46,352.56 (purchase price) = **12.46%**. That's a darned good cap rate. Most investors are buying properties on terms that produce cap rates in the 7 to 9% range...which means breakeven or negative cash flow.

The gross rent (monthly) multiplier is $46,352.56 ÷ $625 = 74.16. Compare that to the gross rent multipliers in the next article in this issue.

Goodfriend's cash on cash return is $160.82 x 12 = $1,929.84 ÷ $11,000 = **17.54%**. Nice work if you can get it.

Appreciation, amortization, and tax benefits are additional.

Plans

Goodfriend hopes to refinance the property in the next six months to the tune of 80% of an appraisal of $55,000 or $44,000 at 11%. That would give him debt service of

$n = 360$
$i = 11\% \div 12 = .92\%$
$PV = \$44,000$

$PMT = \$419.02.$

His cash flow would drop to $481.15 - $419.02 = $62.13. But his equity would also drop from $11,000 to $46,352.56 - $44,000 = $2,352.56. Since his cap rate is higher than his mortgage interest rate, any leverage increases his cash on cash return rate. $62.13 x 12 = $745.56 ÷ $2,352.56 = **31.69%**! QED

Note that many lenders have a policy of lending a percentage of appraisal or sale price, whichever is **less**. In pursuit of that policy they ask when you bought the property and how much you paid for it. You may be tempted to **lie** to avoid bumping into such a policy limit. Resist that temptation. Lying to a lender is a state and usually a federal felony. Goodfriend is confident he can find a lender who will go by the appraisal rather than the **lower** of the appraisal or his purchase price.

Why it worked

The four success factors in this deal were:

1. Less desirable, overlooked area.

2. Seller in need of quick sale and buyer who could buy quickly.

3. Architecture (converted garage) that turns off buyers more than it turns off renters.

4. VA assumption which provided below-market interest rate and avoided loan transaction costs.

Items 1 and 3 can be found in any type or size property. Items 2 and 4 are mainly single-family home characteristics.

Most real estate investors are doing deals which show a much lower rate of return than this. The reason is that they would turn their noses up at the Romeoville kind of neighborhood and especially at the converted garages. If they were nothing down/high leverage type buyers, they would be flummoxed by the need to come up with $11,000 (24%) down and lose the deal as a result...unless they could foresee the refinancing and its resulting $44,000 ÷ $46,352.56 = 94.92% net acquisition leverage.

The beauty of an **investment** lies in its **numbers**, not its architecture. You should not regard investment decisions as an opportunity to demonstrate your good taste in architecture or neighborhoods. You should not regard the affluence of your tenants as a reflection of **your** affluence. Indeed, the opposite is usually true. The investor who chooses acquisitions according to their **return** rather than to impress his superficial friends's judgments, will generally avoid architecturally correct properties and fashionable neighborhoods... and he'll become more affluent for having done so.

Marc Goodfriend is the president of the Chicago Creative Investors Association and co-editor of its newsletter. [*Editor's note*: *Marc Goodfriend has passed away. His wife, Jane Garvey, continues to write and publish the newsletter,* Creative Investment Advisor.] JTR

5
Buy Two,
Get One for 2/3 Off

December 1988

Properties with two houses on one lot are **leper** properties. That is, virtually all prospective buyers shun them.

Such shunning is only an investment problem in rental property when **tenants** also shun them. But tenants do **not** shun two-on-a-lot houses. The investors I've spoken to say such houses rent for the same as a normal house.

If the rent is the same...and buyers shun the properties...you would expect them to have high cap rates. (A property's cap rate is its net operating income before debt service divided by its price.) And my investigation indicates that two-on-a-lot properties do indeed have high cap rates.

Marin County, CA

One Marin County, CA investor said he bought a two-on-a-lot two years ago for $189,000. At the time, each of the two 2-bedroom cottages would have sold for about $130,000 to $150,000 if they were **one**-on-a-lot houses. Taking the median of $140,000, we get an overall value of

$140,000 x 2 = $280,000. So the investor got the property at a $280,000 - $189,000 = $91,000 or 33% discount.

Not side-by-side

I'm not talking about side-by-side properties, each of which has street frontage. Rather I'm talking about properties where one house is **behind** the other.

With side-by-side houses, the obvious solution is subdivide into two lots.

In the case of the Marin County investor, **neither** house has street frontage. **Both** are behind another house on another lot owned by another party. Access to those two cottages is via a 100-yard driveway which is an easement over the other owner's property.

Rents the same

The Marin investor gets $900 a month for the house he does not live in. He says that's normal market rent for a two-bedroom cottage in his area. If he rented **both** out, he'd get $1,800 a month. With a 25% down payment, the mortgage on his property would be $141,750. At 10.5% for 30 years the monthly payments would be $1,296.64. The monthly before-tax cash flow would be about:

Income	$1,800.00
Taxes	$157.50
Insurance	$40.00
Repairs	$90.00
Net op. income	$1,512.50
Debt service	$1,296.64
BTCF	$215.86

or $215.86 x 12 = $2,590 per year. The property's cap rate would be $1,512.50 x 12 = $18,150/$189,000 = 10%...which is darned good for a Marin County single-family (more or less) rental house.

Atlanta example

Atlanta Realtor® Bill Kramer (404-255-8600) has a management client who owns a property which has a house and a duplex on one lot. Like the Marin property, neither has street frontage. Both are reached by an easement over another property.

Kramer says most single-family rental houses in his market have monthly rents which are about .8% to .85% of the purchase price. That means negative cash flow. But the two-on-a-lot he manages rents for a total of $1,000 or 1.18% of its value of $85,000. The .825% median for regular single-family is 1.18 - .825 = .36 lower. In other words, you can buy house rental income at a .36 ÷ .825 = 43% discount in the Atlanta area if you buy two-on-a-lot properties.

Appreciation rates

Two-on-a-lot properties appreciate at the same rate as normal properties. Sure, they sell at a discount off normal. That's good news when you buy and bad news when you sell. But if "normal" goes up during your holding period, so does the price of a property which sells at a **discount** off normal. As I've often said, relative prices (high or low end of the market) mean nothing when it comes to appreciation rates.

Better investments

Two-on-a-lot properties have much better cash flow than normal properties and equal appreciation rates, so they are clearly better investments. When your fellow investors rib you about owning such properties, just smile knowingly.

Liquidity

I doubt you'd have any trouble financing two-on-a-lot properties. Some lenders will refuse because it's unusual. But others will welcome the cash flow and superior debt-coverage ratio (net operating income divided by debt service). And when it comes to borrowing, you only need **one** lender to say yes.

Resale of two-on-a-lot properties will probably take longer than normal properties. That's true of all "leper" properties ...if you don't "cure the leprosy." But you should be able to live with that...especially if bridge financing can be obtained in a pinch.

Home office

To deduct expenses for an office **in** your home, you have to meet strict exclusive-use and principal-place-of-business tests (IRC §280A). But those tests do **not** apply to a **separate** structure. So a two-on-a-lot property offers an owner-occupant home office deducter who can't meet the "**in**-the-home" tests the opportunity to deduct for business use of the second structure, or part of it.

Insurance

Some insurance companies will probably insure your two-on-a-lot property at a **lower rate** per thousand dollars of coverage because the open space between the two structures acts as a sort of fire wall which reduces the probability of total loss compared to a **single** structure of equal square footage.

Two-on-a-lot properties probably violate current zoning but are allowed to remain under the doctrine of **nonconforming use** (complies with zoning in effect at the time it was built). But if one of the structures burns down, you probably would not be permitted to rebuild it. So you should consider getting an endorsement to your insurance policy to cover the loss represented by inability to rebuild. One insurance company calls it a "contingent liability from operation of building laws" endorsement. Check with your agent.

Moving one building

In a few cases, it may pay to move one of the structures to another lot. You're getting the second house real cheap. That's not the zero or close to it cost for to-be-demolished property as described in my August article on building moving ("How to Buy for Half Price and Nothing Down"). But in a few cases, where the new site is nearby, for example, the margin may be enough.

How to find them

The existence of a second structure is generally noted only in the **remarks** section for each listing in the multiple listing (MLS) book. And they rarely give any details about the second building.

You can find them by driving around looking for them. Or by aerial reconnaissance. (No kidding. A lot of my readers are pilots and plane owners. And others could afford to charter a plane or chopper once for this purpose.) Virtually all two-on-a-lots are in **rural** areas or **older** neighborhoods because modern zoning generally doesn't allow them. I checked the first two communities in a recent MLS book for my area and found two two-on-a-lots in Alamo, CA out of 83 houses for sale; one out of 146 in Antioch.

In some areas, county tax records may show when there's more than one structure on the property.

Scan the MLS book looking for new two-on-a-lot listings every time it comes out. Using the county tax records or ownership services, compile a mailing list of all the two-on-a-lot owners and mail them quarterly **post cards** offering to buy their property. Point out that they'll save the real estate commission by selling direct to you and suggest that they put the card with their deed or some such so

they can find it if they decide to sell in the future. Send similar post cards to sales **managers** of real estate offices only point out to them that you are helping them **get** a commission on an otherwise hard-to-sell property.

You may need to search systematically over three or four or more counties to find enough properties to do as many deals as you'd like.

Easement, zoning, etc.

Access and/or parking may be a problem. Check each carefully. When there are tenants, use the interview questions in my book, *Residential Property Acquisition Handbook*. Easements can be tricky. Have any easements checked by an attorney who specializes in real estate. Easements were crucial in both the case studies in this article as well as in a third example which I left out. There's a chapter on easements in my book, *How to Increase the Value of Real Estate*. Make sure the zoning and/or deed restrictions don't limit use of the second unit to family or short-term guests.

Part-time investors

As with most leper properties, a **part-time** real estate investor can pursue the two-on-a-lot strategy. The fact that the market shuns them means they'll still be available in the evening when you get off work or even on the weekend if you can't get to it until then. JTR

6
Two Bargain Houses

Most of the deals I write about are done by experienced investors. Unfortunately, that intimidates the **inexperienced**. This article tells of extraordinary profits made by a **beginning** investor who used a number of sound principles, albeit combined with several mistakes which could have been costly.

In the fall of 1989, Lana Balou had decided she wanted to invest in real estate. She and her husband had owned one home; but no rental property. She became familiar with values in her target market of Richmond, California (on the northeastern shore of San Francisco Bay) and began to look.

An interesting ad appeared in the *Contra Costa Times* classified section. It said:

> *"3 br 1 bath, $133,500, $20,000 below appraisal, nothing down."*

Lana immediately inspected the property and concluded it was **more** than $20,000 below market. She found comparable sales indicating it was worth $170,000 to $184,000.

The seller was an unlikely bargain source. She was a **real estate agent**...but in Oakland. She had apparently appraised the property as if it were in Oakland not realizing it was worth more in Richmond.

Full-price offer

Lana jumped on the property the first day, made a full-price offer which was accepted, and signed the papers. The next day, three back-up offers at **more than** full price came in.

In spite of her beginner status, Balou knew the importance of **speed** in making bargain purchases. (See "Eleven percent cap rates really are attainable" in the 7/88 issue.) She also had enough confidence in her appraisal skills to make a **full-price** offer which is the only sensible course of action when a property is offered at a bargain price. Nevertheless, many investors absolutely **re-fuse** to ever make a full-price offer.

She also knew to stand firm when the seller tried to get out of the deal to take advantage of the later offers. Balou said firmly, "We have a deal." And the seller abandoned her efforts to get out of the agreement.

Financing

The purchase agreement called for the buyer to **assume** the existing adjustable-rate mortgage (ARM) of $115,000 and the seller to take back a second for the balance of $18,500. I asked Balou why she didn't buy **subject to** the first rather than assuming it. She did not **know** about subject to when she made the offer.

However, the first mortgage lender said they would **not** allow assumption unless Balou put down at least 10% or $13,350.

Since the deal was contingent on her getting the first lender's approval, Balou was technically "out of contract" as the seller put it. But citing the classified ad's "nothing down" wording as a promise that had to be kept, Balou said she would come up with the $13,350 if the seller would agree to no payments on the seller second (now down to an amount of $18,500 - $13,350 = $5,150) for the first two years. The seller agreed.

Balou and her husband refinanced their home to get the down-payment money.

Why sold so cheap?

Why did the real estate agent seller, who had just completed renovation of the property, sell so cheap? She fell into one of the categories I listed in "Sellers who are likely to sell cheap" in the 10/87 issue: sellers who have already made a big profit.

Balou's seller had bought the property in question real cheap at a **foreclo-sure** auction. The sale price of $133,500 represented a good profit for the seller in spite of the fact that it was still below market

Many of my case-history articles on bargain purchases have ended with the hero selling at a big profit which was still well **below** market. This article could as easily have been about the **seller** of Balou's property. **Both** buyer and seller did well.

Resale

Balou wanted to flip the property quickly to realize her theoretical $170,000 - $133,500 = $36,500 profit. She listed the property for sale at $170,000. Two weeks later, the World Series earthquake hit. That killed the market because of lack of buyer interest and greatly in-creased lender inspection requirements.

Leasing

Faced with mortgage payments on the first mortgage and no buyers for the property, Balou decided to try to **rent** it for $850 a month while still keeping it up for sale. But none of the prospective tenants looked good enough to be trusted with the just-renovated property.

Balou paid her first mortgage pay-ment (about $1,000 including taxes and insurance) with a credit-card advance.

Lease-option

Faced with no buyers or suitable ten-ants and mortgage payments she couldn't afford, Balou decided to try a lease-option. That worked.

A suitable lessee/optionee was found in **one week.**They moved in in Decem-ber. Plus that family pays **$1,000** rather than the $850 a regular tenant would have paid. The option is for one year at $170,000.

So all was now well with the Balou family's entry into real estate investor land. For about a month.

In January of this year, Balou was laid off from her job as office manager for a casualty insurance firm.

Adjacent property

In February, a real estate agent Balou had met at an open house called to tell her the property **next** to her first acquisition was for sale. Again, the seller was a real estate agent herself... but this time, in Richmond. No bargain there, right?

Wrong. This property was in **very bad** shape.

The roof had been leaking for years. The retaining wall in the back yard was collapsing. The foundation was badly cracked. The interior walls were painted dark brown. Some windows had been boarded up.

On the other hand, the second house was a little **bigger** than the first...two baths instead of one and more square feet.

The asking price was $115,000, all cash for the owner's equity. There was an assumable ARM with an $80,000 balance held by the same lender as on Balou's first rental.

The still unemployed Balou, who had not yet inspected the house, and mindful of the lender's previous 10% down requirement, offered full price, with assumption of the $80,000 first, $11,500 down and the seller carrying back a second for the balance of $23,500.

She got the $1,000 earnest money from another credit card advance. The offer was contingent on inspection by Balou and assorted experts.

"No" was the reply. It had to be $35,000 in cash for the equity.

Balou figured she could, at worst, **assign** her purchase agreement in view of the much below market price. So she agreed to the seller's counter. The seller had also insisted that all contingencies be removed within **three weeks.**

Assign the agreement?

Balou did indeed find a buyer for her purchase agreement. But he only offered her **$4,000.** And even he chickened out when he saw the inside and back yard of the property.

Partner?

Balou then found an equity partner. But she, too, chickened out, saying there was not enough profit in the deal.

At that point, Balou had **ten days** left to salvage her $1,000 earnest-money deposit.

Engineer

Sinking more money into what two experienced real-estate people had now said was a hopeless deal, she hired an engineer for $200 to tell her what needed to be done to the property and estimate its cost.

He said the property was **fundamentally sound.** He estimated the foundation repair at just $1,000 (See "Profit opportunities in bad foundations" in the 6/88 issue.) and said the retaining-wall repair would cost $10,000.

Appraiser #1

Knowing she would need an appraisal to get financing, she threw good money after her earnest money and engineer report by spending $250 for an appraisal. The appraiser said the property should be **torn down** and put the land value alone at just $60,000-$70,000. Balou told him what the engineer's report said, but he was not impressed.

Appraiser #2

Balou then spent **another** $250 to get a **second** appraiser to visit the property. He agreed with the engineer's report and figured the property would be worth $187,500 after fix up.

Financing

Balou, who had no money and was running out of time to come up with $35,000 in cash, then called mortgage lenders listed in the *Yellow Pages.* She told the lenders the details of deal and asked, "How much will you lend me?" She hoped to get enough to pay the entire purchase price then get an FHA Title I improvement loan.

After calling only 5 lenders, she had two bidding against each other for her business. The winning bidder agreed to lend her up to 70% of the $187,500 **post-fix-up appraisal** on a phased basis. This **construction** loan cost eight points, carried a 15% fixed interest rate, and was due in one year.

The deal closed on June 1, 1990. In addition to the $35,000 needed to buy the property, the lender has advanced an additional $16,000 for the estimated $20,000 fix-up cost. Balou was required to put up $4,000. She did that by arranging lines of credit at lumber yards and running up a $4,000 tab of building supplies.

Eviction

One of the **mistakes** Balou made was not insisting that the property be **vacant** at closing. She had heard that the tenants were buying a home and assumed that they would move out as she was told.. They didn't. In fact, they physically threatened contractors who came to the property to give estimates.The seller refused to give Balou the keys at closing.

In the growing confrontation, the tenant threatened to **sue** Balou. She offered to pay them to move out. They agreed to do that for about $1,200...in the form of a cashier's check to be given to the tenants the day **before** they moved out.

To my surprise, she says they kept their end of the bargain and left the place spotless. I would not advise Balou or any other reader to pay tenants **in advance** to move out. Find some neutral third party to verify the move out and turn over the money.

Principles

Balou's two acquisitions illustrate many of the principles of sound real estate investing:

- Move **immediately** when you find a bargain.
- **Persist** in the face of discouragement.
- Don't back down when sellers try to **welsh**.
- Avoid **litigation** when economical settlement is possible.
- If one approach doesn't work, try another.
- Don't hesitate to pay **full price** for a bargain.
- Compared to a **bad tenant**, a vacancy is a delight.
- Don't accept **negative cash flow**.

- **Document** your case with an engineer's report as appropriate.
- Know the **values** in the target area.

The mistakes she made include:

- Using adjustable rate mortgages.
- Not hedging the construction loan with a permanent commitment or an interest-rate-futures option.
- Not trying to buy "subject to" rather than assuming.
- Not calling for each property to be vacant at closing.

It can be done

In this article and the article on Bob Bruss's unfit-for-human-occupancy deal on page 337, the total profit made was in the neighborhood of $157,000 or an average of more than $52,000 per deal. The deals were done in the last year in the San Francisco Bay Area...one the world capitals of investors whining they can't find deals that make sense.

One was done by a nationally known real estate expert and attorney using long-established relationships with bankers and agents; the others by a novice armed only with guts, a credit card, and the *Yellow Pages*. Both succeeded because they employed many of the same principles of real estate investing.

There are always opportunities in real estate...in every market...if you have a sound approach...and you pursue your goals doggedly. JTR

7

"Unfit for Human Occupancy"

August 1990

On January, a working woman in her sixties was released from a hospital on The Peninsula, a generally affluent area directly south of San Francisco. As was standard in such cases, a visiting nurse was assigned to check on how she was doing.

"Unfit"

When she arrived at the woman's house, the visiting nurse was appalled at its condition. The roof had holes in it big enough to allow not only rain but also leaves to come in. More than 20 cats lived in the attic producing the sort of stench you'd expect. As required by law, the nurse reported the condition of the house to the city. A city inspector visited the property and promptly posted a sign reading:

"Unfit for human occupancy."

The city ordered the gas-and-electric company to turn off those utilities and forced the couple to move out immediately.

How he found it

Bob Bruss, an investor and nationally known real estate writer, had been watching the house for some time. In addition to the bad roof, its grass was never mowed and two vehicles sat unmoved and covered by tarps in the driveway for years. Like many investors, Bruss tries to contact the owners of such neglected properties on the theory that they are often willing to sell at bargain prices. In this case, he had left two or three notes for the owners over the years. But he got no response.

Fortunately, he also made it known to all the real estate agents in the area that he bought fixer uppers. One such agent learned of the condemnation of the house and tracked down its owners, who had moved to a boarding house in San Jose.

The owners refused to sign a listing or even state an asking price. Nevertheless, the agent decided to call Bruss in the hope that a specific offer might get the sellers to act.

Offer

Bruss said he was interested, inspected the property, and offered $212,000 including a 6% commission for the agent. Had it been maintained in a normal fashion, the two-bedroom, one-bath house would have been worth about $320,000 in that neighborhood, according to Bruss.

The owners neither rejected nor countered the offer. After waiting two weeks, Bruss called the agent and said if he didn't get an answer in the next four days, the offer would be withdrawn. When presented with that ultimatum, the owners countered at $216,000. Bruss agreed and the papers were signed.

Bruss then introduced himself to the neighbors, told them of his rehabilitation plans, and gave them his card and invited them to call him if they saw any suspicious characters around the property. Shortly thereafter, a neighbor called and said she had seen a man on the property and asked what he was doing. He said he was about to buy the property. She took his name then called Bruss to tell him.

Interloper

Bruss recognized the name as that of an aggressive local real estate investor. Upon investigation, he learned that the investor had agreed to buy the property for the same price as Bruss...only there would be no commission. So the sellers would net 6% x $216,000 = $12,960 more than selling to Bruss through the agent. Of course, that would require them to breach their agreement with Bruss.

Bruss, who is a lawyer, called the investor and told him that he would enforce his purchase agreement against the seller by filing a specific performance suit and would file a *lis pendens* (lawsuit regarding ownership pending) against the property if the owners did not perform at closing a few days later. The investor knew such a suit would probably prevail (See "Sellers who welsh" in the 9/89 issue, Chapter 16.) and immediately abandoned his plans to buy the building.

Gut rehab

The owners **did** sell to Bruss. They owned the house free and clear and had even paid the 1990 property taxes in advance. The closing went smoothly.

The house requires a gut rehab. It's the worst house Bruss ever bought in his many years as a fixer upper. The tax assessor split Bruss's $216,000 purchase price into $215,000 for the land and **$1,000 for the improvements.**

The hardwood floors were destroyed by the rain but the underlayment was OK. The floors will be removed and replaced by carpet. All non-carpeted floors will get new vinyl. Because of mildew, all the walls and ceilings have to be replaced. The appliances and plumbing fixtures were also unsalvageable and will be replaced. The fireplace, on the other hand, was in great shape because it had never been used in the property's 40- to 50-year history.

The house has a 6' x 15' front porch which is under the main roof and is surrounded on three sides by the house. Bruss is enclosing that porch and thereby adding a third bedroom and expanding the living room. (See "One-bedroom houses" in the 7/88 issue and the "Reducing the load factor" chapters in my books, *How to Increase the Value of Real Estate* and *How to Manage Residential Property for Maximum Cash Flow and Resale Value.*) He is also turning part of the living room into a second bathroom.

Bruss's fixed-price contract with the general contractor is for $62,000 and will take four months to complete. Change orders typically add a bit more. When complete, he figures the expanded house will be worth $350,000. Although the papers have not yet been signed, Bruss believes he already has a leasee optionee.

Financing

Bruss financed the purchase and renovation as follows:

- Construction loan of $170,000 at prime plus two percent
- Secured line of credit drawn down $50,000 at same rate
- Unsecured line of credit drawn down $60,000 at same rate.

He says all three loans came from the same local bank. He recommends against banking with more than one bank or with large banks. Rather he says you should cultivate a relationship with a **small bank** in your community ... a bank which only has one or two branches and which is **not** a subsidiary of a large bank... where your business will be more appreciated. Of course, in this age of big banks buying up little ones, one can never be certain that a community bank won't become part of BigCitiMegaBanc next year.

Hedge floating-rate loans

Bruss's loans are all floating rate. I believe it's financial Russian Roulette to finance real estate with floating-rate loans. Rather, the investor should use either **fixed-rate** loans or **hedge** using interest-rate futures contracts or, in this case with its six-month holding period, the simpler interest-rate futures options. Although the use of interest-rate futures hedging is inexplicably rare among real estate investors, it is common among builders. In this deal, Bruss is operating more like a builder.

I explained the use of interest-rate futures **contracts** in detail in "The best of both worlds, a hedged ARM" in the 11/87 and 12/87 issues. And I showed how to use interest-rate futures **options** in "How to lock interest rates even when the lender refuses" in the 7/89 issue.

Ethics

There is no ethical issue for Bruss in this deal. A buyer has the right to make any cash offer he wants and owes no one an apology if the seller agrees to sell cheap.

An **agent** representing a seller has a duty to make a full and complete disclosure of all material facts which might influence the seller. According to *Fisher v. Losey*, 78 C.A. 2d 121, that includes "the price that can be obtained, the possibility of a sale at a higher price, dealing with the property in another fashion..."

Tax ramifications

Bruss plans to keep this property and lease option it as he often does. (For a brief discussion of Bruss's approach to lease options, see "Lease-option defaults, walk aways, etc." in the 5/89 issue, Chapter 76. For more on lease options in general, see "Lease option can mean bigger vandalism," 3/88; "Is option money still not taxed until the option is exercised or expires?", 5/89; and "Lease options: What you need to know," 12/87 and 1/88, Chapters 74, 75.) He can begin depreciating it when the house is ready to be rented. Bruss's **basis** is the sum of:

- $216,000 purchase price
- $4,000 (approx.) in closing costs
- $62,000 (approx.) in fix up costs
- construction period interest.

The fix-up costs are 100% depreciable because they are 100% attributable to the improvements. The other basis items must be allocated to land and depreciable improvements.

Replacement cost

To do that, Bruss will ask his insurance agent for the **replacement** cost of the improvements. That's one of the main methods I advocate in my book, *Aggressive Tax Avoidance for Real Estate Investors*. Furthermore, Bruss says he was audited by IRS a couple years ago and the auditor **liked** the insurance-agent-replacement-cost-estimate approach.

Many investors would use the tax assessor's breakdown. In this case, that would give the absurd result of saying that Bruss got a three-bedroom, two-bath house built for $62,000...on a lot worth $215,000.

The ultimate depreciation schedule ought to have a **personal property** component for the appliances, drapes, and carpet; a **land** component; a **land improvements** component (See "Break out the land improvements" in the 7/89 issue); and a **structure** component. The personal property basis would be simply the cost of the appliances. The closing costs, fix up costs, purchase price, and construction period interest would be allocated into the land, land improvement, and structure categories.

Lessons learned

Bruss regrets that he did not follow the "unfit-for-human-occupancy" notices filed in building inspectors' offices in the cities near where he lives. Had he known that the owners of this property had a new and compelling reason to sell then he probably would have tracked them down on his own. Presumably, he could have split the $12,960 commission savings with the sellers.

He does **not** regret telling that agent and others of his interest in such properties. Doing so enabled him to be the first buyer to make an offer on this property and that was crucial to making the $68,000 or so profit. ᴊᴛʀ

8
Foreclosure Auction Case History

September 1990

When I interviewed Paul Thompson for the July article, "How to buy profitably at foreclosure auctions," I mentioned that I had never been to one. On August 17th, he took me to one.

Stockton, CA

I met Thompson at his Livermore house at 8 a.m. and we drove to Stockton so as to arrive about a half hour early. When we walked up the courthouse steps, I started for the building entrance out of habit. But Thompson just walked over and leaned on the masonry wall. Then I realized these things are **really** held **on the steps.** There we waited under a "No loitering" sign.

Most such auctions are scheduled for 9 a.m. to discourage bankruptcy filings on the day of sale.

If you saw the gathering from across the street, you probably would not recognize it as a foreclosure auction unless you had experience in that area. There were twenty men and women in casual clothes, some carrying clipboards with fold-over covers. Several greeted each other by name. Thompson said five were regulars.

If a layman had to guess, he'd probably figure they were Rotarians meeting informally on their day off.

The auctioneer fit right in. He wore sneakers, an open collar shirt, and a beeper. His clipboard was fatter than the others. And he greeted several of the would-be buyers by name.

The auctioneer volunteered the information he knew everyone was most interested in: which auctions were postponed or cancelled. He announced that only two of the scheduled auctions were going to be held and gave their street addresses. The crowd was very disappointed. Thompson explained that the only properties with enough equity to warrant bidding were all postponed or cancelled.

Five checks

Thompson brought five separate cashiers checks totaling $260,809.

Three of the four properties he was interested in were among the cancelled or postponed sales. This in spite of the fact that he had called as recently as the day before to confirm that the sale was still on.

Just prior to bidding on each property, the prospective bidders were required to show their money. Thompson showed $140,000 worth of checks to prove he was qualified on the property he bought. The checks are shown **only** to the auctioneer so the other bidders won't know Thompson's maximum bid. No one else showed money thereby indicating Thompson was the only bidder.

The actual auction

After checking his watch several times to make sure it was 9 a.m., the auctioneer began reading disclaimers and such from papers in his clip board. Before long, he came to the first property to be auctioned.

Thompson was somewhat confused as to the exact amount of the minimum bid. The auctioneer recognized that Thompson wanted to bid the next dollar amount and said, "You mean $137,639? That's the next even dollar above the minimum."

When no one else bid, the auctioneer spoke the familiar, "Going once, going twice, going for the third and final time at $137,639. [Pause] Sold for $137,639."

A second property was then auctioned off in similar fashion. Only one person bid. (Thompson did not bid because of the neighborhood.)

The entire two-property auction was over by 9:04 a.m.

Elm Street

Thompson bought 123 Elm Street (not the real address) in a small central valley town. The minimum bid on the property was $137,638.23. That's the amount owed including principal, interest, penalties, and costs. Thompson bid $137,639 or 77¢ more than the amount owed. The previous owners are entitled to that 77¢ unless there is some statutory minimum amount of excess proceeds.

Market value

Thompson had **driven by** 123 Elm the day before. He could see it was about two years old, in a decent neighborhood, and apparently vacant (dead lawn, newspaper on driveway). He had not gone to the door.

Based on his knowledge of the market and the windshield appraisal, Thompson figured the property was worth about $160,000 to $170,000. The margin over the minimum bid was only $160,000 - $137,638 = $22,362 ÷ $160,000 = 14%. Thompson usually won't bid unless he can get the property for at least 15% below market for a "good" property; 20% below otherwise.

Delayed exchange

If none of the properties available that day had enough equity, why did Thompson bid at all? He needed a property to complete a delayed exchange. Because of the tax savings, his **overall** margin was larger than was apparent to a person who knew only the value of the property and the liens on it.

He was exchanging out of a foreclosure condo he bought for $63,000. He had received an all-cash offer of $90,000 which he couldn't refuse.

Can you exchange into a foreclosure bought at auction? Sure. Why not? In the event, it was a nonissue.

After the auction was completed, the two successful bidders repaired to the courthouse hall to complete business. Thompson asked the auctioneer if he would mind coming to the office of Thompson's delayed-exchange facilitator a couple blocks away. The auctioneer readily agreed.

It would not have been a problem if he had refused. All that matters is that the auctioneer receive a check from the delayed-exchange escrow and that the exchangor not have unfettered right to the money. That could have been done in the courthouse. Independent Exchange Service's Brandt Nicholson (415-882-4667) says they have handled similar exchanges. All the auctioneer cares about is that it's a cashiers check.

Thompson had $20,000 in the delayed-exchange escrow. He needed more to buy the property. No problem. Just use **two** checks: one for $20,000 and one for the rest.

On to the property

Having completed the transaction, we set out to see what Thompson had bought. On the way, I asked how many bedrooms the property had.

"I don't know."

How many square feet?

"Don't know that either."

Is it occupied?

"I don't think so."

I began to wonder if the neighborhood would offer good avenues of escape should the former home owner come after us with a gun. On the way to the house, Thompson had to pull over to consult a map. "I don't remember where this house is," he explained. This was definitely not the kind of acquisition I was used to.

3br, 2 1/2 ba, fr, fp

But when we pulled up in front, it looked like your basic house. Almost brand new. Dead lawn, but otherwise in great shape from what could be seen. The house is a two story with an attached two-car garage and a deck in the back. The lot wasn't much bigger than the house. But the house was one of the newest in the neighborhood.

The neighborhood was modest working class with the occasional pickup truck or boat in the driveway.

No answer at the door. Drapes all drawn shut. All doors locked. We went to a phone booth to call a locksmith. He showed up in twenty minutes and picked the front-door lock, a dead bolt, in about 10 seconds. He worked on changing the locks, putting all on one key, while we inspected the property.

Immaculate is not a strong enough word to describe the condition of the house. Mint condition would be too strong…but not by much. The property was perfect on the inside except for a pencil line on the wall where a picture had been hung, two torn vinyl spots where the refrigerator had been, and a slight stain in the tub drain caulk. The oven and microwave ovens were spotless. Same for the toilets and other bathroom fixtures. Not so much as a paper clip was left behind. And someone had obviously spent two or three man days cleaning the place.

I was flabbergasted at the condition of the place. My tenants don't leave apartments that clean. And I have a security deposit they want back. I had heard and believed that foreclosees generally leave the house a mess and sometimes spitefully punch holes in the walls and do other vandalism. A new tenant could have moved into **this** house as soon as the locksmith opened the door.

In addition to the two-car garage and deck, the house has three bedrooms, two and a half baths, a family room with fireplace, living room, wet bar, dining room, kitchen with dishwasher, disposer, and microwave, central air-conditioning, wall-to-wall carpet, parquet foyer, and drapes or blinds on all windows and glass doors. It had over 1,800 square feet.

Revised value

Thompson said the house was one of the better ones as far as condition was concerned. But he did not seem as surprised by it as I was. However, upon seeing the condition of the interior, Thompson revised his market value estimate up to $180,000. At $180,000, that would give him profit of $180,000 - $137,639 = $42,361 above his purchase price. That's a $42,361 ÷ $180,000 = 24% discount.

I asked Thompson how many hours he had spent **total** to buy this property. Three. Of course, he had also spent additional hours rejecting properties he did not bid on. Thompson figures he spends about 20 to 30 hours a week pursuing foreclosures. In 1989, he bought 7 properties; 6 so far this year. That's 20 months x 4.3 weeks per month x 25 hours per week = 2,150 hours to buy 13 properties or 165 hours per acquisition. This was an average deal so the pay per hour is about $42,361 ÷ 165 = $256 per hour. Nice work if you can get it. And you can get it if you try.

Thompson bought me the usual tycoon's lunch at Arby's. Then, having made $42,361 between 8 and 10 a.m., he took the rest of the day off.

One of the worst times and places

You should note that all of the above took place at one of the **worst** times and places imaginable. California's central valley has had high appreciation rates in recent years. Sacramento has been one of the very top cities in appreciation in the last year. Those conditions produce the **minimum** number of foreclosures and the **maximum** number of bidders at the auction. In the few years Thompson has been doing this, he has seen the average margin on properties he buys drop from about 35% to 40% to about 20% to 25%. If and when conditions worsen, the margins and compensation per hour of foreclosure buyers should increase dramatically. JTR

9
Gary DiGrazia's Greatest Hit

September 1990

Gary DiGrazia is a teammate of mine on the Padres of the Bay Area Mens Senior Baseball League (hardball for guys over thirty). Journalistic ethics require me to disclose stuff like that.

However, this article is not about baseball. It's about bargain purchases of real estate out of **probates**. When I told him about a deal from a recent article, Gary said he'd done a better one.

The DiGrazia system

Gary is a real estate salesman who works only on probate property. About 40% of his income comes from commissions on probates he lists and sells. This article is about the **other** 60%...in particular...one house bought in April of last year.

Gary pursues probates in Hayward, San Leandro, San Lorenzo, and Castro Valley (southeast of San Francisco).

Stated briefly, Gary's approach is like a lot of other guys. He sends a letter to executors listed in legal newspapers. But there's more to it than that. Subtle shadings involving things like rapport and grieving. Details like being able to read between the lines of probate files.

He also employs a technique which has cropped up several times in recent interviews with professional investors: a **stable of buyers and agents** who will either buy or find a buyer for your property quickly.

No muss, no fuss

Quick **resale** is essential to Gary. He's a deedless real estate investor, a flipper who regards 90 days as long term. He wants no part of either **management** or **renovation**. Local appreciation rates are all but irrelevant to his program. In short, he is a **non**-subscriber whose approach to real estate conforms more closely to my recent writings than do the programs of most of my subscribers.

25 letters a week

Gary learns about new probates from legal newspapers like *InterCity Express*. About 25 new probates involving one- to four-family houses (Gary buys nothing else) are opened each week in his target area. Unlike foreclosures, which increase or decrease in number according to economic conditions, new probates come in a steady stream.

Gary sends **one** letter to the **executor**, **not** the attorney, of each new probate. In the four years he has been doing this, he has learned that executors are generally grieving relatives who must be approached with great sensitivity. After negative responses to the letters he sent when he began, Gary has rewritten the letter several times. It now begins with an expression of sympathy and is extremely "low key."

3 or 4 responses

He follows each probate, whether they respond or not, on hand-written tracking sheets. Gary has a computer. But he does not use it to keep a probate data base. He spends about five to ten hours a week keeping the tracking sheets up to date.

Three or four of each batch of 25 respond. The response may come in a week...or a year. Gary still sends **no follow-up letters**. The typical response is noncommittal, resulting, at best, in his inspecting the property.

Gary buys three or four houses per year in his target area. His average deal produces $20,000 in profit split between him and his investor partner. Plus Gary gets the buyer's broker commission which is typically around $5,000.

Preparation

Before he inspects the property, Gary reads the entire **probate file** which is a public record. He also takes every opportunity to build **rapport** with the executor including face-to-face meeting whenever possible. That rapport often becomes crucial when other actors like attorneys and other would-be buyers later come into the picture with deal-killing on their mind.

Intimate knowledge of the executor's wants and needs also enables Gary to out-negotiate his Johnny-come-lately critics and competitors. As does his general knowledge of what executors want most: things like **speed, cash,** and **minimum effort** on their part.

Offer

As with most real estate investment strategies designed to produce immediate profits, **speed** is important to Gary's. Within 48 hours of inspecting the property, Gary submits an offer from one of the three investor partners he works with. He won't let the investor offer more than 75% of market value. He puts 30% down in order to get a fast, "easy-qualifier" mortgage.

The offer calls for closing in 30 days, a number of inspections, and gives Gary ten days to remove those inspection contingencies.

He uses the ten-day contingency period for both inspections and another purpose: to find a **buyer** for the property.

Buyers

Gary has a stable of regular buyers and agents he calls when he has a property to sell. He wants to sell the property at **quick-sale value** (about 90% to 95% of market value) for **all cash** as fast as possible because the property is **vacant** and generating no income. Meanwhile, the money borrowed to buy it accrues interest. Gary has keys to the property at this point and shows the property to his own buyers or gives the key to selected, cooperating agents.

He generally gets a buyer fast enough that he **could** double escrow the deal if he wanted. But double escrows *per se* antagonize the probate attorneys too much so he closes the resale **separately**. However, the closings are still close enough that he can pass most of his closing costs on to the ultimate buyer. Among other things, he uses the standard flipper technique of paying 110% of a normal title insurance premium to get a "110% binder." That enables him to get back all but 10% of his title insurance premium when the ultimate buyer gets title insurance from the same company (which Gary requires).

Financing

Gary acts as a buyer's broker for the investor who is buying the property in question. The investor typically gets the 30% down by drawing down a **home equity line of credit**.

Partnership agreement

Gary gets the buyer's broker commission at the front end. And he gets 50% of the net profit. This is by **verbal** agreement only. I can't recommend that to subscribers. See "Arbitration" in the April '89 issue for a horror story stemming from a mere **omission** in the agreement, not lack of a written agreement.

One of the benefits of this approach is that Gary's name does not appear on the title. In this era of often ruinous liability for toxic contamination, that's a darned good idea.

Condition of property

Unlike foreclosures, which are generally in rough shape and often occupied, probates are usually **clean, well-maintained,** and **vacant**. Gary agrees with me that renovation is time-consuming and not very well compensated (See "Cost accounting in real estate" in the 1/90 issue).

Resale

Gary is pursuing the **buy-very-low-sell-low** strategy rather than the far more well known buy-low-sell-high approach. Selling for quick-sale value makes sense whenever the property in question is **vacant**. Buy-very-low-sell-low also makes sense when the **investor's time is valuable**. At quick-sale value, you can generally sell in a matter of **weeks**, for **cash**, without an agent.

5835 Hooker

One of the responses Gary got in the spring of '89 was from Fred Cucci (not his real name). Fred was the executor of his mother's estate which included her home, a two-bedroom, one-bath house at 5835 Hooker Street in Hayward (not the real address). Fred, however, was handling the estate from out of state. Gary would have to establish rapport without a face-to-face meeting.

He did...through numerous phone calls. Gary arranged immediately to inspect the property. Then he quickly made his offer: $150,000 with 30% down and a new, easy-qualifier mortgage.

The house came with a lot big enough to build on. The executor knew that but didn't want to be bothered getting approvals. Gary figured the property was worth $200,000.

Court appraisal

The Cucci estate was being handled according to the rules of California's **Independent Administration of Estates Act.** That is the less formal of the two California procedures. It does **not require** a court appraisal. However, most estate attorneys order such an appraisal as a CYA measure. The attorney in this estate ordered such a court appraisal.

The court appraisal is done by the court-appointed estate referee. Estate referees get paid minimal fees. You get what you pay for. Probate experts figure the typical referee does a windshield appraisal. While referee's appraisals are often inaccurate, they can be inaccurate in **either** direction. By law, if the referee's appraisal comes in more than 10% above Gary's agreed-upon purchase price, the deal is off.

Gary held his breath waiting for the appraisal. It came in at $158,000 ... **within** the 10% allowable range.

Interlopers

Theoretically, that should have sealed it. But as with the three bargain purchases I wrote about last month, others quickly recognized the bargain and tried to overbid it.

The attorney recommended that the property be listed with a real estate agent so a **new, better** buyer might be found. Plus, a builder who wanted the property for its extra lot tried to get the executor to sell to him instead.

That builder was building on other lots around 5835 Hooker. One of those lots had been sold to the builder by the deceased who had taken back a mortgage on it. That mortgage was now one of the estate assets the executor wanted to liquidate. Gary and his partner offered to buy that note from the estate for face value. That clinched the deal. As it turned out, the builder got some construction financing and paid off the note so Gary and his partner never had to complete the note purchase.

No court confirmation

Because this estate was handled under the Independent Administration of Estates Act, court confirmation was not necessary. Under the other procedure, the public would have to be given an opportunity to bid more than the amount agreed to privately by Gary and the executor. Such public auctions often wipe out the private bidder's bargain. In California, the public overbid must be at least 10% higher than the private bid or it will be ignored.

Resale

Gary resold the property through one of his "broker outlets" in May of '89, three weeks after he and his partner closed the purchase from the estate. The sale price was $230,000. The investor paid a 4% commission.

Here's a summary of the deal:

Resale price	$230,000
Selling commission	$9,200
Net sale price	**$220,800**
Purchase price	$150,000
Buyer's commission	$8,000
Closing costs	$1,000
Total cost	**$159,000**
Net investor profit	**$61,800**

Gary got half that profit or $30,900.

Attorneys

Probate attorneys are cultivated by real estate brokers. As a result, many probate attorneys have favorite real estate agents. They generally recommend to the executor that he or she list the property with that favorite broker.

Listing with a real estate agent usually eliminates any bargain opportunity. Broadly speaking, the two ways to buy property for at least 20% below market are 1. buy property **nobody wants** or 2. buy property **nobody knows is for sale**. Probate properties are generally not in the first category. So locking them up **before** others find out about them is key.

Gary obtains agreement on the sale price and terms **before** the probate attorney persuades the executor to list it. On a number of occasions, the probate attorney has tried to kill Gary's deal. So far, none has succeeded...primarily because of the rapport he has established with the executor.

Gary has written a manual on probate property for California investors and agents. Call him at 415-276-5331 if you are interested. JTR

10
Discount Lien Releases: Part I

October 1990

I have written about Ted Thomas's system for buying preforeclosures five times (11/88, 1/89, 6/89, 8/89, 3/90). Some might think that's more than enough. But he keeps doing interesting stuff. The July/August issue of John Beck's *Distress Sales Report* (415-523-6115) tells of another of Thomas's deals...involving discounting liens.

Value, $330,000; liens, $405,000

Thomas found a man whose house was being foreclosed. The house was worth about $330,000. I drove by it and confirmed that value with a local Realtor®. John Beck examined the documents relating to the deal at the county courthouse and in Thomas's files. The first mortgage lender was foreclosing on their loan which had a current balance including costs and arrearages of $178,000. The owners said they'd sell to Ted for $52,500 cash above the $178,000. Heck of a deal: a $330,000 property for just $178,000 plus $52,500 = $230,500.

The bad news was that there were really **more** than $178,000 in liens against the property. $405,000 in fact.

The extra $227,000 in liens were **judgment** liens owned by recreational-vehicle finance companies. They had sued the home owner and won judgments in those amounts.

How did Thomas make money on such a deal? He persuaded the two creditors to **release** the property from their liens for $5,000 each or a total of $10,000. That made his total cost $178,000 + $52,500 + $10,000 = $240,500 which is still a good price for a property worth $330,000.

Lien release is not judgment release

If it seems unlikely to you that creditors would do such a thing, you may be confusing lien release with judgment release. Neither creditor forgave the **entire** debt. Rather they executed a "Lien Release and Partial Satisfaction of Judgment." That means the debtor still has to pay the rest of the judgment.

The value of a lien

A lien is worth the discounted present value of the amount the lienholder is likely to receive multiplied by the probability that he will receive that amount. When the lien is about to be wiped out by a foreclosure or other forced sale, there is no need to discount to present value.

In Thomas's deal, the senior judgment holder was owed about $132,000

owners of mortgages are generally **too sophisticated** to sell the mortgage for a big enough discount.

But I **did** write an article entitled "A corporation and its real estate are soon parted." (4/88 issue, See Chapter 21) The point of that article, which **was** supported by my research, was that non-real estate corporations usually lack both real-estate expertise and the motivation to obtain it. As a result, they sometimes stupidly

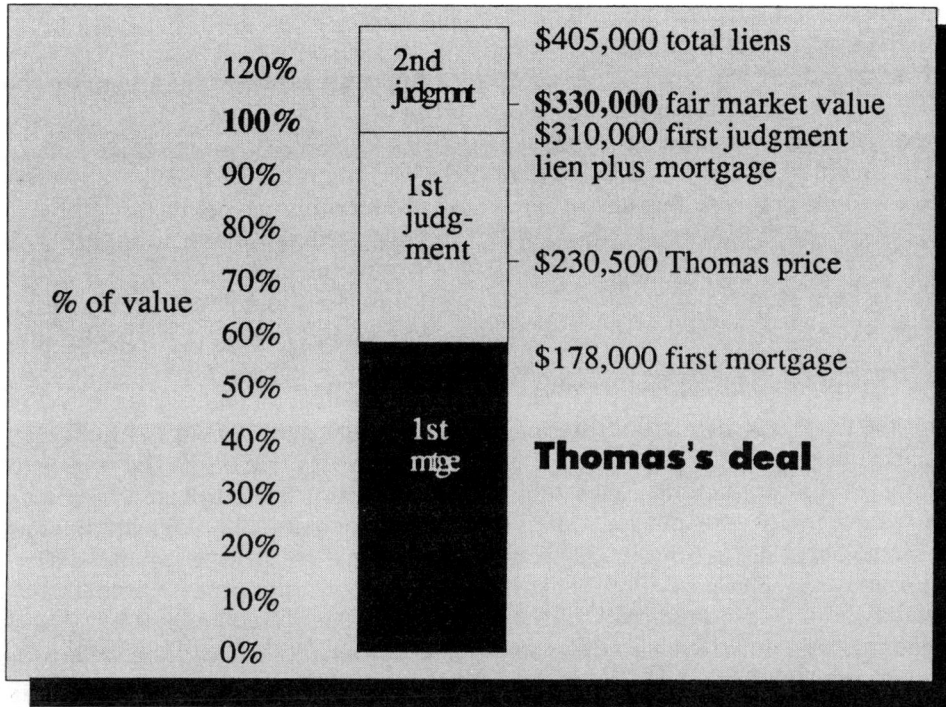

% of value		
120%	2nd judgmnt	$405,000 total liens
100%		**$330,000** fair market value
90%	1st judg- ment	$310,000 first judgment lien plus mortgage
80%		
70%		$230,500 Thomas price
60%		
50%		$178,000 first mortgage
40%	1st mtge	
30%		**Thomas's deal**
20%		
10%		
0%		

and the junior judgment holder, about $95,000. The title report showed an additional $22,000 attachment lien. But it had expired. Since properties rarely sell for more than about 80% of market value at forced sale auctions, the **junior** judgment holder would probably not get anything at all from the auction.

overpay for real estate or sell real estate which they consider "surplus" **too cheap**.

Let's marry those two ideas. Non-real estate corporations not only sell **real estate** too cheap sometimes, they agree to **release liens** too cheap, too. And as I said in the 4/88 article, therein lies an opportunity.

A fool and his lien are soon parted

I once tried to write an article on the subject of deliberately buying **mortgages** which were already in default at bigger-than-normal discounts so you could foreclose and either get a high yield if a third party bought the property at auction...or buy the property yourself for a credit bid which was well below market value. But my research indicated that plan was **not** viable...because the

Assumption is the mother of all screw ups

In the Thomas deal, the two judgment creditors were not real estate investors. The senior judgment creditor was in **Indiana. Sophisticated** real estate or mortgage investors would **not** agree to a lien release for $5,000 until they ascertained the current market value of the property.

In his letter to the judgment creditors, Thomas said the total liens on the property exceeded his purchase price by far more than $100,000. He also told them a senior mortgage was in the process of foreclosing. He told them he had arranged to buy the property but was on the verge of backing out of the deal because of the unexpected liens. He said he would go ahead with the purchase only if the liens could be released at less than face value. He did **not** tell them his purchase price, the amount of the mortgage, or the fair market value.

The judgment creditor apparently **assumed** Thomas was paying approximately fair market value and that their lien was mostly or completely unsecured.

Worth far more

The **second** judgment holder was **smart** to sell a lien release for $5,000.

But the **first** judgment holder should have held out for a higher price to release the lien...or bid at auction. Since they were a creditor on the property, they could have bid as high as $310,000. The amount above $178,000 would be excess proceeds and would be returned to that first judgment creditor. Such a bid would release the debtor from as much of the judgment as the excess proceeds (above the foreclosing $178,000 mortgage) covered...and it would make the judgment holder owners of a property with $330,000 - $178,000 = $152,000 of equity...which is **more** than the amount of their judgment.

If they resell the property for $330,000, they are entitled by well-established precedent to keep the **entire** $152,000 even though they were originally only owed $132,000. By selling to Thomas for $5,000, they blew about $152,000 - $5,000 = $147,000.

Uncertainty for judgment holder, certainty for Thomas

The judgment holder's motivation to deal with Thomas at all is the certainty of his offer versus the uncertainty of what the property will sell for at auction.

From Thomas's perspective, however, there is **no** uncertainty at all. His deal with the debtor is he'll buy the property for $230,500 **only if** there are no liens above $178,000 on the property. So if he cannot get the judgment creditors to agree to big enough discounts, he just walks away... perhaps bidding on the property at the foreclosure auction itself.

"Assumable" liens

Suppose I offered you a loan on the following terms:

- 10% interest
- No monthly payments
- Fully assumable with no credit check
- Nonrecourse
- If I forget about it for over ten years, you don't have to pay it back **at all**.

That's a deal and a half, isn't it? Yet real estate investors **walk away** from such deals every day. How so? They agree to buy a property. The title report comes back with one or more judgment liens as "exceptions" to the title report. The investor and or his attorney automatically tells the seller, "That lien has to be paid off at closing." Your basic kneejerk reaction.

Why would you want to do a stupid thing like pay off that lien? Leave the darned thing on the property! Just pay the seller that much less for his equity and buy the property **subject to** the lien.

State law

In California, a judgment accrues interest at 10% per year. Other states would probably have similar interest rates. Also in California, the lien must be renewed in ten years or it expires. Other states probably have expiration dates. Do corporations forget to renew such liens? Corporations do. Windfall city!

New financing behind judgment liens

Many title companies will even help you get a **new** mortgage without paying off such a lien. They just make you put up

150% (typically) of the lien amount as a sort of security deposit or bond with the title company. They'll then remove the title exception for that lien which makes the new mortgage a first, in effect.

As long as the lien exists, the title company is protected by your deposit. And if the lien **expires** without being renewed, you get your money back. This is analogous to defeasance which I discuss starting on page 165 of my book, *How to Use Leverage to Maximize your Real Estate Investment Return.*

Wipe-out auctions

Junior lien holders are most likely to agree to release liens at a discount when their lien is on the verge of being wiped out by a **foreclosure** of a senior lien or an auction initiated by a **government** tax or other agency which is owed money by the property owner. You find those situations by following notices of the various kinds of forced sales. Continued next month. JTR

11
Discount Lien Releases: Part II

November 1990

In last month's issue, I told you how Ted Thomas bought a $330,000 house for $240,500 by obtaining releases of two judgment liens at a huge discount.

Owners of liens will often agree to release them from a property or sell them for an amount less than the total amount owed. But most real estate investors are either **unaware** of that fact or they **underestimate** how much of a discount can be obtained.

Competitors are the bane of any business person including those who buy properties which are going to foreclosure, tax, or other forced-sale auctions. But those competitors are typically **only** interested in properties which have **equity**...at least 20% equity for most professional investors. That is, they **reject** properties which have liens totaling more than 80% of market value.

That dramatically **reduces** the competition for those properties... which, in turn, dramatically **increases** the bargains which the remaining buyers can get.

Big discounts from mortgage lenders are rare

In general, you **cannot** obtain big discounts from mortgage lenders. Although you can sometimes buy the note from them at a discount. For example, Ernie Kessler, owner of Foreclosure Research of America (301-294-2274), routinely tries to buy notes on properties he owns or is about to own. He approaches the owner of the note through a separate corporation he owns. The corporation does not give any indication it is related to anyone who owns or is buying the property in question. In other words, it's a straw man.

In one deal, Kessler bought a house which was in the process of foreclosure and simultaneously bought the second mortgage on the same house at a discount. The $50,000 **first** mortgage was foreclosing. The owner of the $10,200 second agreed to sell the note for $8,000. Kessler bought the house and the second mortgage then resold the house all on the the same day. Had he not bought the second at a discount, his profit on the deal would have been $4,000. By buying the second at a $2,200 discount, he increased his profit from $4,000 to $6,200.

Author George Coats (*Smart Trust Deed Investing in California* 818-339-0270) says he tried to buy trust deeds at a discount four or five times with no success.

George **did** succeed in getting a discount on a first trust deed on an avocado grove. The property value appeared to be greater than the trust deed, which was in default. But the note holder did not want to foreclose. So George bought the trust deed for a 35% discount off its face value of $80,000. Although the deal turned out to be more difficult than George expected, he made a $20,000 profit.

If there **is** already a default, they may be willing to sell at a discount, even a big discount, if they fear their lien will be wiped out. But mortgage lenders and note buyers will generally do a **competent** job of estimating the equity in the property available to pay off their lien at the auction. Consequently, they will generally **not** release or sell their lien for enough to make it a good deal. But what about lien holders who are **not** competent.

Incompetent lienholders

Are there incompetent lienholders? You bet. Not all lien holders are mortgage lenders or note buyers. Many obtained their lien as a result of a successful **lawsuit**. They are called **judgment** lien holders. It was an out-of-state judgment lien holder who stupidly agreed to release a $132,000 lien for just $5,000 in last month's Ted Thomas case.

Are there a lot of judgment lien holders? You bet. Note buyer Lloyd Walters estimates about 20% of those who default on their mortgages also have outstanding judgments.

"We wrote it off"

It is a basic principle of bill collecting that the longer a bill is outstanding, the lower the probability it will be collected. Consequently, accountants, bookkeepers, and businesspeople are in the habit of "writing off" long-overdue debts. That is, they reduce the value of the debt to zero in their books.

People who have no accounting books *per se* also tend to write off long-overdue debts **psychologically** as well.

Lien is additional security for a judgment

In the case of a mortgage, the lien on the property is of **primary** importance. Owners of mortgages hardly ever agree to release a property from the mortgage lien unless they are paid off **in full**.

But **judgments** are generally the result of an **unsecured** extension of credit (many are the result of **torts** like auto accidents). From the perspective of the judgment lien holder, the lien itself, as opposed to the judgment, is a sort of unexpected bonus. It is viewed as extra or additional security for the original unsecured loan.

I have often noted that many real estate bargain-purchase opportunities arise out of the easy-come-easy-go syndrome. The fact that the original extension of credit was **unsecured**, and that the lien arose **unexpectedly** out of legal procedure, gives the lien an easy-come cast in the lien holder's mind. That, in turn, often leads to an easy-go laziness when you offer to buy a lien release.

Found money

Your offer to pay for a lien release some years after the original judgment was entered seems like found money to a judgment lien holder.

The reaction may well be, "You mean the guy's willing to **pay** us for just a lien release on that judgment we wrote off three years ago?! And we can still go after the rest of the money?! Take it!"

Wipe-out auctions

When there is a wipe-out auction impending, junior lien holders have a powerful impetus to seriously consider any offers for their lien. The following are examples of wipe-out auctions:

- Foreclosure of a mortgage
- Trustee sale (in states which use trust deeds)
- Sales for nonpayment of taxes including:
    - local property taxes
    - state income or other taxes
    - federal income or other taxes
- Sheriff's sale (demanded by an impatient judgment holder)
- All sorts of other situations like resale of property seized because it was being used by drug dealers.

An impending wipe-out auction is **good** news to a junior lien holder if his lien will be covered by the likely auction sale price. But the junior-lien holder can only recognize that fact if he or she is knowledgeable about the current market value of the property and the bidding patterns of local auction buyers on such properties.

Professional auction buyers and pre-auction buyers **do** possess that knowledge. But the lawyers and business executives who decide whether to accept your discount lien release offer generally do **not** possess that knowledge or even know where to get it. That is especially true when they are non-real estate people and when they are not located in the same area as the property in question.

On the other hand, virtually everyone knows that forced sales wipe out liens junior to the lien which triggered the forced sale.

Two case histories

Chicago-area investor Esther Joyal has obtained discount-lien releases twice. She buys foreclosures at or before the auction. If there are liens in excess of 80% of value on the property, she contacts the lienholder, tells him of the impending auction, and asks, "Do you intend to bid?" If they say, "Yes," or "Why do you ask?" she explains that she is interested in buying the property but only if the lien in question can be released at a discount. She then asks if they would like to get "something" for their lien, leaving them to mull over the implicit thought that they may get **nothing** if they **don't** come to agreement with her.

In one deal in 1988, she got a $13,000 judgment lien released for just $1,000. In another, she got the lien holder to agree to release the lien for less than half its face amount. She notes that institutions like retail chains and credit-card companies will often agree to release the lien for 50% of its face value.

Types of lawsuit lien

There are three types of lawsuit liens in California. Other states probably have similar liens. They are:

- Attachment lien
- Judgment lien
- Execution lien.

Each of these has an expiration date. That is, on the anniversary prescribed by law, the lien expires if it is not renewed. In California, judgment liens expire on the 10th anniversary of their being recorded, attachment liens, the 3rd; and execution, the 2nd.

Attachment liens are a sort of advance lien which is granted **before** trial if there is a high probability the creditor will win and a danger that the debtor might dispose of assets before the judgment is entered.

Homestead and other laws

Many states have homestead laws which make it hard or impossible for creditors to execute liens on the debtor's residence. To execute a lien means to get the sheriff to auction off the property to pay the debt. For example, in Texas, which has the homestead exemption most favorable to debtors, a person can declare bankruptcy and exempt from the bankruptcy up to one acre in a "city, town, or village," or up to 200 acres elsewhere. There is no dollar limit on the **value** of the property in question (Texas Property Code Annotated §41.001). That is, the Texan who lives on and owns a free-and-clear 200-acre ranch worth $10,000,000 can emerge from bankruptcy with the entire $10,000,000 ranch even though his creditors had to settle for pennies on the dollar.

By making it harder or impossible to get paid off out of the home owner's equity without his cooperation, these laws increase the probability that you can get a lien released at a discount. So if you want to play the lien-release game, you should become informed on the creditor/debtor laws in your state.

Title companies make expired liens exceptions to title insurance

Distress Sales Report editor John Beck (415-523-6115) says title companies routinely list **expired** liens as exceptions to title insurance. That means, the first mortgage lender insists that the liens be paid off at closing. As do many attorneys.

A smart buyer should post a bond or deposit with the title company covering the lien. Some title companies will accept that, which in turn, causes the lender to make the loan. Since the lien shows up at closing as a charge against the seller, the seller accepts that much less money at closing. The buyer should be able to get his money back from the title company by showing that the lien has expired.

How to find them

In general, this formula involves finding greater-than-80%-lien-to-value-ratio lawsuit-based liens on properties which are about to be sold to pay off a senior lien which is in default. You find them the same way you find all other forced-sale bargains: by following legal notices of defaults and auctions. The fact that a property is overencumbered will come out in your conversation with the seller or in the title report.

Approach

Since the owners of such liens are generally unsophisticated in the ways of real estate, you should educate them **selectively**. That is, you inform them as to the **dis**advantages of their position. For example, that the sale will extinguish their lien, that you won't buy unless they release their lien at a discount.

But do **not** inform them of the **advantages**, like the fact that they might get some excess proceeds from the auction. As always, do **not** do this with widows and orphans. It's OK to take advantage of sophisticated business people who simply disdain real estate expertise. But **not** people who lack any business sophistication at all but who have somehow come into ownership of a lawsuit lien.

When you seek to buy a lien at a discount...as opposed to merely seeking its release from one property ...you are well advised to keep the connection between the current or future owner of the property and the would-be lien buyer secret. Do this by **silence, not** by false statements.

Efficient screening of pre-forced-sale opportunities generally requires you to wait until about a week before the auction to contact owners. But don't wait that long with **overencumbered** properties. You need extra time to contact and negotiate with the lien holder(s). ᴊᴛ̇ʀ

12
Judgment Investing

Even in this time when it seems hardly any traditional real estate deals make sense, there **are** ways to buy interests in real estate for pennies on the dollar. One of those ways is buying court judgments.

Lloyd Walters

Lloyd Walters buys judgments. In the typical case, A sued B in small claims court and won. Then A found out how hard it is to **collect** such a judgment and forgot about it. Walters sends A a letter offering to buy the judgment for 10¢ on the dollar. If there are any unusual problems with the judgment, he offers less.

Walters offers 10% of the **judgment amount** only. The amount that can actually be collected is **greater** than the judgment amount because of the right to get court costs and interest from the debtor.

Sometimes, A counteroffers and Walters will go as high as 15¢. His cost runs from 2¢ to 15¢ on the dollar, averaging 8¢ or so. For example, he paid $50 for a $2,000 judgment in one deal.

Check out the debtor

If the owner of the judgment verbally agrees on the price, Walters checks out the debtor to make sure he owns real estate or other assets that can be levied against. If so, Walters completes the deal.

After Walters buys the judgment, he reports it to the TRW and CBI credit bureaus and records it against real estate owned by B if it's not already recorded. Then he sends B a letter asking that it be paid off.

Death and bankruptcy

In the $50 example above, done when Walters first started buying judgments, he made a beginner's mistake. The debtor had **died** and the probate period of the estate had **expired**. Fortunately, however, the transfer of the real estate had not yet closed. The title company found the judgment Walters had just recorded and sent him $2,000 out of escrow within six months of his purchase.

Dead debtors and those who go **bankrupt** are the big bugaboos in this business. Walters now checks the vital statistics in the county recorder's office for death certificates before he buys the judgment. If the debtor is dead, he checks to see if the probate of the estate has been completed. If the debtor is dead and probate and disposition of the estate have been completed, Walters does **not** buy the judgment. (If the dead debtor had his assets in a **living trust** to avoid probate, you may be able to collect from the trust. The county recorder's vital statistics only cover people who died in the county.)

Walters says that bankruptcy judges generally give short shrift to such "involuntary" liens as judgments. "Voluntary" liens like trust deeds receive more money in a bankruptcy in his experience. Walters says there is little you can do to protect yourself from bankruptcy of the debtor.

Walters tries to avoid the problem by buying only judgments small enough ($10,000 or less) that they are **nuisances** to the debtor; not a debt big enough to throw the debtor into bankruptcy.

Offer to debtor

Walters makes the following offer to the debtor:

If you give me a trust deed (mortgage in eastern states) on your real estate, and agree to pay it off according to a schedule, I will cancel the judgment (by recording a satisfaction of lien) which is currently recorded against you and clear the judgment off your record at the credit bureaus.

He asks for a one-year payoff but will take what he can get. He adds 10% per year since the judgment was entered by the court to the amount of the judgment. That's the statutory rate at which interest accrues on judgments in California. And his installment notes call for 10% interest as well so that Walters is no worse off interest-wise than he was just holding a judgment lien.

If the debtor agrees, Walters has traded an "involuntary" lien for a voluntary one. Then, if the debtor goes bankrupt, Walters believes he'll probably get some of any equity the debtor has in his real estate. In addition, it is far easier to foreclose on a trust deed or mortgage than it is to force the sale of a property to satisfy a judgment lien.

Walters has never had to foreclose on a judgment or a trust deed which the debtor agreed to substitute for the judgment lien.

Unfortunately, the debtor accepts this offer only in a minority of cases.

Wait

If the debtor turns down such an offer, you could just wait. Eventually, the debtor will want to sell, refinance, or just clear their credit rating and the new buyer or lender will almost certainly insist that the judgment be paid off.

If you could match Walters' experience of buying a judgment a day averaging $1,100 at a cost of 8¢ on the dollar, you'd buy interests in real estate worth $110,000 every 100 working days...at a cost of 8% x $110,000 = $8,800.

You'd have no management, no tenants, and no personal injury or toxic liability. You'd never have to deal with real estate agents, loan officers, or prospective purchasers. The value of your interests in real estate would **"appreciate"** at precisely **10%** per year **by law** (in CA...other states may have different interest rates. A decline in the value of the property could make it impossible to get the 10%.)

Initial cash flow

In several years, the buy-judgments-record-them-and-wait approach should produce $100,000+ in annual cash flow. But initially, cash will flow more slowly. To produce more cash flow in the early years, you could pursue the debtors more diligently.

Depending on state law and the facts of each case, you can garnish wages, force sale of property, seize rental security deposits (in the case of tenant debtors), have the sheriff confiscate their car or other personal property, seize the receipts of the debtor's business, force the debtor's own debtors to pay you money they owe him, or levy against the debtor's bank accounts. Essentially, producing initial cash flow in judgment investing is a **collection agency**-like operation.

Special state and federal laws apply to debt collection. Learn them before you act.

Faster payoff

Walters is experimenting with buying judgment liens on properties on which a **notice of mortgage default** has been filed. He figures the judgment lien holder will be eager due to the threat of being wiped out. And if the property sells for a high enough price, Walters will be paid off quickly with no collection effort on his part.

Foreclosure is rare. Only 3% of the default notices actually lead to auction. And completed foreclosure only wipes the lien **off that property**...and then only when the high bid is inadequate to cover the judgment.

Foreclosure does **not** wipe out the judgment entirely. The debtor is **personally liable** for the judgment. It is **not** like a nonrecourse trust deed...even in California where virtually all trust deeds are the sole security for the debt.

You can leave the abstract of judgment in the county records thereby attaching a lien to any other property the debtor owns or buys in the future. You can record it in as many counties as you wish as long as you pay the recording fees. And you can still use such collection methods as levying against bank accounts or garnishing wages.

How he finds them

Walters works with small claims and municipal court records. He does not buy judgments held by landlords against tenants (because evicted tenants rarely have assets). Most of the judgments he buys involve bad debts between friends, car accidents, and contractor or repair work which was done unsatisfactorily.

There are no data bases or printed summaries of the cases where Walters operates (Alameda County, CA). He or his assistants have to look at the case files. (There are, however, statewide data bases which can be used for **tracking down** the debtor.)

Walters conducts his business with both the owner of the judgment and the debtor almost entirely by mail. In spite of that, he says the one-a-day pace he achieved was very hard work.

In California, judgments are good for ten years. And they can be "revived" routinely for additional ten-year periods.

Walters has never tried it but I am intrigued by the possibility of buying judgments against former **college student** tenants. Let's say four guys rent a house. They don't pay the last several months rent and do some damage. The landlord sues and wins. But the students are judgment proof or go off to grad school or the army or whatever.

Years later, they come back as lawyers, doctors, businessmen, etc. I presume you can buy such forgotten judgments real cheap. And that the former students will have had both an attitude adjustment and a loss of their judgment-proof status.

Gotcha!

Walters' manual

Walters (415-829-2939) has a $59, 180-page manual called the *Complete Guide to Judgment Investing*. It's based on his experience in California and on California laws. ⬛

PART TWO

FINDING DEALS
THAT MAKE SENSE

13
Buyers Who Overpay: Part I

October 1989

In the 10/87 issue(See Chapter 15), I wrote an article called "Sellers Who are Likely to Sell Cheap." If you were waiting for the other shoe to drop, here it is.

Two categories

Two kinds of buyers are willing to pay more than normal market value for some properties:

- Lazy and/or incompetent buyers.
- Buyers who have a unique relationship to the property in question.

There is a large element of secrecy with these buyers. The lazy, incompetent ones don't want anyone to know that for obvious reasons. And those who have a unique reason to want a particular property strive mightily to keep that unique reason quiet.

You can represent the prices various buyers are willing to pay on a graph. One buyer will be willing to pay more than any other...let's say $100,000. He is the **high bidder** and he gets the property. The price he pays is the fair market value.

Perhaps two other buyers will pass at $100,000 but would have been willing to pay $99,000. Maybe four other buyers would have been willing to pay $98,000. At $97,000 there might have been seven buyers and so forth.

But this article is about situations where the graph would be **different**. In addition to the folks willing to pay $100,000 or less, there'd be a guy who'd be willing to pay, say, $110,000.

The trick is to systematically buy at market value or less...then sell to one of those few who will pay **more** than market value.

Case history

Listen to this disguised deal (amounts changed somewhat) which really took place recently. Investor spots piece of land next to hospital he knows wants to expand. Seller is in a hurry to sell. He gets the seller to agree to sell it to him for $400,000 putting a mere $8,000 deposit up. Then he offers it to the hospital for $790,000. They know they could have had it for $400,000 if they had been ready to act quickly. But their board requires months to approve such things so they just accepted the higher price. Aaaagh!

To we results-oriented entrepreneurs, that's insane. But in the narrow timid world of the process-oriented bureaucrat, following the policy manual...no matter how far astray it leads...is the way to survive.

Systematically tying up property in the path of expansion-minded bureaucracies is easier said than done but worth the detective work it requires because it can lead to spectacular profits.

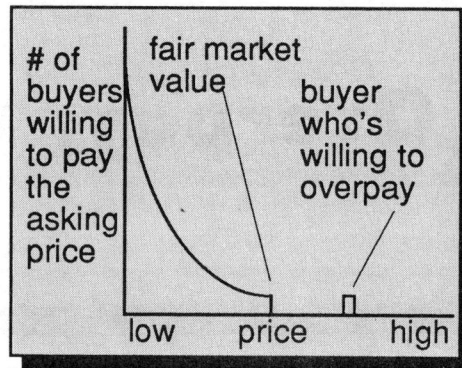

Value in use

Sometimes, it's logical for a buyer to pay more than market value...although it's **never** logical for him to **let the seller know** that. For example, when I sold my first duplex, the buyer said he did not want to inspect the inside of the property. Today, if a buyer said such a thing, I'd turn into a private investigator and find out who he was and why he **really** wanted my property. Back then, I sold him the property for market value.

Turns out he was a front man for a savings and loan whose branch was adjacent to my property. They needed my property to build a drive-thru window. It was sensible for them to overpay by real estate standards because they had **non-real estate reasons** for wanting the property. Their alternatives were to continue to lose business or to move the entire branch to another location. Paying an extra $10,000 or so would have been no problem. That's why they concealed the true identity of the buyer.

Moving is very expensive for most businesses. So they will often overpay by real estate standards to avoid it. You could specialize in scoping out which businesses in your area want to expand

and tying up property in their way. The owners might even go for options rather than forcing you to take title.

Many nonresidential rental property owners who would not normally agree to a straight option will agree to an option-to-purchase clause being inserted in a lease. I don't know why they reject the one and accept the other. Maybe the lease-option sounds like an afterthought whereas the straight option sounds like you're playing some angle.

So you might lease a property in order to get an option to purchase clause in the lease (the clause must be very detailed to be enforceable). You could sublease the property to a regular tenant at breakeven, a profit, or small loss while you waited for your sale.

Business and emotion

In "Partial Interests: Part I" in the 2/89 issue I quoted a study which said that tenants in common buy out their fellow tenants in common at a **premium** over market value 19% of the time. The premiums ranged from 6% to 35%. Those buyers paid more than market value because they had some business or emotional tie to the property. They very much opposed its being sold away from them or even a share of it being sold to an outsider.

Landlocked land

Bob owns landlocked land which is useless. If he had road access, it would be worth $70,000. George owns the land between Bob's land and the road. To everyone but Bob, George's land is worth $100,000. But Bob could afford to pay as much as $150,000 or so. Because having it increases the value of his **first** property by $70,000. And putting a road across George's old property would probably not diminish its value by more than $5,000 or $10,000.

You could systematically seek out land which is the best access to landlocked land and try to sell the land or part of it or an easement to the landlocked owner at a premium over its market value. In the alternative, you could option the access property then buy the landlocked owner out at the low landlocked price then resell the property with road access for the higher **un**landlocked price.

Assembly

Property can often be made more valuable by **combining** it with adjacent property. That's called assembly. It's the opposite of subdivision.

The value-increasing effect of combining smaller lots into a larger property more valuable than the sum of its parts is called **plottage**. Plottage creates buyers who overpay and logically so.

More famous examples of plottage occur in New York City. In his book, *Land Rush*, Mark Stevens, tells how New York developers acquire adjoining city parcels in great secrecy. For example, they have a different straw buyer for each parcel. Each straw buyer uses a different law firm. If the property is a restaurant, the developers hire a retired restauranteur so he can talk ovens with the seller and operate the restaurant after purchase until the needed parcels are all bought.

The assemblers are deathly afraid that the owners of the parcels they have not yet bought will **find out** that they are assembling them into a larger, much more valuable parcel. Then they will demand far higher prices.

The acquisition of the land for DisneyWorld was an example of a huge assembly conducted in utmost secrecy. Disney's disguised front men acquired 27,443 acres in the Orlando area for about $5,000,000 ($182.20 per acre) in the early sixties. On 11/15/65, Walt Disney revealed the plans to build DisneyWorld to the public. The land acquisition cost was just 5% of the total Disney expected to spend building the park. Clearly, they would have paid more than $182.20 for parcels they could not do without.

In its December 25, 1965 issue, *BusinessWeek* said more than 50 parcels had changed hands "…some at prices twelve times greater than before the Disney move was revealed." One 1965 investor offered $300 each for Orlando area lots that had sold at tax auction for $11 to $25 in '64. A property that was on the market in '64 for $10,000 was marked up to $70,000. The price increases didn't stop in '65 either. After DisneyWorld opened on October 1, 1971, a 2,500 acre tract that was worth $2,000 an acre in '67 went up to $130,000 an acre.

Even Disney is not a sure thing in the assembly business. The U.S. Forest Service awarded Disney the contract to build the Mineral King resort in Sequoia National Forest in '67. But the Sierra Club filed suit to stop it so neither Disney nor anyone else built Mineral King.

The assembly principle applies not only to mega developments like DisneyWorld. It appears in every nook and cranny of the U.S. on all sizes of deals. The bank drive-thru window acquisition I described above was a small-scale assembly which I could have profited from had I been smart enough to recognize it.

If you can spot an assembler, you can beat him out for one or more of the needed parcels. Then bargain hard when he gets to you. This is a tricky game because developers can sometimes build **around** holdouts who overplay their hand. Continued next month.JTR

14
Buyers Who Overpay: Part II

Ponderosa syndrome

In an episode of *Bonanza*, Hoss was escorting a man to the Ponderosa on horseback. The man asked, "How long till we get to the Ponderosa, Hoss?" "We've been on it for the last two days," said Hoss.

Many people are enamored of such empires and have a compulsion to own land...even if it's just a little land.

Slivers, vertical land, etc.

Distress Sales Report (415-523-6115) editor John Beck often writes about buyers who buy useless parcels of land at tax sales. For example, in his April/May 1989 issue he tells of a parcel that sold for $4,000 at a tax sale. According to the assessor's records, the parcel's "use code" was 003 which means "*vacant residential lot—totally unusable (incurable)*."

In March, real estate educator Ron Starr and a partner (who spotted the deal) bought a 25-foot-wide useless parcel on a steep hill in Alameda County, California (Oakland area). They paid $500 the day before it was scheduled to be sold by the county for nonpayment of taxes. They let it be sold at the tax auction and it went for **$4,600.** After the back taxes and costs were deducted, they got $2,139.89. (By California law, excess proceeds above taxes owed and costs are refunded to the persons who owned the property when it was sold at tax auction. Other states may have different laws.)

At that same auction, Starr saw two other lots sell for $20,000 each. Those lots were useless because their soil was unstable. A house on one had previously been demolished by a slide.

In a 1981 deal, Starr and a partner bought a to-be-auctioned property for $275. No one bid at the first auction. But within five years they got excess proceeds of $9,430.73.

This does not always work, however. Starr bought two to-be-auctioned lots in El Dorado County, CA (South Lake Tahoe area) for a total of $880. They ended up selling for less than the taxes owed so Starr got nothing for his $880. (Western Land Bank, which is discussed below, bought one and resold it, price unknown.)

10' x 150' lot

Several years ago, an acquaintance of Starr's bought a 10 foot by 150 foot sliver (It was created by a surveyor's error.) in Mill Valley, CA, an expensive suburb of San Francisco. He paid about $800 then resold it for about $3,000 all cash through a classified ad.

In another deal Starr witnessed, a man bought two Oakland lots on an earthquake fault for $1,000. He did not pay the property taxes thereby deliberately letting them go to sale at the tax auction. He received excess auction proceeds of about $21,000 seventeen months later.

These parcels are unsuitable to build on. But the compulsion to own land...and the notion that "you can't go wrong with real estate"...cause some to buy anyway.

Real estate can be useless because it's too small or the terrain is unbuildable or it's in a floodplain or odd shaped or lacks access, etc. Since it's useless, you'd think it's worthless...or at least that's the **logical** conclusion.

Too-small or odd-shaped parcels generally came about in the days before zoning (which arrived in the 1920's) or through surveyor error or as a result of the building of roads or other eminent domain proceedings. You can spot them on tax maps.

Cost, $500; resale price, $2,000

It appears that metropolitan-area, non-slum real estate doesn't sell, when advertised to the public, for less than about $2,000...**no matter how useless it is.** So if you can buy it before the public knows about it for, say, $500, you can probably sell it at a profit.

You can often buy useless property for $200 to $500. The typical seller is someone who finally realizes the property is useless and that its usefulness isn't going to improve. You are alerted to this fact when the property is listed as being in arrears on its property taxes.

As with foreclosures, you can buy **before** the auction, **at** the auction, or **after** the auction from the successful bidder. And as with foreclosures, buying before the auction generally provides the best bargains. As with partial interests, title problems, bad foundations, etc., the market for these properties is extremely thin. That's why you get a bargain. Two hundred dollars seems to be the minimum amount that's large enough to get the owner to go to the trouble of deeding it to you.

Now how do you resell it for $2,000 or more? A **classified ad** has worked for some. If you had a bunch of these properties, you might prepare a **catalog** with a title like "Own a lot in the Bay Area for less than $5,000." Offer it in ads.

Western Land Bank

Peter Bogart and his wife Punty are apparently doing quite well with a variation of this approach. Roughly speaking, it appears they gross about $2,000,000 a year on the sale of about 650 properties. The minimum bids printed in their catalog appear to be more than they paid for the property.

According to Beck, the Bogarts frequently buy property at tax auctions then hire an auctioneer and hold their own well-advertised, resale auctions in Los Angeles area hotels. The ads carry the name Western Land Bank. Beck says Punty Bogart bid on virtually every property at the August 31, 1989 Sonoma County, California tax auction, buying ten properties out of the 25 offered. Although their ad in the 4/10/89 *Daily Commerce* says "liquidation at 50%-60%-70% even 90% below market," she paid 128% to 322% of the assessor's fair market value estimate on nine properties and got one for 85% of assessor's appraisal. Beck says the Bogarts "can afford to pay 'crazy' prices because they can resell the same properties at even 'crazier' prices."

If you buy these properties from the owner **before** the auction, you should kiss the Bogarts for driving up the sale prices and thereby, the excess proceeds you'll receive. However, if you buy **from** the Bogarts or bid **against** them at auction, kissing may not be what comes to mind.

"Natural growth abounds"

A reliable source says Western Land Bank described one of their properties with the phrase, "natural growth abounds." He visited the property in question and says that while "natural growth abounds" was certainly an accurate description, most people would simply call the property a marsh.

The Western Land Bank offers 6% seller financing and fills its ads with bargain-connoting words like "foreclosures, tax deeds, R.E.O.s, probates, estates, bankruptcies, liquidation, depression priced." I surmise they feel it's appropriate to use those words on the grounds that that's where **they** got the properties. However, some buyers may be confused into thinking the Western Land Bank auction is an event where you can buy R.E.O.s **direct** from the lender or probates **direct** from the estate, etc.

The Bogarts did not return my first phone call and were reportedly on vacation the second time I called.

Let it go to tax auction

You might "market" the property through the county tax sale auction if the pertinent state law requires that excess proceeds be paid to the owner. Unlike private auctioneers, the county often charges little or nothing for this service. In California, the charge is $186.50. This let-it-go-to-tax-auction sale method is also the only one I know of where you don't have to sign a contract, get title searched, prepare a deed, etc. Check local law and observe several tax auctions before you assume you can profitably do this in your area.

According to Beck, every one of the twenty-five properties sold at the 8/31/89 Sonoma County auction produced excess proceeds. The excess proceeds ranged from $441.88 to $40,754.04. The average excess proceeds was $8,182.24. Had you bought **all** the properties **before** the auction for an average purchase price of, say, $1,000, you'd have made $8,182.24 - $1,000 = $7,182.24 x 25 = $179,556.

Environmental audit

In the environmental audit article in the last two issues, I said you should not buy real estate without making sure it's not contaminated. And that such audits cost from $500 to $30,000. In general, you cannot afford such audits on useless properties. But you'd better at least do a self-help, on-site inspection.

Another advantage of selling through the tax auction is that you don't have to make any of the usual disclosures, warranties, etc. However, local, state, or federal laws may require that you notify the government if you are aware of contamination. Such a sale would not absolve you of all liability. But it would at least immunize you against any **misrepresentation** charges.

Ethics

There is nothing wrong with selling a property for more than its market value as long as you do **not represent or imply** that the sale price is **at or below** market. You should limit the information you provide to such things as the legal description, the dimensions, the assessed value. You can say, "I'll let you have the property for $10,000." But do **not** say things like, "It's worth every penny of the price I'm asking."

Don't even imply that it **can** be used. For example, describing a lot as having a **view** implies that one could put a building on it. If building is not feasible, the word "view" could be attacked as deceitful.

In my opinion, you must also give the other person **fee simple** title. No oddball lesser rights like a lease-option unless the buyer is financially sophisticated.

I also would not use, in an advertisement or elsewhere, any name, word, phrase, or emblem that might cause people to think I was anything other than an individual, private seller. I would **not** use words like "R.E.O., tax deed, bankruptcy, etc." unless I made it clear that the seller was **neither** a lender or government or court or whatever...nor **representing** a lender or government or court or whatever.

Is it right to sell a product which is useless or largely useless? A vast number of common products are.

A guy made a million selling pet rocks. Surely, you are permitted to make yours selling pet lots.

And who is to decide the usefulness of the things people buy? Shall we deny the "bow wow" her bottle of Obsession? The wimp his pack of Marlboros?

The world is full of nobodies yearning to be somebodies. Owning real estate, even useless real estate, makes some people feel better about themselves …gives them a chance to drop lines like "I own some property up in Sonoma County" into conversations. Attention must be paid to these real estate Willy Lomans as they strut and fret their hour upon the stage. Let he who is without foible cast the first stone at them and the people who sell them their props.JTR

15
Sellers Who are Likely To Sell Cheap

October 1987

"Make your money the day you buy the property."

That's an often heard albeit easier said than done real estate investment admonition. The purpose of this article is to tell you ways you can **increase your chances** of buying property below market value.

Like a gold mining engineer working with low-grade ore, you need to produce tons of "tailings" (rejected properties) for every ounce of real estate "gold" you find.

This article, then, is a lesson in real estate "geology" to help you find the most promising, but nevertheless still low-grade real estate "ore."

The bell-shaped curve

You learned about the bell-shaped curve, also known as the normal distribution, in basic statistics. It says that in most things there is a large average contingent and much smaller contingents of above- and below-average.

In stocks, bonds, and commodities, there is **no** bell-shaped curve when it comes to buying something below market value, above market, or above market. All transactions are done **at** market. But in real estate, some properties **are** sold below market.

In general, those are the **only** ones you should buy. In other words, about 98% of the properties on the market are **off limits** to you.

Long-time owners

Positive cash flow makes you lazy. That's the title of an article I wrote a few years ago. The same principle applies to **resale gains**. The bigger the gain as a percentage of the original down payment, the less diligent the seller is about getting fair market value. In other words, guys who bought a property for $20,000 with $4,000 down sometimes aren't very concerned about the difference between a $200,000 offer in hand versus a possible $220,000 offer in the bush.

They're making a big profit no matter how you slice it. And in their laziness, they may fail to find out that the market value isn't the $220,000 they don't mind not chasing, but $230,000 or $240,000.

Only a small percentage of deals make sense

buyers pays **less** than market value but not **enough** less for adequate profit

buyer buys for **much** less than market value

buyer pays market value

buyer pays **more** than market value

Profit at close

NO profit the day you buy the property

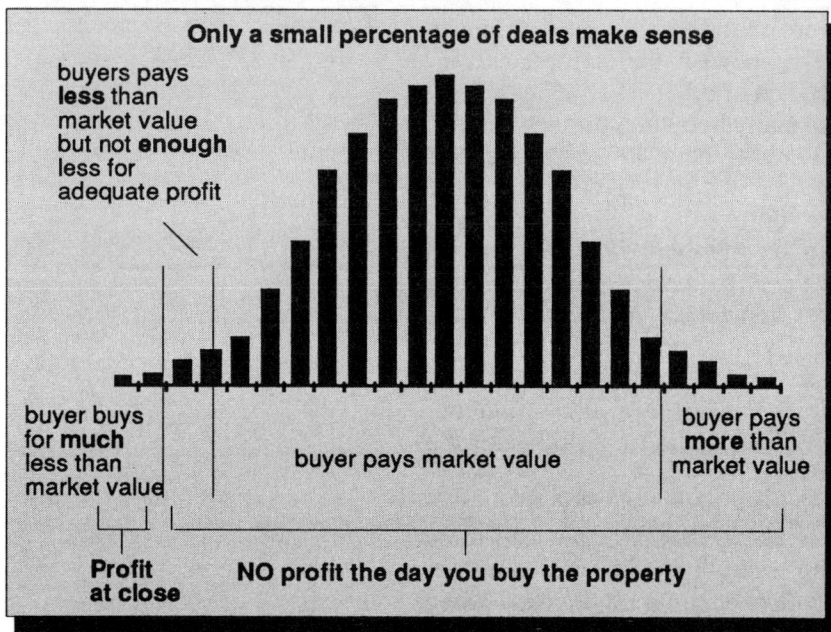

Sellers who have not been in the market for many years often do not realize the value of their properties. That's when you can get a bargain.

Indicated action: Systematically search property ownership records and make unsolicited inquiries to the owners with the longest tenure.

Not yet on the market

The vast majority of sellers are **out of date** and **behind the market** when they first contemplate selling. But most of those out-of-date people **suspect** that they are out of date and take steps to get **up to date**...like consulting with several Realtors®. Or if they are for sale by owners, they ask for the moon and get educated by the lower offers...or lack of offers.

That's why Dwain Sachs, a St. Louis investor, tries to make a deal with an owner **before** the property actually gets on the market. Sachs, who is also a Realtor®, pursues owners the way a real estate agent pursues listings. (He does not buy his own listings at bargain prices.)

At the first hint of the possibility that a property might be sold, Sachs is Johnny on the spot asking, "What'll you take for it?" To make the deal as quickly as possible and before the rest of the market starts educating the seller, Sachs pays **all cash** and closes this afternoon if you

need to. He gets his financing, if any, **after** he ties up the deal or buys the property.

To move with utmost speed, Sachs is wired. He's got portable phones in his home, a cellular phone in his car, and a beeper on his hip. He returns deal calls immediately. Seven days a week.

"His Accidency"

In a take-off on the royal title of "His Excellency," President Gerald Ford referred to himself as "His Accidency"...in light of his becoming President by the unexpected resignation of Richard Nixon. There are a lot of "His Accidency's" in real estate, too.

Accidental owners include:

- Lenders who foreclosed
- Heirs
- Donees (gift recipients)
- Surviving spouses
- Tax authorities

With lender and tax authority owners, the decisions are made by **bureaucrats** who do not own the property. They get paid the same whether the property sells for market or **less** than market. One REO ("Real Estate Owned" by banks as a result of foreclosure) officer told me that if he were on the outside, he could make a lot of money off the laziness and incompetence of other REO officers.

With many **heirs** and **donees** there is an "**easy come, easy go**" syndrome. The typical heir was not involved with the property **before** the death and does not wish to be involved **now**. He or she simply wants to know, "How much cash do I get and when do I get it?" This behavior is more true of children of the deceased than **surviving spouses**. But surviving spouses are also often not diligent about getting top dollar for the property.

Sometimes heirs sell cheap because they are **leaderless**. If mom had three children, each typically inherits a one-third tenant-in-common interest when she dies. In order to sell the property, **all** three must agree on everything. In many cases, the three siblings live far apart, are not close friends, and fought with each other as children. So **nothing** gets done. Especially true with **raw land**, which can be ignored more easily than improved property.

If one of the siblings cannot or will not take charge, **you** should. By doing the organizing and leading, you can often present the heirs with an opportunity to liquidate that has not occurred since they became owners...and is not likely to occur again. They may prefer your **below-market** offer in the hand to an unlikely market value offer in the **bush**. JTR

16
Sellers Who Welsh

As closing day approaches, sellers and optionors often find that they made a bad deal. The property is worth more than they agreed to sell it for.

No guarantor

In the options portion of stock and bond markets, the optionor has to eat the losses whether he likes it or not. The various clearing houses guarantee the optionee's profits. And the parties are required to put up cash in advance to cover the possible losses.

Not so in the real estate business. There is no clearinghouse guarantee. No cash or deed is put up in advance. Human nature being what it is, real estate sellers and optionors who made bad bargains often simply refuse to sell. This happens far more often than most investors seem to realize. As a result, buyers/optionees are often unprepared and lose their profit.

That's the **bad** news. The **good** news is that the needed preparation is straightforward and victims of seller/optionor reneging who sue generally win a lucrative judgment or settlement.

Case history

Bill Carrithers lease-optioned a house in Scarsdale, NY (the actual town was in the same region) in December of 1984 from Del Fuller (names changed to protect privacy). Here are the details of the deal:

- twenty-year old, four-bedroom, three-bath ranch house with a two-car garage
- Carrithers to occupy the house as his residence
- one-year lease with option to renew for one more year at $1,800 per month
- fair market rental value was $1,800
- lease includes fixed-price option to purchase house for $230,000 until December 1986
- fair market value of house was about $255,000 in Dec. '84.

No response

The New York area market appreciated rapidly in early '85 and Carrithers told Fuller he wanted to exercise the option in April of 1985. Fuller, who cashed Carrithers' rent checks every month, did not respond.

After Fuller ignored numerous demands to set a closing date, Carrithers' attorney sued Fuller for specific performance in the Spring of 1986. Carrithers suit also alleged that the optionor had forged his mother's signature on the option agreement and named as defendants the real estate agent and firm that had handled the deal and notarized the mother's signature

Carrithers had stopped paying rent in January of 1986. Fuller tried to evict Carrithers for that but Carrithers' attorney was able to prevent it (presumably on grounds that Fuller owed Carrithers far more money in the form of option profits and attorneys fees than Carrithers owed Fuller).

$120,000 profit

Carrithers moved to California in September of 1986 and the case was moved to federal court on "diversity" grounds (parties live in different states and amount in dispute greater than $10,000).

Trial was set for August, 1988. At that time, the house was worth about $350,000 to $400,000. As often happens, the trial's approach triggered serious negotiations and Carrithers settled for $100,000.

His attorney had taken the case on a contingency basis for a 30% fee so Carrithers netted $70,000. Carrithers does not know how the $100,000 was split between the defendants and their errors-and-omissions insurance carrier, if any.

Another case history

In 1976, a San Francisco Bay Area investor agreed to buy an apartment building there for $1,000,000. The seller signed the purchase agreement then refused to go through with the deal.

He had agreed to do an installment sale then said it would cost him too much in taxes. So the buyer accommodated him by going out and getting a new, institutional mortgage. But the seller still refused to perform.

That ticked the buyer off and he sued. He won the trial in '82 and got the property, which by then had risen in value to $2,800,000. The seller appealed but lost.

The buyer's **attorney fees** were about $500,000. But the court ordered the seller to pay about half that. Plus the buyer received the property's **net income** for the six years that elapsed between 1976 and 1982.

Attorney key

I often proceed in real estate matters without an attorney. A poll I took indicated you readers do, too. I generally **disagree** with the most successful advertising slogan of all time: "A man who acts as his own attorney has a fool for a client."

But when it comes to options or purchase agreements which call for closings more than 90 days hence, I strongly recommend that you have the documents drawn up by an attorney who has special expertise in that area.

That's because of the high incidence of reneging and the critical importance of properly drawn documents and buyer performance in winning a favorable resolution

Perform on your end

The attorney should also handle the attempt to **close.** A layman or underqualified attorney may feel that there is no point in going to closing if the seller or optionor states unequivocally that he or she will not perform.

But in order to prevail in a specific performance suit, you must prove that you fulfilled your end of the deal including **actually tendering the money.** If you fail to do that, the seller or optionor will win the case easily. (*Goodale v. West*, 5 C 339)

The money need not be set aside after the seller or optionor refuses to take it (except that you will need it again when you win the case if the court orders specific performance).

If the purchase agreement or option has a "time is of the essence" clause and deadlines or windows for closing, you must scrupulously comply with them.

Defenses against you

You must **not** have obtained the option by:

- Misrepresentation
- Concealment
- Circumvention
- Unfair practice

and you must show that you:

- Acted in good faith and
- Had "clean hands."

"Unclean hands" means you have "violated conscience or other equitable principle."

Title insurance

If you were going to **buy** a property, you would have a title search done and obtain a commitment to insure title from a title insurance company. But I surmise that lessee/optionees generally don't do that. **Do it** whenever possible.

An option, like a deed, can have great value. But as with a deed, an option is worthless if it's not signed by all the owners of the property. Furthermore, make sure the signatures are **notarized**.

Suing

As a general rule, you can sue **either** for **specific performance** (force the seller to deed you the property) or for **cash** damages. Cash damages would be better where the property had not appreciated much...or had gone down in value ...since the agreed upon closing date.

Furthermore, you are generally entitled to and should seek **additional damages** for the delay and litigation expenses...above and beyond the market value of the property at the time you had the right to buy it.

For example, you would normally be entitled to **rent** or **net income** from the time the seller illegally refused to sell to you until the time you actually receive the deed as a result of court decree. You can also get **injunctions** to prevent the seller or optionor from taking action that would adversely affect your interest in the property or for failing to take action that would protect it.

Buyers/optionees only

Buyers or optionees who sue for specific performance usually win. Make sure you understand that does **not** apply to **sellers.** To win a specific performance suit a you must prove that there was a valid agreement and that you lived up to your end of it.

For the **buyer or optionee,** that usually means just proving that you offered the money. **Sellers,** on the other hand, would have to prove all sorts of things. A buyer can find endless fault with the property and thereby legally get off the hook.

No one has the **right** to specific performance *per se.* The court has discretion (in California at least) to decide whether specific performance or cash judgment is the appropriate remedy.

Valid contract

An option to purchase must be as **detailed** as a regular purchase agreement. The usual well-drawn lease option is a lease with an attached purchase agreement. If it is not detailed enough, it may not be enforceable.

A one-sentence option to purchase in a lease is laughably inadequate...unless the lessor/optionor is willing to honor it. In the case history above, Bill Carrithers' lease option, which was drawn up by his attorney, had 37 addendums.

As with purchase agreements, an option must be **in writing** to be enforceable.

Fight back!

I am no fan of tv consumer reporter David Horowitz. But his slogan, "Don't get ripped off. Fight back!" applies in spades to sellers or optionors who renege.

Neither am I fond of litigation. But the belief among businesspeople that litigation is "not worth it" generally does **not** apply to suits against reneging sellers or optionors where the purchase agreement or option has significant equity (agreed-upon purchase price is less than current market value).

You'll probably win

In the typical business lawsuit for bad debt or breach of contract, the probability of winning is in the neighborhood of 50%. But the probability of winning in the typical buyer/optionee's specific performance suit is **higher**.

The San Francisco area investor above was advised by his attorney at the outset that the probability of victory was 80%. Some litigation pays you well for your time and for your investment in its cost.

Business opportunity

One might even be able to profitably engage in the business of buying the right to sue reneging sellers or optionors from buyers and optionees who don't want to be bothered. That'd be a sort of high-stakes cousin of the judgment investing I wrote about in the July issue.

To insure that the buyer/optionee provided the testimony you needed, you should probably make at least part of the money he gets from you contingent on his cooperation in the litigation and on its outcome. JTR

17
WSJ Article Says Fixers Rarely Profitable

An article in the April 13, 1989 *Wall Street Journal* ("This Old House May Not Be Worth Fixing These Days") casts doubt upon the current viability of the classic cosmetic renovation strategy advocated by William Nickerson in his book, *How I Turned $1,000 Into $5,000,000 in Real Estate in My Spare Time.* The *Journal* article quotes remodeler/investors in Boston and Seattle and the editor of the *Old House Journal* as saying the prices of fixers are generally too high these days to allow for renovation and profit.

The only profitable remodeler/investor the *Journal* found was a guy who adds a second story to tiny one-story houses in Arlington, VA. (I advocated that on page 84 of my book, *How to Incerase the Value of Real Estate.*)

Some markets still offer profitable renovation opportunities. I wrote about Lancaster, PA subscriber Jim Muldoon's sucess with the Nickerson method in the 10/88 issue. (See Chapter 18. Muldoon was the only one of about 3,000 subscribers nationwide who responded to a request in the newsletter that Nickerson practitioners contact me.)

But my impression is that most fixers sell too high these days. A fixer which would be worth $100,000 after $30,000 worth of renovation seems to sell for $87,000 or so. The buyers are newlyweds and other amateurs who are entralled with the opportunity to get into a $100,000 neighborhood for just $87,000. They plan to do most of the work themselves, place little or no value on their time, and grossly underestimate the time and money required to complete the job.

In fact, fixers sell so high, I recommend that you **not** follow the traditional advice to fix a run-down house up before you sell. Clean it, yes. But leave the bad roof, worn carpet, outdated electrical system, etc. to the idiot newlyweds. Indeed, it may even make sense to defer maintenance in single-family houses which you plan to sell. That sounds anti-social but the plain fact appears to be that pre-sale fixing does not make economic sense in most single-family situations.

JTR

18
The Nickerson Formula Lives

October 1988

Last month, I asked any readers who used the Nickerson formula to call me. Jim Muldoon (215-267-0187) of Lancaster, PA did.

The Nickerson formula, which is set forth in William Nickerson's classic book, *How I Turned $1,000 Into $5,000,000 in Real Estate in My Spare Time*, says you buy well-located, structurally sound houses or apartment buildings which need cosmetic renovation. Then you renovate them and raise the rents as a result of the renovation.

Nickerson says you should get $2 of property value increase for every dollar you spend on renovation. And his typical example has you putting 25% down and raising the value of the property through renovation and rent increases by about 25% over two years. Since he pays for the renovation out of the property's cash flow, the formula has you about doubling your money every two years.

The keys

I know more people who have **tried** it...including myself...than **succeeded**. Based on my interview with Muldoon, it appears it's working for him because:

1. Property can **normally** be bought on 11% cap rates in his market.
2. He spends **long hours** on weekends doing the work and supervising his helpers.
3. He buys labor and materials at substantial **discounts** below normal rates.

Nickerson would criticize Muldoon's doing all the work himself with just helpers. Nickerson said you can move faster if you subcontract. But Muldoon estimates that he would **not** be able to achieve Nickerson's two-dollars-of-value-increase-for-each-dollar-of-renovation standard if he had to use outside contractors.

Lime St. 5-plex

In 1983, Muldoon bought a five-unit apartment building for $75,000. It needed much clean-up and painting. Because of its condition, rents were depressed. Here are the before and after rents:

Unit	Before	After
1	$220	$220
2	$235	$285
3	$235	$300
4	$235	$325
5	$215	$350

To achieve this, Muldoon:

- Rrefinished the hardwood floors
- Wallpapered the bathrooms
- Replaced the kitchen cabinets with assemble-yourself versions and
- Replaced the kitchen counters with post-formed countertops.

Except for hiring guys to help with the painting at $4 to $5 an hour, Muldoon did all the work **himself**. He estimates 100 manhours per renovated unit. (#1 was just painted.) Muldoon's out-of-pocket expenses were about $4,000. If we value his time at $10 an hour, that's another 450 hours x $10 per hour = $4,500 for a total of $8,500. He agreed sell the building for $106,000 in February of '85.

Prospect St. 19-unit

Actually Muldoon **exchanged** out of Lime Street. Nickerson advocates that. So do I. Muldoon's attorney said it was probably the first exchange ever done in Lancaster County. I doubt that. But I'm not surprised that a tax attorney in that part of the country would **think** that.

Muldoon got excited about the 19-unit when he heard that the rents were about $250 on average. That's about $110 or 30% **below** the going rate for such apartments in the area. That $110 discrepancy provides the margin Muldoon needs for costs and profit.

He paid $235,000 for Prospect Street. $41,000 down, a $100,000 first from a bank, and a $94,000 second from the seller (fully disclosed to the first lender). Closing day numbers were:

Gross income	$57,924
Operating expenses	$24,270
Net operating income	$33,654

That's a cap rate of $33,654 ÷ $235,000 = 14.32%. And that's **before** renovation/rent increases.

Muldoon described Prospect Street as a, "Dirty, dirty old place. Hadn't been painted for twenty years. Terrible dirty. Grossest fingerprints you ever saw around the light switches." He attributes the high cap rate to the neglected condition. Although, he says **normal, clean** apartment buildings in his area would sell at 11% caps...which is unusually high by national standards.

The renovation

Prospect Street had old kitchens with cast iron sinks. Muldoon gutted the kitchens leaving only the plumbing. He got a "builders price" of $600 per apartment from a cabinet distributor on 19 kitchen and 19 bath cabinets. For the kitchen, that gets him a 96-inch kitchen cabinet unit with overhead cabinets, countertop, stainless steel sink, and lower cabinets. For the bath, the $600 includes 24-inch vanities with marble-like tops.

He got that discount even though he told the distributor he would only be buying one unit's worth **every two months**. Muldoon says the distributor's price is about 30% to 40% below normal. Lumberyards would only give him a 10% to 15% discount.

Muldoon buys his faucets, sink traps, and light fixtures from Maintenance Warehouse (800-431-3000) which he learned about from my book, *How to Manage Residential Property*... He likes them for such small items because they have decent prices and offer one-stop shopping by phone... which saves his time.

In addition, Muldoon also:

- Painted the exterior, hallways, and apartments
- Removed two evergreen trees which were growing up through some sycamores
- Refinished the floors and
- Cleaned dirty but intact tub tile with a product called "Bathroom Renovator."

Muldoon replaces most refrigerators with **used** friges he buys for about $200 from classified ads in the local weekly shopper newspaper. He buys new 20-inch **ranges** for about $300 which represents a small volume discount.

Time expenditure

Muldoon figures each unit in the 19-unit is taking about **330 manhours** to renovate...110 hours each for him and his two helpers. He found the helpers by running an ad in the classified which said simply,

"Work weekends renovating apartments. 267-0187"

He pays one relatively unskilled guy $5 an hour. The other guy, who is skilled, gets $65 a day or $8.13 an hour. Muldoon works side-by-side with them.

Rent increases

The average rent **before** renovation was $253; **after**, $359. His out-of-pocket costs are $1,400 for labor and $1,700 for materials for a total of $3,100. At a 10% cap rate, the $106 per month increase in rents increases the unit value by ($106 x 12) ÷ 10% = $12,720.

Nickerson said you should get two dollars of value increase for every dollar you spend on renovation. Muldoon is getting $12,720 ÷ $3,100 = $4.10 for every dollar. If you value Muldoon's 110 manhours at $10 an hour, the cost to renovate goes from $3,100 to $4,200 which is still $12,720 ÷ $4,200 = $3.03 for every dollar.

But Muldoon says if he contracted out the work as Nickerson prefers, the total cost per unit would rise to about $7,300. Then, the ratio would be $12,720 ÷ $7,300 = $1.74 for every dollar ...which is **below** Nickerson's two-for-one criterion.

Boiler windfall

A control device on the Prospect Street hot water heating boiler failed, allowing the boiler to crack. Turned out that was covered by his hazard insurance so he got a new boiler for free. One bidder said the **old** boiler had been **too big** for the building. So Muldoon got a new boiler which was much **smaller** but adequate ...as well as **more efficient** because of its modern design. The gas bill dropped from $12,000 a year to $8,000 as a result. That increases the value of the property $4,000 ÷ 10% = $40,000.

Binge strategy

Muldoon, by his own admission, is pursuing what I once called a "binge" approach. That is, he works long hours during which he focuses intently on his real estate formula. Binging generally brings people to their peak efficiency. And that's necessary to succeed with the Nickerson formula.

An old farmers saying holds,

"The best fertilizer is the shadow of the owner."

By working side-by-side with his helpers and diligently searching for bargains on materials, Muldoon makes extensive use of "owner's shadow fertilizer."

Move up to delegating

It's possible that if Muldoon **forced** himself to subcontract, he'd **learn** how to get the work done for a little less and cut his contract total cost enough to hit Nickerson's two-to-one ratio. That would, as Nickerson points out, speed Muldoon's progress. He now takes two months to complete **each unit** working weekends.

We all tend to have difficulty delegating. And delegating...or more precisely in this case...finding and supervising good contractors... is a skill which can be learned as surely as carpentry.

Workable; not easy

The main lesson of Muldoon's real world experience applying Nickerson's teaching is that Nickerson's formula still works... but it ain't easy. You really have to concentrate on acquiring the renovator's skills of buying labor and materials at prices **much lower** than normal. And getting adequate quality work at low labor rates requires close supervision.

I called William (now 80) and Lucille Nickerson and read them this article to get their reaction. They think Muldoon is working too hard. They'd have him contract out **all** the work thereby getting each job done **quicker** and freeing up time to find **more deals**.

Muldoon is pleased with his discovery that cabinet distributors are cheaper than lumberyards. But Nickerson was less impressed. "We bought from the **factory**."

The Nickersons had no tricks for finding general contractors though. They say they simply got three estimates from guys who advertised in the Yellow Pages, classified section, or apartment association magazine. And they found the very cheapest contractors generally offered **false** economy in that they were less efficient and required more supervision.

Muldoon's $1.74-for-one result using **contractors** is only 26¢ away from the $2-for-one Nickerson criterion. So they thought he might be able to meet the $2 standard by focusing more energy on finding slightly better **prices** on materials, slightly better **bids** from contractors, and especially getting slightly better **properties** on slightly better **terms**.JTR

19
Fourteen Who Outperformed Their Market

August 1988

Fourteen Syracuse, New York area buyers beat the pants off the other buyers in their region according to a study by a Syracuse law professor. Those fourteen each bought one of the many varieties of "leper" properties: **foreclosures.** Leper properties are properties which virtually all of those in the market shun. As a result of that shunning, some good deals get overlooked. The investors who are the heroes of this article selectively bought the best of the overlooked pile.

The Spring issue of *Real Estate Educators Journal* (312-372-9800) mentions a study of foreclosures which was written up in the *Cornell Law Review* (volume 70, page 850). I got the Cornell article and reanalyzed its figures from an **investment** standpoint. (The author wrote the article from a protect-the-consumer standpoint.)

Amateurs

The study of all the foreclosures in Onondaga County, New York (Syracuse area) which commenced in 1979 followed each property until August 1, 1984. According to the article's author, Steve Wechsler, only one of the twenty-seven non-lenders who were successful bidders bought more than one of the foreclosures. Thus I conclude that they were amateurs, rather than professional foreclosure buyers. Although when you see how much money they apparently made you'll agree they lost their "amateur status."

All but one of the **non-lender** buyers (77% were bought by the foreclosing lenders) made a surprisingly high gain on resale. The study does not say how much, if any money, was spent on **fix-up** by the buyers before resale. But the **most** spectacular gain was made in a property that was resold so fast...42 days after foreclosure... that fix-up seems unlikely.

1,115% appreciation

The indicated **annual** appreciation rates on the fifteen resold, nonlender deals in the *Law Review* article (see box) ranged from 18.74% to 1,115.81%...with

Foreclose Date	Foreclose Price	Resale Date	Resale Price	Resale Profit	Daily Apprec.	Annual Apprec. %
7/18/79	$14,965	5/8/80	$28,250	$13,285	$45.03	109.84%
7/20/79	$23,300	3/18/80	$34,250	$10,950	$45.25	70.88%
8/1/80	$21,000	6/6/81	$35,750	$14,750	$47.73	82.97%
7/3/79	$6,970	2/3/81	$14,750	$7,780	$13.39	70.12%
7/5/79	$33,500	4/14/81	$45,750	$12,250	$18.88	20.57%
9/27/79	$84,500	10/29/80	$101,766	$17,266	$43.38	18.74%
7/15/80	$23,500	3/20/81	$35,250	$11,750	$47.38	73.59%
10/9/79	$4,200	5/13/81	$19,750	$15,550	$26.72	232.19%
9/4/80	$17,500	1/21/82	$34,750	$17,250	$34.23	71.39%
12/4/79	$15,500	11/11/80	$22,750	$7,250	$21.14	49.77%
5/7/80	$12,150	6/18/80	$27,750	$15,600	$371.43	1115.81%
2/8/80	$16,600	10/16/81	$39,750	$23,150	$37.58	82.63%
1/9/80	$70,000	11/21/80	$67,250	($2,750)	($8.68)	-4.52%
8/15/80	$26,800	3/25/83	$68,750	$41,950	$44.07	60.01%
8/15/80	$24,400	3/27/81	$78,750	$54,350	$242.63	362.96%

a median of 71.39%...at a time when the Northeast region existing house appreciation rates were:

Year	Appreciation Rate
'79-'80	13%
'80-'81	5%
'81-'82	-.3%
'82-'83	14%

Most lenders lost

The **lenders** in the sample did less well. They **lost** an average $14,000 per foreclosure. Keep that and lenders' traditional conservatism in mind next time you are tempted to rationalize taking back a mortgage with the line,

"The worst that can happen is that I get the property back."

Twenty-two percent of the lenders in this study were **individuals** who had sold the properties and taken back mortgages. The lenders were made whole by foreclosure and subsequent resale in only 44% of the cases. And the study includes no amount for carrying costs. So one can assume that net of carrying costs, the made-whole percentage was even **lower** than 44%.

Some lenders won big

Some of the lenders did almost as well as the nonlenders though. On the deals in which the foreclosing lender resold at a profit, the annualized appreciation rates ranged from 56% to 1,067%.

Any surplus over the foreclosed lien and costs goes to the **borrower** at foreclosure. But when a lender profits by reselling the property **after** foreclosure, the lender can not only **keep** all the profit...they can still go after the borrower for a **deficiency judgment** if the foreclosure proceeds were less than the loan plus costs...where deficiency judgments are allowed under the terms of the loan and state law. A deficiency judgment is a decision by a court forcing the borrower to pay the lender, in cash, the shortfall between the amount realized at the foreclosure auction and the balance of the loan and costs at the time of the auction.

Other observations

Other interesting facts in the study:

• When lenders bought the property, the foreclosure price was less than the mortgage more than ninety percent of the time. But when **nonlenders** (investors or home buyers) bought the property, less than 39% of the sale prices were below the amount owed.

- Only one lender sought a **deficiency judgment** even though there were apparent deficiencies in 80% of the foreclosures and both the mortgages and state law allowed deficiency judgments. The lender in question won the judgment but could not collect it.

- Author Wechsler who is a lawyer and MBA expressed the suspicion that the nonlender buyers "...*were snapping up the most attractive properties at foreclosure and leaving the depreciated and neglected parcels for the [lenders]*." What the heck did he expect?

- The median amount owed (for costs, fees, real estate taxes, etc.) above the loan balance was **7%** of the loan balance.

- About a third of the **nonlender** buyers **still owned** the properties at the end of the study period.

- Lenders in Onondaga County who were interviewed as part of the study insisted that lenders **never** made money on resale of foreclosures. When confronted with examples, they dimissed them as flukes.

Doable but not easy

I pounced on this study because it purports to show the **entire** foreclosure market in that county for one year. The success of the fourteen nonlender buyers who resold proves that the high returns I urge you to insist on are actually **available**. The fact that there were **only** fourteen shows how rare such deals are...another point I've been trying to make lately. And finally, had I just told you about **one** of these deals, you might have wondered if it was a one in a thousand shot.

Nope. It's a 14-in-118 shot. That was the actual incidence of this particular variety of deals that make economic sense during the 1979 study period. (The nonlender buyers who **held** their properties may also have bought at bargain prices.)

Not in *today's* market

Whenever I use an example from the **past**, some readers grouse that:

"Those days are gone. It's much harder today."

Not according to Ernie Kessler. He's been buying foreclosures in the Maryland-DC area since 1981. And he publishes a listing service (*Foreclosure Hotlist* 301-294-2274) for other foreclosure buyers. He won't consider buying a foreclosure property unless it has at least 25% equity. The percentage of foreclosures in his area that **meet** that criterion has been as low as 10% of the 250 to 300 that come up there each month. But lately, it's been **40%**...the **highest** he's ever seen.

"Not in *my* county"

Citing an Onondaga County, New York study will also undoubtedly inspire some to utter those words which are the bane of all nationally-oriented real estate gurus:

*"Well, **sure**, you can do that in Onondaga County. But this is _____ !"* [insert your county]

According to the *Almanac of American Politics*, Syracuse is ,

"...sufficiently middle American that for many years it was a favorite test market site."

To hear the typical "It-won't-work-here" heckler tell it, you'd think his local real estate market was Mars compared to where the technique you talk about was used.

John Beck, foreclosure buyer, author of several books on foreclosures, and publisher of the *Distress Sales Report* (415-523-6115) newsletter is thoroughly familiar with the California and Texas foreclosure markets. Plus he has lectured on the subject all over the country and spoken to foreclosure buyers nationwide. He says the Onondaga County figures are representative of what he sees **nationwide**...in **today's** market.

Foreclosures are tricky

Switching from buying regular properties to buying foreclosures is not the same as switching Realtors®. Even **experienced** real estate investors need re-tooling to enter the foreclosure market. It's a very complicated game...where the rules vary from county to county and state to state. Success requires meticulous record-keeping, efficient investigation of values and liens, willingness to buy buildings you are not allowed to inspect inside, etc.

So you should use this article as a springboard to **study** foreclosure investing...not as instruction on how to **do** it. Both Beck and Kessler do local seminars which interested investors in the MD-DC or California areas should attend. Also Beck's books on the subject are excellent. (Kessler has not written a book.)

The fact that some **lenders** who foreclosed made big profits ...and that they seem unaware of it...suggests buying mortgages which are in or about to be in default as a strategy. (See "Back-Door Vulture Strategy" in the October '87 issue. See Chapter 51.) JTR

20
Alcoholic and Drug Addict Sellers

June 1988

In January, Jeff Griffin went to Darlwin Britt's Gary, IN house to board it up for the mortgage company that had foreclosed on it. The heat, water, and electric had been off for several days. It was littered with drug paraphernalia. And in a padlocked second-floor bedroom barricaded from the outside with a refrigerator, he found 9-year old Darlwin Carlisle, Britt's daughter. Her frostbitten legs had to be amputated at mid-calf.

The girl's mother, who was charged with felony neglect of a dependent, left the house to buy milk and cookies and never returned. That's an extreme example of the generally unrecognized connection between alcohol or drugs, and real estate.

Millions of addicts

Fourteen million Americans are addicted to alcohol; two million, to cocaine; and half a million, to heroin. Many of those addicts own real estate. They either bought it **before** their addiction got bad... or they **inherited** it. And sometimes, they sell real estate they **don't own**.

You are **more** likely to run into an addict if you buy **foreclosures**.

Few in their right mind would let a property in which they had equity be foreclosed. They'd either find a way to make the payments or sell it, right?

But the addict property owner is **not** in his right mind.

Capacity

Capacity is the key **legal** issue when buying from an addict. The sale can be voided if the seller was "...entirely without understanding..." or had an "unsound mind" at the time he or she signed the necessary documents. (*Deering's California Civil Code* § 39) The seller's right to rescind is not dependent on the buyer being **knowledgeable** about the seller's unsound mental state or having fraudulent intent. (*Weseman v Latham*, 153 CA 2d 841) The law in your state may be different.

Fidelity National Title executive Zana Bata says the one time she handled an addicted seller she made sure there were:

• Extra witnesses

- That every aspect of the closing was explained in great detail, and
- She and the witnesses took great care to observe signs of the seller's mental condition.

Notaries are supposed to refuse to notarize the signatures of persons who appear to lack legal capacity as a result of being under the influence.

It is **not a crime** to buy from a seller who lacks capacity. Nor is the sale void. But it is **voidable**. That is, the seller or his guardian, conservator, heir, etc. may sue to rescind the sale and will prevail if they can prove the seller lacked capacity at the time of the conveyance.

Guardians and conservators

If a person is "substantially unable to manage his own financial resources or resist fraud or undue influence," a court is supposed to appoint a guardian or conservator. (*Deerings California Probate Code* §1701) Thereafter, the addict's property can only be sold if the guardian or conservator signs the appropriate documents. In most cases, the guardian or conservator **also** needs a specific order from the **court** to do something as important as sell real estate. If you buy from a person who has a court-appointed guardian or conservator, make sure you get copies of:

- Court order appointing the guardian or conservator
- Court order authorizing the sale
- Signature of the guardian or conservator on all the necessary selling documents.

A notice of guardianship or conservatorship should be **recorded**. It should turn up when the title company searches the records under the name of the seller. But it's possible that the seller may have a guardian or conservator who does **not** show up in the title search.

Fraud

Underwood says industrywide title fraud claims are up 13% over last year. He attributes the rise to a general decline in morality of which drug abuse is a part. Most title claims involve **forgery**. Drug-related examples include an addict son who sells his mother's house without her knowledge or an addict who forges his or her spouse's signature.

Trend

Contrary to the impression the media have created in recent months, drug abuse is **not** increasing. The number of coke and heroin addicts has been steady for a number of years. Marijuana use is declining. Crack is the only category that's increasing.

Mortgage industry groups have no statistics on the relationship between alcohol or drug abuse and mortgage foreclosures. Their studies show divorce, excessive debt, job loss and such as the main causes of mortgage default. Of course, those events are, in turn, often caused by alcohol or drug abuse. It's hard to come up with statistics on the role of alcohol and drug abuse in foreclosures because of the inherently embarrassing and/or illegal aspect of the problem.

John Beck, publisher of the *Distress Sales Report* (415-523-6115), says one of his properties was burned to the ground. The fire department blamed **free-basing** cocaine. Beck believes that a "substantial percentage of those properties with considerable equity which come up for foreclosure sale are drug- or alcohol-related."

In John's May issue, he tells how foreclosure buyer, Ted Thomas made a quick (six weeks) $38,000 profit on a pre-foreclosure purchase of a house in the best neighborhood in Alameda, California. Thomas had to remove four truck loads of beer bottles as part of his clean up. Neighbors thanked him for buying the place.

Dealing with addicts

Burt Sanders (name changed to protect the addict's privacy) was hot after a property which was in foreclosure. It was owned by an addict. Sanders left note after note for the seller...whose gas, electric, and water had been turned off for two months...but who was still living in the house.

When the addict finally responded, Sanders negotiated with him at 11 pm under a street light in front of the house (no electric, remember?) and agreed to pay the seller $10,000 cash the following morning... just hours before the auction. But the addict didn't show on auction day.

You get in touch with an addict the way Kojak gets in touch with a snitch.

"It was 11:13 am. Raining buckets. I was nursing my third cup of coffee at a window seat in Marge's Diner. Reading a dog-eared copy of Real Estate Investor's Monthly *when I spotted him. I tossed a sawbuck on the table and ran across the street. 'Who loves ya, baby?'"*

And you make **appointments** with addicts the way you would respond to a call from a lost four-year old. *"Where are you right now? Stay right there. I'll be there in ten minutes."*

Sanders ultimately bought that property at the foreclosure auction November 5, 1987. He paid $80,700. Spent about $7,000 cleaning (including drug paraphernalia removal) and fixing it up. And, in May, a refinance appraisal put the value at $165,000.

The addict got $567.98 (the excess of the $80,700 bid over the foreclosed loan balance). Had the addict shown up the day of the auction, he would have received $10,000 cash net direct from Sanders... in effect, a sale price of over $90,000.

In December, Ernie Kessler, publisher of *Foreclosure Hotlist* newsletter (301-294-2274), went to a foreclosure auction. A house with multiple mortgages was being foreclosed by the first lender who bid $30,800. Kessler bid $30,900...and won. Tenants living at the property subsequently told Kessler that their landlord had recently become a cocaine addict. The property was worth $85,000.

You say you don't want to hang around the kind of neighborhoods where alcoholics and drug addicts live? I agree. You should not even **drive** through...let alone buy property...in neighborhoods **dominated** by alcoholics and drug addicts and other undesirables. This article is not about buying in druggy **neighborhoods**. Rather it's about buying from druggy individual **sellers**. There are alcoholic and drug addict sellers in **your** neighborhood. In **all** neighborhoods. The property Burt Sanders bought was in a perfectly nice San Francisco suburb.

Before or after foreclosure?

If you buy an addict's property **at** the foreclosure auction or from a **lender** who took deed in lieu of foreclosure, you generally don't have to worry about the problems described above. Those problems come up only when you buy **direct** from the addict **before** foreclosure has been complete.

In general, you get a **better price** dealing with the owner than with the lender or at auction. Remember that while foreclosure wipes out all junior liens, deed **in lieu** of foreclosure or selling the property to you **prior** to foreclosure do **not** wipe out **any** liens. And that it is common for an addict who is delinquent on his mortgage to also have liens for nonpayment of taxes, alimony, child support, judgments, water, you name it.

Always get title insurance when you buy real estate. And **especially** when you buy from an alcoholic or addict. Most of the problems that can arise are then the title company's worry.

If you buy from an addict or anyone else after a notice of default is filed in California, make sure you comply with the **Home Equity Sales Statute** (California Civil Code §1695).

Ethical?

Is it ethical to buy real estate from alcoholics and drug addicts at less than market value? Yes, as long as you abide by the law. The discount arises from their neglect of their responsibilities and their inability to fulfill the duties of the owner in a normal sale, e.g., keep the place presentable, give the real estate agent reasonable time to find a buyer, etc. Those problems, in turn, arise from a decision they made when they were definitely **sober**…the decision to get high using chemicals known to be ruinously addictive. In effect, they decided to risk such eventualities as selling their property for less than market value each time they got high.

The discount is also partly compensation to you for the extra effort you have to make…and extra risk you have to take…to buy from these people.

When inspecting or cleaning up a drug addict's property, look out for **needles**. They are one of the prime ways **AIDS** is spread.

Let's be careful out there.JTR

21
A Corporation and Its Real Estate are Soon Parted

April 1988

We're not in the real estate business.

That's the "Mating Call" of the businessperson who owns real estate as part of a **non**-real estate business. And therein lies an opportunity.

Non-residential users

This article is about non-residential users of real estate. A user is an owner-occupant. For example, a printing company may own and occupy an office-warehouse building. A chain of clothing stores may own some or all of the buildings it occupies. Etc.

When it comes to real estate, most non-residential users are **dumb**. Not because of low IQs. Rather they aren't interested.

The printer's balance sheet may show that his office-warehouse is 25% of his assets...but he thinks he's a **printer**, not a real estate investor.

Disdain for real estate

Not only are users ignorant of real estate. They **disdain** it. The real estate department of many large corporations is where they send you when you are derailed from the fast track. The elephant's graveyard of corporate bureaucrats. Career Siberia.

Smaller company executives and entrepreneurs bristle if someone hears that they own a building and says, "So, you're in real estate?"

"Oh, no. I just own the building as part of my printing (or whatever) business. I'm a printer (or whatever)."

Only when they get to their true profession does their chest pop out again. Therein lies an opportunity.

The opportunity

People who "aren't in the real estate business"...but own mucho real estate...probably don't know what what their real estate is worth. And if they don't know what it's worth, you may be able to buy it from them for **less** than it's worth.

Mind you, these guys are rarely **total** fools. If you make them an offer, they'll probably make some effort to find out if it's a fair offer. Especially entrepreneurs. Corporate bureaucrats may just get a CYA appraisal...or less.

Appraisal not enough

But asking an appraiser and a friend in the real estate business often is not enough to ascertain true value. Case in point: Steve Roulac (415-433-0300) is a consultant who, among other services, tries to help large corporations **avoid** selling their real estate for less than market value. One of his clients had a piece of surplus land. They had it appraised by an M.A.I. and were about to sell it for the appraised value of $4,000,000.

Roulac's firm looked into the deal and said the present value of the property was **$16** million if developed as Roulac recommended.

From $1 to $1,000,000

One of Roulac's competitors, Hoffman Associates, had a client in the Northwest in the '70s. They had a surplus warehouse with 100,000 square feet as I recall. The client tried to sell it. No offers. They tried to lease it. No tenants. Finally, they tried to give it to the city for one dollar. No dice.

Hoffman Associates talked to other industrial tenants in the vicinity of the building. Many of them wanted to expand. But none needed 100,000 square feet.

So the client followed Hoffman's recommendation to divide the space into bays of the size the nearby tenants needed. The property leased up so that it had a capitalized value of about $1,000,000.

School boards are users. One of my seminar attendees told me of a case where the board declared a school surplus. Two appraisers said it was worth $220,000 and $280,000. Fortunately for the school board, state law required them to **auction**

the property. It sold for $475,000. So the typical user behavior of hiring an appraiser does not preclude bargains.

Sale-leasebacks

If you make users an offer to **buy** their building, you inspire them to make sure the property's not worth more than the offer. I suspect you'll have more success offering **sale-leasebacks**.

Let's say a company owns a building worth $1,000,000. You offer them a sale-leaseback on terms which give you a 12% yield. To the seller, the deal looks like **financing**. Only it's a **better** deal than their banker will give them.

The banker wants a floating rate, short-term note. You are willing to give them a long-term, fixed-payment lease subject only to cost-of-living increases. And your "loan-to-value" ratio is higher than what the bank is willing to do. So the seller gets more cash to put into his non-real estate business.

He may not see himself as being in the real estate business. But he sure sees himself as being in the business of getting **financing**. And you've just offered him a better deal than the financiers are willing to offer. So he evaluates the deal as a financing opportunity...not as a sale.

Not even an appraiser

Do businesspeople hire appraisers to make sure the value the lender's using in his loan-to-value ratio is correct? Of course not. So a sale-leaseback may enable you to buy for 20% or more below market by increasing the chances that the seller will not get up to speed on real estate values.

I oppose the use of unusual finance techniques to fool widows, orphans, and other unsophisticated folks. But I have no such qualms about successful businesspeople who disdain real estate. They are fair game.

Become bilingual

You speak real estate. But that's not the language of the user. They're not in the real estate business, remember? You'll need to learn to speak **their** language. Do that by geting belly to belly with user decision makers. Keep your eyes and ears open. After you've tried to buy real estate from a half dozen or so users, you'll start to speak their language and understand what makes them tick.

Campeau & Federated

The recent takeover of the Federated department store chain by shoping mall developer Robert Campeau assisted by Edward DeBartolo, another shopping mall developer, is a manifestation of the user-and-his- money opportunity. Department stores are users of real estate... extremely important users because of their anchor tenant role.

Department store people knew that...or thought they did. But they apparently did not realize just **how** valuable they were to real estate developers. So now they **work** for real estate developers.

"Surplus" real estate

Big corporations, school boards, and others often have "surplus" real estate. I have never regarded any of **my** real estate as surplus. Nor have I ever known a real estate investor who did.

Calling valuable property "surplus" is a telling manifestation of the attitude of the institutional bureaucrat toward property under his control. And it is one of the words you need to learn in order to speak the user's language.

Help these folks who are "not in the real estate business" rid themselves of their annoying "surplus." JTR

22

How to Make Money By Splitting Off Excess Land

July 1986

Buildings need a certain amount of land. If you have too little land, your building value will suffer. But **more** than you need rarely adds to the value of your property. When you have more land than you need, you should consider splitting off the excess. If you can sell the excess, the remaining property typically will not drop in value at all...or will drop less than the amount you got for the excess. In other words, the value of the parts may be greater than the value of the whole.

Double lot

You often find a single-family house on a double lot. The extra lot may even be on a separate deed. The obvious solution is to sell the lot to someone who wants to build a house there. But if the vacant parcel is buildable, the guy who sells you the property will probably either split it off himself...or demand that you pay the price of the house plus the price of the lot.

The more common and more useful circumstance is that the double lot no longer meets zoning standards. That is, when the homes were originally built, a house could have been built on that lot. But zoning has since changed so that the lot is **too small** to build on.

Get a variance

If a variance is required to make the lot buildable, the guy who sells you the property will generally **not** expect you to pay anything...or at least not very much...for the excess land.

The trick to getting a variance is usually to hire the local attorney who is known as **the** guy to use to get zoning variances. Frequently, he's well-connected politically and may even be a former city councilman or mayor or some such. If the cost of getting the variance (attorney's fee) is less than the value created, you'll make a profit when you split off the excess land.

What if no variance?

What if you can't get a variance? Is excess land which is too small to build a house on worthless? Maybe not.

Often, you can sell it to an **adjacent property owner**. He may want it to add to his building. Or for parking. He may want to put in a swimming pool or patio or tennis court. Or maybe he just wants it to feed his Ponderosa complex. "When do we get to the Ponderosa, Hoss?" "Shucks, Sam, we've been on it for the last three days."

The reasons is no concern of yours…unless it would decrease the value of your property. All you need to know is to approach adjacent property owners and ask if they'd be interested. You should have a price in mind. Make it reasonable. We're talking about an awfully small market here. And you may need some patience. The adjacent property owner may never have thought about it before. The seed you plant may take some time to take root.

Identify a specific use

Ask a knowledgeable person in the area what specific uses would be allowed to your neighbors if they added the excess land. For example, local law may require an acre in order to have a horse on the property. If your excess land is enough to raise the adjacent property owner over an acre, you might approach him with the line, "Would you have any interest in buying part of my property if it would enable you to have a horse on your property?" Parents of 11-year old girls are especially good targets for that one.

It's never a good idea to rely on your customer's imagination when you're selling something. That's why builders have furnished sample homes. So do some research so you know what **specific** benefit your neighbor would get from buying your excess land. Draw up a plot plan showing the current borders and your proposed borders and give it to him.

Or maybe *you* should add

If your excess land is too small to build on…and you can't get a variance…maybe *you* can buy more land from an adjacent property owner so that your excess land becomes large enough to build on. That'd be a case of the value of the whole being greater than the value of the sum of the parts. It's called plottage or assemblage.

If turning your excess land into a buildable lot is not possible, you might consider adding to your building. Be careful, though. It's easy to overimprove for the neighborhood. Adding a garage in a neighborhood which does not have garages may not add to value because people who pay more want not only a garage but also a higher priced neighborhood and a larger, higher quality house.

Works for income property, too

Split off works for **any** kind of property…not just single-family houses on oversize lots. Apartment buildings, office buildings, shopping centers, and industrial buildings often have lots which are larger than they need. Lots which could be trimmed with little or no effect on the value of the remaining property.

Again, the adjacent property owners are the primest customers. I sold my first duplex to an adjacent (catercorner) savings and loan which needed my property to construct a drive-through window.

Look at your survey or plot plan. If you don't have one, create one with graph paper. Ask yourself if any of the sides can be partially or completely cropped with little or no harm to the remaining property. If so, see if you can sell off the unnecessary portion.

One of the few legitimate nothing-down techniques

Split off of excess property is one of the few legitimate nothing down techniques.

Let's say you find a property selling for $1,000,000. The seller wants $180,000 down. It's an office building next to a thriving shopping center. The office building originally was to be one of two structures on the land. But the builder went broke before he could start the second phase. Then the zoning was changed to prevent buildings more than two stories high in that location. Attempts to get a variance have failed.

What about the shopping center owner? He's thriving. There's an excellent chance the shopping center owner would jump at the opportunity to expand by buying your excess land for more parking or more stores or both.

If you could sell the land to the shopping center owner prior to closing for $180,000 or more, you'd have yourself a nothing down deal. And a profitable one at that. Because your building would be worth $1,000,000 or close to it without the excess land. But your loan balance would be just $1,000,000 - $180,000 = $820,000. So you got in for nothing down yet when closing is over you have $180,000 **equity**.

If you do just **one** deal like that as a result of reading this, you've paid for 1,875 years worth of **Real Estate Investor's Monthly**.乃ℝ

23
Property Wanted Ads

November 1988

You've seen "property wanted" ads in the newspaper all your life. Did you ever wonder if they work?

They do. The fact that they **continue** to run in the paper is proof of that. Advertising is funny that way. When it comes to ad copy-writing, it's hard for your competitors to keep any secrets because, by definition, it's publicly displayed. You can even figure out which copy works best by watching which ads run longest.

Wording of the ad

There aren't many variations of a property wanted ad. Virtually all seem to offer the same things:

• Quick action
• No commission
• All cash
• Will take anything
• No inspections.

Many ads specify interest in foreclosures (**pre**-foreclosures actually) or in a particular property type. One foreclosure-seeker ad in the *LA Times* began, "Save your credit."

The general idea of most of the ads is that the guy who's running it has **cash**, will close practically **overnight**, and is not **choosy**. A property-wanted ad which appeared in the August 26, 1988 *Wall Street Journal* seemed to claim the **ultimate** in lack of choosiness:

"Fed up with due diligence buyers? Call us."

Due diligence buyers are people who check out a property before they buy it. Another advertiser in the *San Francisco Chronicle* claimed to represent "foreign buyers."

The quick action property-wanted advertisers offer is worth something to a guy who's in a hurry. And that's why these ads run. The advertisers are looking to buy at a discount off fair market value. They want to buy at **quick sale value**...or less.

Fair market value is the highest price a property will bring when exposed to the market for a **reasonable** period of time...like three to six months. Quick sale value is the highest price a property will bring when exposed to the market for a **short** period of time...like a week. Some property-wanted ads in the *LA*

Times offer to close in two or three days. An ad in the *San Francisco Chronicle* said the buyer was in a hurry because of "Several Starker accounts." [Starker is the name of a court case (602 F2d 1341) which approved delayed exchanges and is now often used as a generic term for such exchanges even though the Tax Reform Act of 1984 superceded the Starker case in large part.]

In addition to the quick-sale discount, property-wanted advertisers hope to share commission and other **transaction cost savings** with the sellers. Finally, property-wanted advertisers hope to find sellers who **underestimate** the value of their property before those sellers learn the actual market value from a real estate agent or other buyers.

Bob Allen

You'll rarely find me recommending Bob Allen's books. He wrote *Nothing Down* and *Creating Wealth*. But in reading *Creating Wealth*, I found one chapter which had the ring of competence to it: Chapter Seven describes Allen's property-wanted ad experience.

Allen was too eager to buy for nothing down. But the same techniques which helped him find sellers dumb enough to sell for nothing down will help **you** find sellers dumb enough to sell for significantly **less than market value.**

Allen's ad read,

"FULL PRICE. We will pay full price for your property if you are willing to sell on flexible terms (little or no money down). Call Spencer 555-1234"

He says that ad, which only ran once a week, generated four to ten calls per week. Only two or three calls per month had potential. And of those, there would only be one property every other month which was good enough to "get excited about."

Allen's advice was that you should buy just one no-money-down house per year...that's one of the six "excited about" houses. (His theory was that inflation would increase the property's value enough to compensate you for the negative cash flow or negative amortization...plus adequately reward

your effort and risk. In fact, that would only work in times of extraordinary appreciation.)

How much?

A two-line classified ad in the *San Francisco Chronicle* or *Examiner* costs $8.48 per day if you run it for at least 12 days or 365 x $8.48 = $3,095.20 per year.

If you only ran it in the weekly real estate section, it'd cost $21.50 per week or 52 x $21.50 = $1,118 a year.

Is it worth it? If it enabled you to get one property a year for 10% less than market...and the property in question was worth $31,000 or more...you'd be ahead as a result of running the ad.

Does it pay?

I was unable to find anyone who kept detailed books on the results of their property-wanted ads. But I found several investors who believed their ads were cost effective even though they did not have **detailed** proof. The Starker advertiser above, who turned out to be one of my subscribers, told me they were well-pleased with it. *"Tremendous response. Three or four calls on Saturday morning, which is high for a classified ad."*

Jay Kaplan used to be the head buyer for Consolidated Capital, a major syndicator. He said they only got **one** of their 400 acquisitions as a **direct** result of their property wanted ad in the Friday *Wall Street Journal*. But that another 200 resulted from **relationships** begun by those property wanted ads. Most of Con Cap's callers were brokers...which was fine with Con Cap. They tried other newspapers and magazines but found that only the Friday *Wall Street Journal* worked.

Experiment

Whether a property wanted ad will work for the kind of property you seek in the market you have chosen remains to be seen. You need to experiment with:

• Different newspapers
• Different wording

• Different ways of screening and responding to callers

Also, ads get stale after a time. When that happens, experiment again.

I'd like to hear from any subscriber who is making a property-wanted ad work in his or her real estate investment program. Please call me at 800-635-5425 or 415-820-6292 in CA. JTR

PART THREE

THOUGHTS ON
INVESTMENT STRATEGY

24
How Real Estate Investing *Really* Works

March 1988

To invest in stocks, bonds, or commodities, you pick up a phone and call in your purchase instructions to a securities broker. No muss, no fuss. Maybe you read some analysts' reports before you decide.

Real estate investing is the same, right? Except that you go to a **real estate** broker instead of a securities broker...and you look at the **property** instead of analysts' reports.

Wrong.

Real estate is **quite different** from securities investing. Real estate investing bears more resemblance to shopping for the best deal on an expensive stereo than it does to securities investing.

One from many

Successful real estate investors typically look at five to ten properties for every one they buy. Many look at far more properties. The more you look at per purchase...the better...except that the value of your **time** becomes a factor.

In effect, the value of the time you spend finding a particular property is part of the **down payment and purchase price**. And the bigger the down payment and purchase price...whether in the form of cash or time...the lower your return.

Unacceptable real estate

You reject many of the properties because the **real estate** is unacceptable. Bad location. Structural problems. Deferred maintenance that would require you to get deeper into general contracting than you want.

Some people say **all** real estate is a good investment if you can buy it on the right terms. In theory, perhaps. But in reality, we all have some non-monetary criteria. Like Donald Trump's horror at collecting rents at his father's apartments. The experienced rent collector Trump accompanied would stand off to the side of the door when he knocked. Trump asked why. The collector said the tenants often fired guns through the door.

I'm with Donald on that one. I'm not going to risk my life to invest in real estate...even though one can earn a premium for doing so. I also do not wish to get involved with extensive renovation even though I know there's money to be made in it.

"I vant to be alone"

And there are risk factors I won't stand for. Like I will not buy an apartment building which is adjacent to another large apatment complex...for fear that if the owner of that complex lets it deteriorate...it'll take mine down with it and I won't be able to do anything about it.

In your typical property search, you will find that about half the properties you look at will be unacceptable to you on **any** terms.

Unacceptable terms

The other half of the properties you look at will not be available on acceptable **terms**. That is, the seller's asking price and the likely sale price...which you arrive at by deducting 5% or 10% from the asking price are such that you would have negative or breakeven cash flow if you paid it.

You must reject those properties. As will virtually all other buyers. Those sellers aren't really sellers. They have a fantasy value in mind. A value that would indicate that they really made a shrewd investment when they bought that property. Only if you play Ricardo Montalban (of *Fantasy Island*) to their fantasy, will they sell you the property. And you'll have made a lousy investment.

Qualify quickly

Salespeople are trained to qualify prospects quickly so they don't waste time with people whose probability of producing a sale is low. Real estate investors need to do the same.

Rank your criteria in order of their importance to you. Then screen the properties in that order. I check **location** first. That requires a drive by the property if I don't already know the area.

Then I find out if the amount I want to put **down** is acceptable by telling the real estate agent or seller, "Look, this is what I plan to put down. Is that enough for this property?" No beating around the bush. If he wants more, the sooner I find out the better. Because I need to move on to other property.

Then I crunch **numbers** at high speed using the rent, tax and utility figures the seller gives me and estimates of the other expenses based on my experience and regional studies of apartment expenses. Working backwards from the net operating income, I arrive at a price that gives me 10% cash on cash return. Then I ask the seller if that price is close enough to continue negotiating. Again, if it's not, I want to know as soon as possible so I can move on.

A lot of buyers and sellers put off dealing with the tough issues in a negotiation hoping they can finesse the other guy when they finally get to the hard part. Don't do that. It's amateurish and a colossal waste of time. In order to conserve your valuable time, you must cull out the time wasters who are unwilling to give you the terms you need as soon as possible.

Real estate investing is mainly a **finding** process. Not negotiating or analyzing. The outcome of negotiations is usually predetermined by the **starting** positions of the parties. Find out the other guy's position as fast as you can so you can get on with the search. JTR

25
Real Estate Investing: How Hard? How to?

May 1988

When most real estate investors bought their first home, they probably looked at about five before they found one that satisfied them. But when you look for **investment** real estate...even if you invest in single-family rental houses ...looking at just five properties generally does **not** produce a satisfactory deal.

Just how hard is it to find a good deal? And how do those who find them do it?

Degree of difficulty

For a guy who has previously only bought a home, it's as if a 100-yard dash runner were switched to the mile. As he hits the half way point, he pulls up and says to the coach, "This race is **impossible!** I've been sprinting for a **long** time and I still haven't hit the tape."

Your home would run negative cash flow

Why is it much harder to find a good investment than to find a home you're happy with? Because you are willing to buy your home on terms that would produce **negative cash flow** if you rented it out.

The typical home sells for 150 to 300 times its gross monthly rent. You want to invest at 100 times gross rent or less in single-family houses and at about an 11% or higher cap rate (net operating income/purchase price) in income property.

The difficulty of investing increases **exponentially** the lower you try to push the gross rent multiplier or the higher you try to push the cap rate.

What investors say

An investor friend says he looks at about ten to twenty properties for every one he buys. That's about what my experience has been as well. But he and I are only occasional rather than full-time acquisitors.

Jay Kaplan has been a full-time acquisitions man for many years. First with Consolidated Capital, one of the largest syndicators, and now for his own account. Jay says his complaints that, *"There's nothing out there. We should get out of the business,"* were a standing joke at ConCap. His older and wiser superiors would exchange knowing glances, sympathize, and send him back out on the acquisition trail. Where he would "get lucky" and manage to scrape up two or three decent deals a month.

"But I got lucky."

Interesting how that word "luck" keeps coming up in my discussions with subscribers. After I listen to their tale of

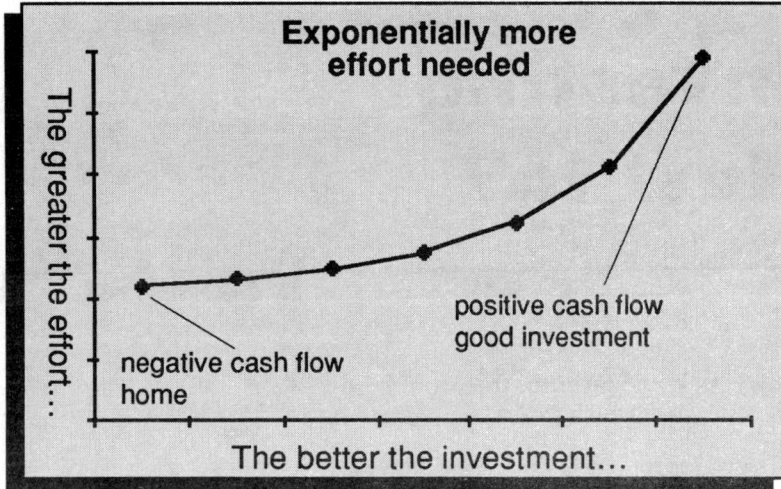

Exponentially more effort needed

The greater the effort...

negative cash flow home

positive cash flow good investment

The better the investment...

market woe, I say, *"So you haven't been doing any deals lately?"* "Well, actually," they answer, "I'm closing on one this week. But that was pure luck." I had roughly that exchange in recent conversations with a subscriber from Palm Springs and another from Chicago.

E pluribus unum

Jay Kaplan says ConCap looked at 200 properties for every offer they made. Atlanta investor, Bill Manley, who is a full-time rental house buyer says he runs the numbers on 50 to 100 properties for every one he buys. In **bad** times, Manley says that gets up to 200.

Investor Dan Kinter considers the entire Sacramento multiple listing service (MLS) book each week. He looks at the **new** listings and at properties who **rejected** his offers three to four weeks ago. Hundreds of properties flow thlough the MLS. About 20 will meet Kinter's very

restrictive location and existing mortgage tests. He makes offers on about four of those. About two accept.

St. Louis investor Dwain Sachs, who keeps precise records, says he looked at 167 properties in the last three months; made **two** offers...one of which is still open.

Anyway, you get the idea. Successful investors...in today's market...consider between fifty and two hundred of properties to find one or two to buy.

How to find them

The standard effort includes:

- A "property wanted" ad
- Scanning MLS (house buyers)
- Relationships with Realtors®
- Relationships with mortgage lenders (who may offer foreclosures)
- Contacting owners whose properties fit requirements but are not for sale

Speed is a necessity. When successful investors hear of a property which meets their requirements and may be available on terms they need, they are on the phone **immediately**. If they can set up an appointment, they are out the door within fifteen minutes of hearing about the place. In their car, they carry blank purchase offers. If they like what they see at the physical inspection, they make an offer on the spot. If it's not accepted, they make a note of the property and resubmit the offer or a modified offer several weeks later. They continue to contact the seller in question as long as they have money to invest.

Twelve-unit buy

One of my acquisitions was typical. I found out which Realtor's® office was first to receive the MLS books for our area. (This was before computerized MLS.) Every week, on the appontied day, I would wait there for the MLS book truck. As soon as it arrived, I would scan the new listings and look to see if any properties I had made offers were still available.

This day, I found a new listing of a twelve-unit apartment building in an acceptable town. I needed one-bedroom rents of $135 or less. This place was at $125.

I called to make an appontiment from a nearby pay phone rather than wait until I got to my office. After inspecting the property, I made an offer. It was **rejected**. The seller had just put the property on the market and thought he could do better. Shortly thereafter, the property was listed as sold.

Persistence

Then it came up in the "**back on market**" category, and I resubmitted my offer. It was accepted. But I was concerned about the roof and had a roof contingency. The roofer said the roof was no good. I asked the seller to credit me the appropriate amount. He refused. It was back on the market **again**.

I still wanted the property. So I visited the owner at his home. We struck a deal.

I raised the rents up to $185 and sold the property for 29% more than I paid for it three years later. "But I was lucky." JTR

26
Formulas That Stop Working

November 1989

You finally found a real estate investment formula that works. Now all you have to do is repeat it until you're rich, right? Not so fast.

Some formulas stop working and never come back. Condo conversion is a good example. It died because apartment building owners got too greedy about how much the converter should pay them. And because governments passed numerous anti-condo-conversion laws.

Other formulas more or less in real estate's graveyard:

- Syndication
- Construction and development REITs
- Timeshares
- Sale-leasebacks of gov't. property
- Recycling gas stations
- Numerous government programs
- Recycling schools
- RV parks
- Oil Patch prosperity riding
- Historic rehab

I will get "rumors of our death are greatly exaggerated" letters from various trade associations representing the above. That's evidence of the fact that many don't realize when the party is over. Executives of trade associations who find themselves writing such letters ought to check the wall to see if there's any handwriting on it.

Rent-raising formula

I hit upon a rent-raising formula in the '70s. Inflation was high then: averaging 6.8% a year from '70 to '75 and 8.9% from '75 to '80. To keep pace with inflation, apartment owners needed to raise rents $15 to $30 each year. But the vast majority of landlords didn't have the guts. They wouldn't send out an increase of more than $10 no matter what.

So I bought their buildings and I raised them to market value. That increased my cash flow and building value...frequently by 25 to 30%.

But in the early '80s, that ended in most markets. Inflation slowed to 5.5% per year in the first half of the '80s. Landlords made up for lost time in the '70s. And overbuilding caused rents to **fall** in many markets.

The **nothing-down** formula was profitable when appreciation was high in the late seventies. But it's a formula for disaster in most times.

Cyclical formulas

Some formulas wax and wane. For example, the supply of "Other Real Estate Owned" (property owned by lenders as a result of foreclosure, OREOs) goes up and down. But the number of investors willing to invest in those properties is relatively constant. So when OREOs are plentiful, they often sell at **bargain** prices. But when there are fewer of them, they get bid up to market value...or higher.

Another example is getting raw land ready (zoning, permits, etc.) for building. When interest rates are high, building usually shuts down.

Most investors don't recognize when a formula stops working. They view the change in the market or law as **temporary** or **insignificant**. And they foolishly continue to buy in accordance with the old formula.

If you've found a formula that works, good for you. But you should come up with **"ejection"** criteria. Air force pilots have criteria which tell them when to eject. Yours should tell you when to abandon a real estate investment formula. Failure to "eject" when the ejection criteria are met can have dire consequences for both air force pilots and real estate investors. I know that some of you are right now frustrated by inability to employ a real estate formula which worked in the past. Consider looking for a new formula if you are one of the currently frustrated.ЈТR

27

The Never-Sell-or-Exchange Strategy

May 1986

Many investors buy only. They never sell. Never exchange. They still have the first property they ever bought.

Is that sensible? It has its advantages.

Disadvantages of selling or exchanging

Selling is a hassle. Exchanging is a bigger, albeit worthwhile, hassle. It's also costly. Costs include:

- Real estate commissions
- Transfer taxes in some locations
- Deed preparation
- Attorney fees
- Title insurance (where paid by seller)
- Termite inspection and repairs.

If you sell rather than exchange, there are taxes. Installment sales don't eliminate taxes...just delay them. Possible taxes on sales include:

- Long-term capital gains tax
- Recapture of excess depreciation
- Recapture of investment tax credits
- Alternative minimum tax

Emotional strain

Selling is a **hassle**. The stress quizzes you see in magazines usually give "selling a house" a high number. They're right. I used to be a real estate salesman. Normal people get hyper when they're buying or selling real estate. And that applies to big time investors, too.

During the time before closing, you ride an emotional roller coaster...**up** when a buyer seems pleased...**down** when he demands that you lower the price because the asphalt has some cracks. Almost every sale includes several seemingly **insurmountable obstacles**. And in almost every deal, you overcome those obstacles through heroic efforts. But by the time you close, you feel like you've been through the wringer.

If you **never** sell or exchange, you **never go through that.** An appealing prospect, no?

Dealer status

Nearly all real estate investors who understand dealer status, fear it. If one of your properties is declared dealer property, you can't:

- **Depreciate** it,
- **Exchange** it, or
- Get **long-term capital gains** treatment on it.

Dealer property is defined by §1221 of the Internal Revenue Code as:

"property held by the taxpayer primarily for sale to customers in the ordinary course of his trade or business."

That's not clear. Nor are the various court decisions on the subject. So about the only way to **guarantee** that none of your property will be declared dealer property is to never sell or exchange.

Refinancing

Never sell or exchange does **not** mean never refinance. If it did, your leverage would drop way down. The never sell or exchange strategy I have in mind in this article means refinancing whenever the proceeds would be large enough to warrant the transaction costs.

The never sell approach with refinancing generally does **not** permit the high loan-to-value ratios you can achieve by selling and reinvesting or exchanging.

That's because institutional lenders are generally more conservative on refinancing than on purchases. They may loan 80% of value on a sale and only 75% on an equivalent refinancing. And the **appraisers** tend to be more conservative on a refinancing. So refinancing may shave 5% or 10% off the loan-to-value ratio you can get.

But you can still get seller financing on the property you **buy** with the refinancing proceeds. And the amount you save in costs and taxes by not selling may compensate for the inability to get higher leverage on the already-owned properties.

If you **exchange up** and get seller financing at, say 85% of value, your **entire portfolio** will be leveraged to 85%. But if you **refinance** a building and use the proceeds to buy a seller financed-building with the same 85% loan-to-value ration, your **overall** loan-to-value ration

will only be about **75% or 80%**. So the never sell or exchange strategy will tend to reduce your leverage a bit.

Upgrading

There are two kinds of real estate investors: those who just buy and hold and those who buy properties with unrealized potential, then make the necessary changes to realize the potential. The latter I call "upgraders." They may renovate, or improve tenant mix on commercial properties, or improve zoning, or one of many other techniques. However they do it, they make properties go up in value **faster** than the general appreciation rate in the area.

Normally, an upgrader would not want to adopt the never sell or exchange strategy. Because once he's upgraded a particular property, that property has no more potential. To keep all his equity at work, he needs to move it to another property with unrealized potential.

But an upgrader **could** follow the never sell or exchange strategy. It's just that it would be a bit **schizophrenic.** Because to continue to own a property is the same as to buy it. And an upgrader would never buy a property with no unrealized potential.

So an upgrader who adopted the never sell or exchange approach would be like **a race car pulling a trailer.** Strange, but it'll get you where you're going reasonably fast.

Property type and size

Another problem with the never sell or exchange strategy is that it would typically stick you with **little properties.** Can you imagine Trammel Crow still owning his first duplex or whatever his first property was? Hey maybe he does. For all I know, he could be parked in front of it right now waiting for some no-show who called about the upstairs vacancy.

Apartment buildings large enough to support **resident managers** are much more efficient than smaller properties. As are non-residential buildings large enough to interest local **leasing agents.** So if you adopt the never sell or exchange strategy, you may want to do it **later in your career** after you've sold the initial small properties.

Deteriorating neighborhood

If you adopt the never sell approach...and the neighborhood where the property is located deteriorates...abandon the never-sell strategy **fast.** The three most important things in real estate are location, location, and location. And to hold is the same decision as to purchase. So you should only continue to hold as long as the location looks like it will continue to meet your criteria.

Who should use the never sell or exchange strategy?

Investors who are especially vulnerable to dealer status...like real estate brokers and builders...might want to use the never sell strategy. It absolutely guarantees protection against dealer status. Nothing else can.

Otherwise, it sounds like a strategy that would be best for **intermediate or advanced** investors. **Beginners** need all the leverage they can get. And upgrading tends to be predominantly a beginner's game. The never sell or exchange strategy tends to emphasize **less hassle** at the expense of **maximum return**. If you've reached the point where you prefer that, you may want to adopt the never sell approach.JTR

28
Comfort Levels and
Real Estate Investing

February 1987

During the **down** part of the cycle, you see quotes like, "Good management really pays now."

But when times were **better**, I don't remember reading, "Bad management is the key to success in today's market."

The Comfort Level

This notion that the benefits of good management rise and fall with the business cycle is really a manifestation of the **comfort level** phenomenon.

Everybody has a comfort level. When they reach it, they slack off. A typical real estate investor wants to earn a return of at least 20% or so. Once he reaches that level, he slacks off. In other words, he doesn't manage as diligently as he should or could.

"Boy, are we fast?"

Alan Parisse of Consolidated Capital recently said of real estate investors, "We were like bicycle riders who thought we were going fast because we were great athletes...but it turns out we were going fast because we were going down hill." In a bicycle race over a hilly course, you go fastest by pedaling as fast as you can **all the time**. If you slack off pedaling...at any time...whether you are going **up** hill or **down** hill...you will arrive **later** at the finish line.

Management in real estate is analogous to pedaling in a bicycle race. Good management **always** makes sense and **always** pays dividends. The fact that appreciation and tax shelter are producing high returns does not mean it's a good idea to slack off on management any more than passing through the down hill section of a bicycle race means the way to win the race is to coast when you're going down hill.

Good management always pays the same dividend

A well-managed building produces a higher return than a poorly-managed building. Let's say that the cash-on-cash return of a **well**-managed building would be **11%** and that of a **poorly**-managed building, **7%**. When you're getting an additional 25% from appreciation and tax shelter...as we often did in recent years…the incremental 4% you'd get from good management seems not worth the effort. But when you're getting, say, 0% from tax shelter and appreciation…as is the case in many markets today, that 4% improvement looms large.

So comments that good management really pays **now** are incorrect. Good management **always** produces the same incremental improvement to the bottom line. What's different **now** is that overall returns have dropped below the comfort levels of formerly coasting real estate investors in many markets…and management is the only variable under their control.If they had managed better during the "down hill" portion of the course, they'd be better off.

Management loaves and fishes

The other side of the coin is that management has a finite ability to turn a property around. I wrote about that in "Should You Use The Vulture Strategy?" (March '86 issue, See Chapter 50) and "Should You Walk Away From a Building if Packwood's Bill Becomes Law?" (July '86 issue). Many owners whose returns have dropped below their comfort level are trying to extract from management **alone**, the same **overall** return that they used to get from appreciation, tax shelter and management combined.

It can't be done. About the best you can get out of management alone is a net operating income equal to 11% to 12% of the building value.

Always manage well

Attention to management always makes sense. It will pay the same dividend in any market. Attention to management will raise your return a bit. But it cannot overcome such huge problems as lower rental market value caused by overbuilding.ᴊᴛʀ

29
The Way We Were

May 1989

Return with me now to those thrilling days of yesteryear... thirty years ago...in this imaginary "interview" with a 1959 real estate investor. I'm doing this to make a point about how different real estate is from then...and how different our approach **ought** to be as a result.

Reed: "Hi, I'm the editor of *Real Estate Investor's Monthly* and I'd like to talk to you about your investments. So what's your biggest problem now?"
1959 Investor: "Interest rates."

Reed: "What's the matter with them?"
1959 Investor: "They're too high. They just went up"

Reed: "To what?"
1959 Investor: "The VA rate is 4 3/4%, FHA is 5 1/4% but those rates are actually too low to attract lenders. The market rate is 5 1/2% on houses and 6% on apartment buildings."

Reed: "Could be much worse ...like 16%."
1959 Investor: "Never."

Reed: "Why not?"

1959 Investor: "The government won't let it. All building and home sales would stop if mortgage rates were that high. We'd have another depression."

Reed: "So you're not worried about rates going above, say, 7%?"
1959 Investor: "Nah."

Reed: "And you're not taking any precautions in case they do?"
1959 Investor: "Like what?"

Reed: "Avoiding adjustable rate mortgages."
1959 Investor: "What's an adjustable rate mortgage?"

Reed: "A mortgage where the lender adjusts the rate and your payment every six months according to the market...with limits of about 1% per six months and a lifetime limit of 5% or 6%."
1959 Investor: "What! That's outrageous! It violates the usury laws."

Reed: "You're not concerned that Congress might wipe out all usury laws."
1959 Investor: "The voters will never allow such a thing."

Reed: "On another subject, are you concerned about your apartments becoming rent controlled?"

1959 Investor: "No. They only have that in New York City."

Reed: "What about tax reform? Are you concerned that Congress might drastically reduce your ability to deduct losses on rental properties...even to the point of not allowing you to deduct cash losses?"

1959 Investor: "Congress won't do that because there are millions of real estate investors. They'd be voted out of office if they did something like that.

Reed: "Are you concerned that asbestos or toxic chemicals might be found on your property and that you will be required by law to remove it at enormous expense?"

1959 Investor: "Why would any of that stuff be at an apartment building?"

Reed: "Asbestos is a common component of various building materials. Oil is toxic and underground oil tanks are common. As is the practice of dumping waste solvents and such."

1959 Investor: "Why would I have to pay to clean it up if I didn't put it there?"

Reed: "The law might be changed to say that you have to pay to clean up previous owner's messes.

1959 Investor: "That sounds unconstitutional."

Reed: "Are you afraid your expenses...like gas or electric or insurance might explode upward?"

1959 Investor: "Gas, electric, and insurance rates can't 'explode' upward because they're state regulated."

Reed: "Can I see the ad you run in the paper for your vacant apartments?"

1959 Investor: "Sure. Here it is."

"Adults only. Deluxe automatic dishwasher built into every apartment means extra hours for fun and recreation. No more messing with dirty dishes ever. Just load the dishwasher and relax. Optional air-conditioner in the master bedroom. Turn the knob

and get just the temperature you want. Muzak in lobby and elevators." [taken from actual 1959 ads]

Reed: "What would you do if the federal government told you that you had to rent to families with children?"

1959 Investor: "The day the federal government tells me who I can rent to is the day I get out of the apartment business."

Reed: "Do you have any black tenants?"

1959 Investor: "You mean black-listed for being Communist?"

Reed: "No. Black-**skinned**. Negroes."

1959 Investor: "I don't think they'd like you calling them black. They're more brown. Anyway, no, I don't. They prefer to be with their own kind. They go to colored schools, sit in the balcony with the other negroes at the movies, and live in the colored part of town. They don't want to live in white apartment buildings any more than the whites want to live in colored apartment buildings."

Reed: "So you're not concerned that a rejected negro applicant will allege racial discrimination in a costly lawsuit or complaint to a government agency?"

1959 Investor: "What are they going to do: send in troops? My building's not government property like Little Rock High School."

Reed: "Are you concerned that you might be sued by a person who suffers some personal injury and that the resulting multi-million dollar judgment might bankrupt you?"

1959 Investor: "My insurance agent says you only need a million dollars of liability coverage if you plan to drive your car into a parade of the major league All Star teams"

Reed: "What do you think will be the biggest problem facing real estate investors thirty years from now?"

1959 Investor: "Let's see. That'd be 1989. Oh, I don't know. Having a place for tenants to park their helicopters, I guess."

Government action

The main changes since 1959 are essentially massive government intervention into the real estate business combined with massive deregulation of the forces which are real estate's "enemies" (like energy, insurance, and interest costs).

The massive government changes in the last thirty years have clearly made investing in real estate **far more risky**. One would expect that investors would have responded to that increased risk by structuring their investments more **conservatively**. But they've actually gone the **opposite** direction.

On the come now

In 1959, investors bought a building on **positive cash flow** terms and held it five or ten years for its income. Now investors buy a building on **breakeven** or **negative cash flow** terms and hold it five or ten years in the hope of benefitting from appreciation. The preferred forms of ownership were sole proprietor or partnership in 1959. They still are.

The '59 investor wanted a cash-on-cash return which was about double the 5% to 6% first mortgage rates of the time, i.e. about 10% to 12%. Today's equivalent would be a cash-on-cash return of about 22%. You can see why 1959 investors were content with no appreciation and very few tax benefits.

2019

Relying on market-wide appreciation instead of income, bargain purchase, or upgrading potential is extremely speculative and presumes you can forecast the market's future. But look at how poorly my imaginary, but arguably realistic, 1959 investor was able to forecast **his** future. And remember Alvin Toffler's observation in *Future Shock* that the rate of change is **accelerating**.

If there were **ten** major changes in real estate investing between 1959 and 1989, there'll be **thirty or forty** between 1989 and 2019. We investors of 1989 will appear far more naieve and out of it to a 2019 investor than the 1959 investor appears to us.

The last war

The typical real estate investor's strategy today resembles too much the "fighting-the-last-war" syndrome often seen in military leaders. The investment environment has changed dramatically... but investment strategies have changed far less. And what change **has** occurred in strategies... away from income toward appreciation...has **compounded** rather than counteracted the increased risk in the environment.

Instead of relying on market-wide appreciation for all or most of their return, investors should be buying properties on terms which yield substantial **positive cash flow** and/or buying for **less than market** value and/or buying properties with **potential for increased value** as a result of actions taken by the owner rather than events in the market. I've written about ways to do that in numerous issues of this newsletter. Given the many **differences** between today's market and 1959's, the many **similarities** in holding periods, property search methods, ownership form, area selection, etc. are overdue for review. JTR

30
"All You Need are The Right People"

During my brief military career, I observed a phenomenon I call the "**Real Army Carrot.**" Whenever a group of us got to griping about some recent, local, idiotic policy, a career guy would always end the discussion by pointing out that, "Yeah, but this isn't the real army. This is the airborne (or Vietnam or Ranger School or whatever)."

The idea behind this comment was that the army was a great place, but it **did** have a few unrepresentative assignments which were undeniably bad. "Just hang on," was the message, "and soon you'll get back to the real army."

But after hearing that same this-isn't-the-real-army statement at every single one of ten different duty stations, I concluded there is no "real army." The "real army" is a myth...an unreachable, motivational carrot that takes the eyes of career military people off the chicken manure through which they trudge.

In business, the "right people"

Lately, I've noticed that business managers have a similar myth: "**the right people.**"

Most management problems are **people** problems. At any given moment, a landlord might be confiding to his or her spouse,

"Kendall's got to go. The vacancy rate is high because she's never there. They charge too much for cleaning. And they're too lenient on collections. All we need are the right people. Then the place will be full and run smoothly."

The **wrong** people...tenants, resident managers, suppliers...vex the owner. And the behavior of those wrong people belies the image of an executive's job that causes young persons to aspire to the prestigious profession of management.

The **image** of an executive is that he or she assembles a winning team then leads those wonderful folks on to victory in the Superbowl of business. The **reality** of an executive career...including ownership of income properties...is that a significant percentage of the people you deal with are incompetent or dishonest or both. And those people take up a disproportionate amount of your time.

If the truth be told, the executive job description is generally **not** leading a team of great employees. Rather it is trying constantly to **assemble** and **keep intact** such a team...which keeps coming unglued as a result of inevitable turnover. While at the same time spending too much time on the few problem people who are causing trouble.

You hear executives complain, "I'm spending all my time putting out fires." Or they put up a sign saying,

"When you're up to your neck in alligators, it's hard to remember that your original objective was to drain the swamp."

Occasional brief, shining moments

Slot machine owners program them to pay off occasionally...to keep the players interested. So do army and executive careers have their brief payoffs. Army officers get to go to "gentlemen's courses" (army schools with light workloads) every now and then and executives actually do assemble the "right people" for occasional brief periods.

The point of this article is that most executives harbor a mistaken notion that presiding over those brief shining moments is what they do for a living. In fact, an executive's job and high pay stems not from his "swamp draining," but from his "alligator fighting."

To mix in another metaphor, the executive is like a maintenance man in a factory. He does not have time to admire the smooth-running machinery. If it always ran smoothly, he'd be out of a job. Rather he's there to jump in and clear up problems when they foul up the machine's smooth running. As such, he spends most of every day not with smooth running machinery but with **fouled-up** machinery. And executives, including landlords, spend their days mainly dealing with the problem employees, problem suppliers, and problem tenants.

The bigger, the more brief the shining moments

I figure you will get about one bad **tenant** out of every ten and about one bad **employee** out of every three...even

if you screen them carefully. The percentage of bad employees is higher because the role of employee is more demanding than the role of tenant. Those ratios, in turn, mean that the bigger your operation, the more brief will be the times when you are free of problem people.

The landlord of a four-family has no employees, so no employee problems. With 75% turnover, he'll have three new tenants per year. If one in ten is bad, he'll only have a problem tenant every three years or so. But the four-unit owner aspires to 100 units. At that level he'll average **ten** problem tenants at any given time. And he'll have a staff of three employees which will average one loser at any given time.

In short order, he will utter the oft heard lament of the newly-arrived, big-time manager,

"It was a lot more fun when I only had four units. But everything will be fine when I get rid of this lemon of a maintenance man and this crop of deadbeats."

No, it won't. The parade of lemon employees and deadbeat tenants never ends.

Not long after that he will muse about,

"hiring a good general manager who will allow me to devote my time to strategic issues."

Hah!

How good people vex you

On those rare occasions when you are free of problem people, you will **still** be vexed by your **non-problem** people. How do good employees, tenants, and suppliers vex you?

They die. They get sick or injured. Employees go on vacation. The tenant or the resident manager's spouse gets transferred. They get an opportunity to move up that you can't match. Resident manager couples get separated and/or divorced. They are not long the days of wine and roses and the "right people."

What's it all about?

Recognize the true nature of the landlord's job. It is to fight a neverending battle with tenants who do not abide by the lease, subcontractors and suppliers who don't keep their end of the bargain, and employees who don't get the job done. To be sure, **most** tenants, subcontractors, suppliers, and employees are good people. But "most" and "all" are two different words.

As my wife has progressed in her career as a bank executive, I have noticed that her conversation about work has changed. Early on she talked about customers. Then customers and subordinates. Then, when she had 100 subordinates, she talked almost exclusively about the successes and failures and comings and goings of her employees. The higher up you get, the more your job description becomes:

1. Recruiting
2. Training
3. Retaining the good people
4. Counseling and motivating the mediocre people, and
5. Firing the bad people.

When you read books, subscribe to periodicals, and attend seminars to improve your professional skills, you should include, in addition to the real estate stuff, information on the personnel-type skills listed above. Because, **that**, not leading a neverchanging winning team, is really what you do as a real estate executive. And if you're still small, that is where you are heading. JTR

31
Making a Million
In One Year

March 1989

"Make no little plans. There is nothing in little plans to stir men's blood." Daniel Burnham

Instead of slogging your way to your first or next million, why not swing for the fence? A legal, ethical real estate deal which makes $1,000,000 in one jump.

It seems eminently plausible in view of the many bargain purchase and upgrading strategies I've written about over the years.

Working example

Let's say you have a net worth of $75,000 and your goal is to make it $1,000,000 within one year. You're going to have to do it with one or two properties in the $1,000,000 range.

You can do:

- a bargain purchase or
- an upgrade or
- both.

I've written about actual bargain purchase case histories with discounts in the 20% to 97.5% range which...in turn...

implies that you'll have to acquire property worth ($1,000,000 ÷ 97.5% =) $1,026,000 to ($1,000,000 ÷ 20% =) $5,000,000 range. How do you mess with one- to five-million dollar properties with only $75,000 in cash?

- Options
- Contingent purchase agreements
- High-leverage financing techniques.

I will not consider partnerships in this article.

Upgrading strategies I've come across have increased property value as much as 300%. That implies that you'll have to deal with property worth at least ($1,000,000 ÷ 300% =) $333,000.

Big versus little deals

The higher the price range, the more efficient the market is. And the harder it is to make bargain purchases or find overlooked potential. In last month's issue, I noted that appraiser Martin Healy, Jr. found that tenant-in-common interests sold for discounts ranging from 3% to 52% with an average of 23.5%. His study was limited to **high-priced commercial property.**

In contrast, I found discounts ranging from 50% to 97.5% among investors who bought tenant-in-common interests in single-family **houses and apartment buildings.**

Ways to do it

In the "More Appropriate Size or Shape" chapter of my book, *How to Increase the Value of Real Estate,* I tell of a "surplus" 100,000-square-foot industrial building in Portland which could not be rented or sold. The corporation that owned it finally offered it to the City of Portland for one dollar. Portland turned it down.

If you had stepped in at that point...and the corporation was willing to make you the same offer...you'd have been on your way to a quick million. That building, which could not be leased or sold, was worth about $1,000,000 (call it a 99.9999% discount).

When the real estate consulting firm of Hoffman Associates looked at the situation, they found that many industrial users in the immediate neighborhood needed more space. They just didn't need 100,000 square feet. So Hoffman recommended they partition the property with walls and new doors to create bays of the size the market wanted. The owners did and after lease-up, the property generated $100,000 of net operating income per year. When you capitalize that income at 10%, you get a market value of $1,000,000.

Flip it

Because you only have $75,000, you need to sell at a higher price your right to buy the property at the bargain price... before closing. So you would try to get as far off an expiration date as possible. The $75,000 would serve as earnest money and liquidated damages or option consideration. You probably cannot close on the property with just $75,000, so don't put yourself in a position where you could be sued for specific performance.

You may be able to borrow the money to go ahead with the purchase from a lender if you can convince them that you did indeed get a bargain price.

Binge

The program I envision in this article is a one-year **binge** on real estate. That is, you eat, think, and sleep your big deal until you've pulled it off. People achieve a much higher performance level... albeit at the cost of a balanced life...when they focus all their energies on one task. But since this is only a one-year project, you should have plenty of time to restore balance in subsequent years.

Prime candidates for such a binge include the recently laid off, divorced, or widowed, or anyone who has enough money to live for a year without a job and enough fire in his or her belly to want to make a million in one great leap.

Workable strategies

Here are some scenarios based on actual case histories that could produce the one-year, one million dollar leap.

Upzoning: The *Texas Monthly* article "Sherwood Blount's First Million" (10/79) told of a deal in which a land owner succeeded in getting the zoning on 46 acres changed from single-family to multi-family...thereby raising its value from $30,000 an acre to $73,913...and making a 46 x ($73,913 - $30,000 = $43,913) = $2,020,000 profit.

The 46 acres was part of a larger parcel which was offered for $8,000,000 with $50,000 in earnest money which would be forfeited if the zoning change was not obtained. $50,000 is well below the $75,000 I posited as your working capital at the beginning of the article. And $8,000,000 is well above the $1,000,000- or $2,000,000-size deals you need to do to have a shot at making a million. But don't forget that if you had put the $50,000 up to do this deal...and failed to get the zoning change...you'd be out the $50,000. No guts, no glory.

Lease-Option and Rent Raise: I once gave a man a piece of advice which made him $6,000,000 in five months. He had mentioned that all his apartments had waiting listis. I told him that meant his rents were low and explained how high he should raise them. He followed my advice and his rents were 28% higher five months later. Since he owned $20,000,000 worth of apartments at the outset...and apartment building values are based on their income...that meant he increased the value of his apartments by about $6,000,000.

He owned those $20,000,000 worth of apartments. With just $75,000 to work with, you generally can't own the $3,000,000 worth of apartments needed to make a million with a 28% rent increase. But you might be able to **lease-option** them. You'd rent the whole complex then sublease it to the tenants.

An option would give you the right to buy the property for a year either at a fixed price or at a price that went up no more than inflation.

Controlling millions with $75,000

Making a million in one deal is not the hardest part of this. Deals with a million or more profit are done every day...by people who already have millions. The trick is doing it with only $75,000.

Bill Tappan, Jr., the Albuquerque real estate broker who wrote *Real Estate Exchange and Acquisition Techniques*, says options in his market usually sell for roughly equal the interest the seller loses on his equity during the option period. For example, if a seller sold a free-and-clear $1,000,000 property now and put the money in a six-month CD, he'd earn about 8.33% which is $83,300 per year or $41,650 for six months. That's well within our $75,000 working cash in this article and leaves over $30,000 for other costs of doing the deal.

Seattle income property broker Mike Scott says sellers of income properties want an average of about 2% as earnest money and that many agree to fixed-price (no escalation during the escrow period) closings as long as six months hence. That 2% would be $20,000 per million which is also well within the $75,000 we have to work with in this article. And six months is long enough to make some value-increasing changes to the property.

You can typically get a seller to agree to let you show the property to contractors, inspectors, insurance agents, prospective tenants, or buyers before closing. That's enough access to allow you to do a deal like the asbestos bargain I wrote about in the 9/88 issue ("Big Profits...and Big Losses...From Toxics Panic" See Chapter 88). The buyers got certified asbestos-removal contractors into the building to give estimates. The estimates indicated the seller was selling $3.6 million too cheap.

Making a million in one year starting with $75,000 is neither easy nor risk-free...but it's doable.

"I bargained with Life for a penny,
And Life would pay no more,
However I begged at evening
When I counted my scanty store.
For Life is just an employer,
He gives you what you ask,
But once you have set the wages,
Why you must bear the task.
I worked for a menial's hire,
Only to learn dismayed,
That any wage I had asked of Life,
Life would have willingly paid." JTR

32
The Wisdom of Making Less Money Per Deal

January 1989

Investors virtually always try to sell their properties for the highest possible price...to renovate for the lowest possible cost. Only a fool would do otherwise, right?

Not so fast.

Return on Investment

Return on investment equals the **profit** you make over a certain **time period** divided by your **investment**. Virtually all real estate investment writing focuses on either increasing the profit or minimizing the investment. But, reducing the **time** period can increase return just as much as increasing profit or decreasing investment. And some successful investors have done just that.

Ted Thomas

Last month I mentioned that Ted Thomas did four deals in November, making $5,000 each on three of them and $10,000 on one. He did that by buying them (pre-foreclosures) at less than market value.

What I **didn't** say was that he also **sold** those properties at less than market value...although not **as much** below market value as he bought them.

You've heard that the key to investment success is,

"Buy low, sell high."

Thomas prefers to,

"Buy very low, sell low."

The people who bought those properties from Thomas in November got them for about $15,000 to $20,000 under market. (That's market value **before** renovation...which foreclosures typically need.) In other words, **they** made more money than **he** did on each deal.

Is he crazy?

No. Those buyers will have to lease, manage, and renovate those properties. All time-consuming, low-profit activities. While they're doing that, Thomas will be doing more deals.

He got the **fast** buck. They'll get the **last** buck. They have higher profit margins per property. He makes more money per **year**.

Most important of all, he has a higher return on the investment of his cash and time.

Jim Stephenson

Thomas is not the only investor to favor speed over profit margin. In his book, *The Stephenson System* (out-of-print as far as I know), Jim Stephenson outlined a system he used to get rich in raw land. (He sent letters to out-of-county owners asking if they wanted to sell and only bought when he could get the property at a substantial discount.)

In one deal, he found an out-of-state trust company which wanted to sell land for $325 an acre. It was worth $750 per acre. Stephenson agreed, then offered the land for sale himself at $525 per acre. He found a buyer and both sales closed the same day. Stephenson made $20,500 on the deal.

Other Stephenson deals ($/acre):

Buy	Sell	Market
$250	$525	$725
$1,500	$2,100	$3,000
$550	$1,650	$2,000

Stephenson said, *"Don't get greedy"* by way of explaining why you should sell cheap.

"Do get speedy," is a better reason.

Speed and expense

Land normally takes a long time to sell. **Six-month to one-year listings are** common in the land business. Commissions are more likely to be **10%** than **6%**. And since bank loans are rare in land, **seller financing** is the rule. But at Stephenson's low selling prices, he usually found an **all-cash** buyer, **before** he bought, without a real estate agent.

Speed and Nickerson

In the October issue (See Chapter 18), I told of Jim Muldoon. He's using the Nickerson method (buy, renovate, exchange up, and repeat) in the Lancaster, PA area with great success. His profit margins are especially noteworthy. **Four** dollars in profit for every dollar spent on renovation versus the two dollars for every dollar Nickerson said to shoot for.

But the main reason for Muldoon's high margins is he does all the work **himself** (with a couple helpers).

One recent 19-unit renovation was taking 110 hours per unit of Muldoon's time. And when I asked William Nickerson, himself to comment on Muldoon's application of the Nickerson formula, Nickerson said he thought Muldoon was doing **too much** himself...thereby reducing the number of deals he could do per year. In other words, if Muldoon could do, say, three times as many deals...making half as much profit on each...he'd be better off.

The big money in this business is in finding bargain purchases and spotting hidden potential. The **chores** that unavoidably accompany real estate investment in most people's minds...leasing, management, renovation...are nickel and dime producers. Extracting profit from a property becomes exponentially more difficult the closer you get to market value.

Don't assume that performing the chores is an unavoidable part of real estate investing. Rather spend your time where it will produce the **most income**. By giving more profit to the others in the deal, you can rid yourself of most of real estate's time stealers.

Get the fast buck, not the last buck. JTR

33
Ranger Real Estate Investing

February 1989

U S. Army Ranger units were among the most effective in the Vietnam war…while suffering remarkably few casualties. American forces in general inflicted ten enemy casualties for every American casualty. The Ranger ratio was fifty to one.

Some of the principles under which the Rangers operated in Vietnam can be applied to real estate investing in the chaotic '80s.

Small units

Rangers operated in six-man, lightly-armed teams. They would attack as many as forty enemy…but not more. They helicoptered into remote landing zones then silently searched on foot for trails along which to set up ambushes. When the enemy walked into the ambush, the Rangers opened fire and simultaneously radioed for waiting helicopters to extract them. In other words, the military equivalent of ringing a doorbell and running like heck.

"Enemy" forces

Real estate investors operate in small groups…usually "groups" of one. And their capital is dwarfed by such "enemy" forces as:

• Higher interest rates
• Overbuilding
• Rent controls
• Recessions
• Toxic waste liability, and
• Tax reform.

Yet unlike the Rangers, real estate investors don't seem to have figured out that they are no match for such forces. Investors can neither control nor forecast the events which can reduce the value of their properties. By buying and holding properties for years at a time they expose themselves to the great financial harm which can come to them if:

• Interest rates increase significantly
• Too many competing buildings are built

- Their uncontrolled apartments become rent controlled
- A recession or depression occurs
- Their property is found to contain dangerous substances
- Congress changes income tax laws adversely.

Real estate quick hits

Can money be made in real estate without exposure to such uncontrollable, unpredictable risks? Yes.

In Ranger real estate investing, the investor keeps his holding period to a minimum and does not risk all his capital in any one deal. In fact, the holding period can be reduced more or less to zero if the investor does double-escrow deals (buys and sells at same closing).

Most people who think of themselves as real estate investors seek their profit by holding property during a period in which they assume that **all** property values in their market will rise. They are actually **speculators** since appreciation rates are determined in part by the above list of factors and the future behavior of those variables is unknowable.

The Ranger real estate investor would make his profit in one of three ways:

- bargain purchase
- profitable improvements
- combination of both.

Because of his short holding periods, market-wide appreciation rates would be **irrelevant** to him.

Bargain purchases

In the three years this newsletter has been in existence, I have written about many ways to make bargain purchases. To wit:

- Correctable title problems 10/86
- Homeowners association problems 3/87
- Bad tenants 4/87
- Sellers who sell cheap 10/87
- Back-door vulture strategy 10/87
- Loan workouts 2/88
- "Surplus" corporate or government real estate 4/88

- Alcoholic/drug addict sellers 6/88
- Bad foundations 6/88
- To-be-demolished buildings 8/88
- Foreclosures 8/88, 9/88, 11/88
- Asbestos 9/88
- Probate 1/89
- Partial interests 2/89

And my "Article Ideas" notebook contains the beginnings of many more bargain purchase articles.

In the bargain purchase strategy, you simply buy at a bargain price and resell for a higher price.

Profitable improvements

My book, *How to Increase the Value of Real Estate*, contains eighteen chapters, each of which covers a category of ways to increase the value of a property. They include:

- Raising rent
- Upzoning
- Cosmetic renovation
- Moving the building
- Escaping rent control
- Improving access, etc.

Articles on increasing value in this newsletter have included:

- Excess land 7/86
- View liberation 6/87
- Tax Reform Act of 1986 Countermeasures 10/87
- Convert one-bedroom houses to two- 7/88
- Nickerson Formula 10/88

In the profitable improvements approach, you buy or acquire control (by option or contingent purchase agreement) of a property that has some unrealized potential, realize the potential, then get out within months.

Tax ramifications

Ranger real estate investors are generally **dealers**. They claim no depreciation and do no exchanges. They do something which was unthinkable to real estate investors of the pre-Tax-Reform-Act-of-1986 era...they pay taxes on their profits. Ranger investors use corporate pension plans, health insurance, etc. to reduce their taxes. Generally, they properly focus on maximizing after-tax income... rather than on minimizing how much the government is getting.

Management

The typical real estate investor spends about 80% of his time on property management...even though he makes about 80% of the money he makes on purpose (as opposed to speculation profits) from **other** activities like finding

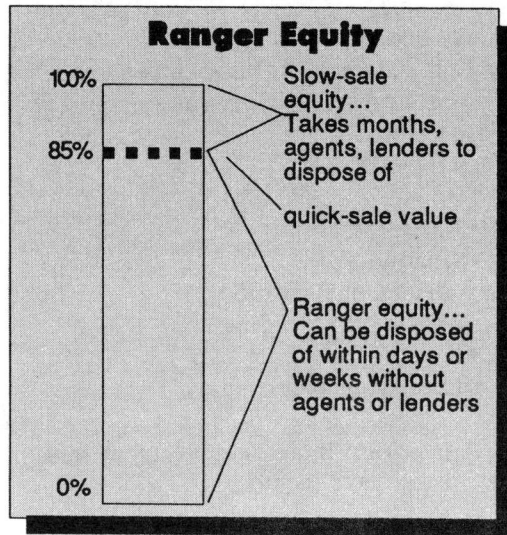

```
                Ranger Equity

  100%                        Slow-sale
                              equity...
                              Takes months,
  85% ■ ■ ■ ■ ■               agents, lenders to
                              dispose of

                              quick-sale value


                              Ranger equity...
                              Can be disposed
                              of within days or
                              weeks without
                              agents or lenders




  0%
```

properties. Ranger real estate investors hardly ever spend any time on management.

Financing

Most real estate investors periodically go hat in hand to lenders asking them to, "Please give me a mortgage." It's frustrating, time consuming, and they hate it. Ranger investors generally deal only in high speed, all-cash transactions... both when they buy and when they sell.

They know that real estate's supposed lack of liquidity applies only to the top 15% or so of the value of a property. Ranger investors don't mess with the top 15% of value. They **sell** at quick sale prices which are about 15% below market...after having bought for even less.

The bushes

Army Rangers hide in the bushes rather than expose themselve to enemy activity by establishing visible base camps. Ranger **investors** hide in short-term, federally-insured certificates of deposit. In a given year, a ranger investor may have been the owner of real estate other than his residence for only a few weeks. But in that same year he may have made hundreds of thousands of dollars from his real estate activities.

In hard times

Millions of real estate investors have seen hard times in recent years. From the Farm Belt to the Oil Patch to Silicon Valley to office buildings and condos almost everywhere...property values have dropped significantly. Investors in those areas have wondered, "What strategy could have prevented these losses?"

The Ranger strategy would have. None of those value drops occurred overnight. With their quick-hit tactics, the Ranger investors would have gotten their profits and been out before any adverse market factors could hurt them. Market-wide value **drops** are as irrelevant to what they do as market-wide **increases** in value are. They survive and prosper by their **wits**, not by hoping for price increases.

Lean and mean

Regular infantry units in Vietnam were plagued by booby traps, ambushes, and mortar attacks from an unseen enemy who knew exactly where the Americans were. Rangers, on the other hand, almost always saw the enemy and, because the enemy did not know where the Rangers were, almost never encountered booby traps, enemy ambushes, or mortar attacks. It was if the regular and Ranger units fought in different wars.

Likewise, Ranger real estate investors operate in a real estate world unknown to most real estate investors. A world largely without tenants or loan officers or real estate agents. A world without fear of dealer status or exchange audits. A world without concern for marketwide appreciation rates or interest rate movements or rent control or tax reform or whatever.

Yet it's still very much the world of real estate. Ranger real estate investors spend virtually all their time on those actions which make deliberate, big bucks; hardly any on the low-profit minutiae that consume most real estate investors' lives...while they wait for their appreciation ship to come in.

Just as the Army Rangers were far more efficient at their jobs, yet took far fewer risks in Vietnam than regular units, Ranger real estate investors are far more efficient at extracting the maximum profit from real estate at minimum risk and with the minimum outlay of time and money.

More skill, nerves

If you are unhappy with the profits you've made of late...or uncomfortable with the risks you've been taking ...consider switching to the Ranger approach. As in the Army, it requires a higher skill level and stronger nerves than the run-with-the-mob approach. But as in Vietnam, the mob is paradoxically less secure and less effective than the quick-hitting little guy who knows his limitations. (Note: I am a reluctant graduate of the U.S. Army's Ranger School.)JTR

34
The Real Estate
B.S. Artist
Detection Checklist

Readers often ask me what I think of a particular guru's seminar or home-study course. In many cases, I don't know the work of the guru in question. But I can make general observations about the B.S. artists which you can use to spot them.

1. Emphasis on luxurious lifestyle. Gurus I respect, like Bill Tappan (author of *Real Estate Exchange and Acquisition Techniques*) and Bob Bruss (nationally syndicated real estate columnist) rarely mention the life-style you will enjoy if you buy their products or follow their advice. Although they are successful real estate people, they see no need to write about being rich or to wear their affluence on their sleeve (or around their neck or pinky).

On the other hand, the B.S. artists feature the **lifestyle** of the rich in their tv ads, come-on speeches, and "how-to" materials. They also accessorize themselves with flash like ostentatious jewelry and rented limousines.

2. Subjective self description. The "about-the-authors" of the gurus I respect are generally written in Jack Webb style: "Just the facts, Ma'am." Leigh

Robinson, for example, describes himself in one sentence: "Leigh Robinson is landlord to 360 tenants and lectures in Landlording for University of California Extension."

Bill Tappan's bio contains not a single laudatory adjective. Just a handful of relevant facts about his exchanging experience and the first edition of his book.

In contrast, the B.S. artists tend to have book jacket or ad copy which describe them as the "leading real estate expert in the United States today" or the "Number One, most-sought-after..." Their bios are full of baseless, subjective adjectives and nouns, like "innovative," "famous," "spectacularly successful," "authority," etc.

B.S. artists often use photographs or videotape of themselves hanging around executive jets, limos, yachts, mansions, five-star hotels, exotic resorts, or expensive cars to imply that they have achieved great financial success.

3. No pitfalls or corrections. There are dangers in everything. But you rarely read about danger in a book by a real estate B.S. artist... or hear about it in one of his cassettes or tv "infomercials."

Everybody makes mistakes. But you rarely read about a guru's mistake or see a correction in a B.S. artist's newsletter.

The B.S. artists are self-proclaimedly big on being "positive." And one of the things they're positive about is that the dream world they depict will not be marred by unpleasant reality.

On the other hand, worthwhile gurus like John Beck (*Distress Sales Report*), are as likely to write about mistakes made (often by the guru himself/herself) and dangers overlooked as about spectacular profits achieved. And all ethical periodicals writers run corrections when they make a mistake.

4. No bad news. In addition to teaching **techniques**, real estate investment gurus have to respond to **news** like court decisions, legislation, economic trends, and so forth. Of course, some of the news is **bad**. But the B.S. artists invariably respond to bad news in Pollyanna fashion. They **always** see "opportunity." The closest they come to acknowledging the unhappy truth is to describe a situation as a "challenge."

The Tax Reform Act of 1986 was a good litmus test. Any investor whose IQ exceeds his body temperature knows that was the worst tax law for real estate investors since the income tax was invented. But when it passed, the B.S. artists called it "the best thing that ever happened to real estate"...or words to that effect.

Why do they do that? For one thing, they fear bad news will depress sales. With good reason apparently. A bunch of real estate newsletters have gone out of business since the late '80s real estate depressions hit many markets and the Tax Reform Act of '86 passed.

Another reason B.S. artists don't acknowledge bad news is that they simply cannot shut off their slinging mechanism. They are B.S. kinda guys.

There's nothing wrong with looking for opportunity in ostensibly bad situations. Many of my recent articles have done just that. You only become a B.S. artist when you look for it, can't find it, but claim it's there anyway.

(**Special interest groups** tend to be B.S. artists, too, although in the opposite direction when it comes to laws. They're always claiming that "civilization as we know it will cease" if such-and-such law is not passed or repealed.)

5. Universally-applicable techniques. The various techniques one can use in real estate investment are like mechanic's tools. The one you use depends on the situation and your goal. Just as **no** tool is appropriate for **every** mechanical job, neither is any real estate investment technique appropriate for every situation. Each has advantages and disadvantages and most are only useful in a narrow range of circumstances.

The B.S. artists trot out one obscure technique after another in an effort to impress the customer with all the "new" material they are getting. But rarely is a word spoken about **when** the technique is appropriate. The reader or listener is left with the impression that the technique is appropriate for **any** and **every** acquisition.

6. Emphasis on motivational material. Every successful person I know has benefitted from motivational books like *The Power of Positive Thinking*. Many of us have had life experiences like emotional high-school football pep talks which gave dramatic evidence of the power of focused motivation. I would not diminish the role of motivation in success in real estate or any other field.

However, motivational material ought to be packaged as such. When books or tapes are described as containing how-to information on **real estate investment**, they ought to contain little or no motivational material. The protest that the customer "needs" to be motivated is beside the point. It is dishonest to promise how-to information then deliver a bunch of "You-can-do-it" platitudes instead.

The motivational business, like patriotism in Samuel Johnson's memorable phrase, is one of the last refuges of scoundrels. Although there are many who approach the field of motivation with rigorous scientific discipline, there are more for whom the motivation business is merely a **con**...a chance to sell yet another cure-all "elixir" without having to get FDA approval.

7. Claim to do lots of deals. Virtually all the B.S. artists say, "I don't just teach these techniques. I use them every day in my own investment program."

Baloney. There aren't enough hours in the day.

Gurus get the same 24-hour days as you. Being an expert takes time. They have to read many trade journals, loose-leaf services, and books to keep up to date. They have to spend hours on the phone interviewing sources for their articles and books...and hours in the library researching legal cases and other relevant facts.

As experts, gurus get interviewed by the media on the phone and in radio and tv studios and they make speeches to investors.

Finally, they have to manage the guru business itself. That means designing brochures, responding to customer-service problems, checking proofs from the printer, indexing books, negotiating with printers and recording studios, going over the income and expenses of the guru business, and so forth.

Obviously, they do **not**, after all that, have as much time as non-gurus do for investing. But in the financial guru business, the question, "Are you **using** these techniques yourself or just **teaching** them?" is ubiquitous. And any answer but, "Oh, yes," seems devastating to the credibility of the guru. (It shouldn't be but that's another article.)

In fact, real estate gurus (other than those who just dabble in guruing) who do a deal a month or more are extremly rare. Or they are buying garbage properties by the dozen...with little or no analysis or due diligence...mainly so that they can **claim** they do lots of deals and be technically accurate.

No angels here

In pointing out some of the revealing habits of the B.S. artists...and the gaps in their information...I do not mean to imply that I am Simon Pure. Among other faults, I am often tactless and sometimes speak with more conviction than my knowledge of the subject in question warrants. "I'm often wrong but never uncertain," is the phrase I jokingly use to describe that tendency.

But when it comes to B.S., be assured that I am **trying** my best to avoid it. Apparently, I often succeed because the most common comment I get from readers is, "I don't agree with everything you say but I like your no-B.S. approach."

My main complaint about the real estate B.S. artists is that they appear **not** to be trying to avoid B.S. Indeed, they seem not to **care** whether they sling it or not. Rather their only criterion appears to be, "Will the suckers swallow this and send me more money as a result?

Note: The four guys I mentioned in this article are **not** the **only** real estate gurus who are non-B.S. artists. JTR

35
Investors in a Time Warp

January 1990

I frequently talk to subscribers on the phone. Recently, however, I made a couple speeches and thereby got to talk to many **non**-subscribers who are real estate investors. Their questions and comments surprised me at first. Then I realized where they were coming from. **When** would be more accurate. Their thinking on real estate is what was appropriate back in about 1982.

When I realized how far behind the times they were, I began to worry if my subscribers are similarly out of date. To make sure you are not, here's a little summary of the out-of-date thinking along with what I believe the current thinking should be.

1982 mentality: Dealer status is a fate worse than death.

1990: Tax benefits are a much less important factor in choice of real estate investment strategy than they were in the early eighties. Now, doing what makes the most money **before** tax is generally what makes the most money **after** tax as well. Do not reject dealer strategies out of hand the way we used to because of their inability to exchange.

1982: Wow! I got the property for **5% down!**

1990: It blows my mind that there are still people who see high leverage as an end in itself...see buying a property with a low down payment as an accomplishment. This is clearly the residue of the something-for-nothing-down movement.

Leverage is a mere **means to an end**. Either the deal makes sense or it doesn't. A high-leverage deal can be, and probably is, a **worse** investment than a low-leverage deal. You don't buy leverage, you buy bargains, unrealized potential, or positive cash flow.

1982: Real estate will always be a **good investment**.

1990: It ain't been that simple for a long time...if it ever was. Nowadays, you have to inspect each property to avoid toxic problems, you have to analyze each market to avoid overbuilding, rent control, etc., and you have to pray that you are spared such nationwide problems as higher interest rates, more tax reform, and so forth.

1982: What's an **environmental audit**?

1990: See my articles on the subject in the 9/89, 10/89, and 11/89 issues.

1982: I'm **pyramiding** up to my goal of owning a hundred-unit apartment building.

1990: Apartment buildings now have considerable **political risk**. Political risk is the risk that the government will pass laws which lower the value of your property. In recent years, there have been an increasing number of such laws, e.g., rent control, tax reform, the substantial penalty increases under the Fair Housing Amendments, increased liability for toxics. Rental houses, on the other hand, are largely immune from political risk. Plus they are small enough to let you diversify against some risks like toxics being found on your property.

Nothing down, pyramiding, you-can't-go-wrong-with-real-estate, due diligence that stops at a termite inspection, and all that are history. It's the '90s. JTR

36
Properties, Properties Everywhere, But Not a Deal Worth Doing

July 1987

In the July '86 issue of Real Estate Investor's Monthly ("Post-Tax Reform Act of '86 Investment Strategy"), I said that the Tax Reform Act of 1986 would cause income property values to drop. But I added that you would **not** see income property sellers lower asking **prices**. Rather, I said they would:

1. Refuse to sell.
2. Take back below-market mortgages.
3. Give cash-flow-guarantee mortgages.
4. Take back higher loan-to-value ratio mortgages.

I was right about number 1. Reports I've received from around the country are that income property sellers are refusing to sell for less than 1985 prices. But buyers are refusing to **pay** 1985 prices. Except for pride-of-ownership properties. Which is more art collecting than real estate investing.

Speculate on double-digit appreciation?

So whatcha gonna do? You've got money burning a hole in your pocket. You want to buy income property. But every deal you look at is priced as if the Tax Reform Act of 1986 never happened. Negative cash flow. The numbers don't work unless you assume double-digit appreciation. But double-digit appreciation in income property values ultimately requires double-digit appreciation in **rents**. And rare is the market where that's happening. Rarer still is the market where it can **continue** for very long.

In the October issue ("Can You Assume Inflation When Deflation Is So Widespread?" See Chapter 56.), I said that continued high appreciation rates in Boston would ultimately cause job offers for, say college professors, in Research Triangle, NC to look more attractive. Last month, I attended a grad school reunion in Boston and darned if the dean didn't tell us he was having a hard time recruiting professors...in part, because of high housing costs in the Boston area.

Publishers Business Services, the Boston firm that once processed orders for this newsletter and my books, said that they were having a dickens of a time trying to hire a part-timer because of the extremely tight job market...which was, in part, due to the lack of affordable housing. So much for any notions some might have had that Boston appreciation rates would stay **permanently** in double-digits. Or any other market. It can't happen because that market will quickly price itself **out of** the market for the workers who are needed to sustain such growth.

Hold your fire

Don't pay the '85 prices and rationalize it by giving yourself some Chamber Of Commerce speech as to why appreciation rates in **your** area will stay in double-digits. You're kidding yourself.

You've got to do deals on **better** terms than in '85 in order to make up for the lost tax benefits. You should no more pay pre-'86 prices for a post-'86 income property than you would pay a tax-**exempt** bond price for a **taxable** bond...which is roughly how real estate's tax situation has changed.

But how do **you** do better if the sellers won't **offer** better?

You might try making 1985 **price** level offers but on the **terms** I predicted in numbers 2, 3, and 4 of my July '86 prediction...i.e., low interest rate, high loan-to-value ratio, seller mortgages with cash flow guarantees.

Try low ball offers

Buyers tend to assume that if a property's on the market for $1,000,000, it can't be bought for less than $900,000 to $950,000. Assumption is the mother of all screw-ups. Maybe it **can** be bought for $750,000 or $800,000. You'll never know unless you ask. In other words, make the offer you **have** to make in order for the deal to make sense. If it's rejected, move on.

Revisit the market

Mike Scott says some sellers have lowered their prices...but they get no response because the buyers got discouraged and stopped looking. If you're one of those, get out and look again. Maybe some of the sellers either **have** to sell or have figured out that wishing won't make the Tax Reform Act of 1986 go away.

Go fishin'

A builder where I used to live once said, "Sometimes, in real estate, the best thing to do is go fishing." Hardly any real estate newsletters will ever give that advice. Because you don't need a newsletter for that. Seems to me, however, that there's a kernal of truth to the notion that the acquisition market isn't always attractive. And that if you acquire when it isn't, you may hurt yourself.

Focus on managing

One non-fishing thing real estate people do when the market's not so hot for dealin' is to clean up their **management** act. That's more productive than fishing. For example, if you have any weak employees, run a blind ad to see if the labor pool offers a better selection than when you hired Mr. or Ms. Not-So-Hot.

Parking places for your cash

If you have a lot of cash burning a hole in your pocket, and you can't find satisfactory deals to do, consider **paying down debt**. To pay down debt faster than required by the terms of the loan is the same as investing the money at the loan interest rate for the remaining term of the loan.

A year or so ago when money market rates fell, I began paying off various car loans, personal loans, education loans, and credit card balances. In effect, I was investing the money at 12% to 18%...much better than the 6% or so the money market checking accounts were paying.

Where to get a 12% return

Mortgage debt should **not** be excluded from such pay downs. Think twice about paying down a mortgage, though. Because it costs so much to get it back...transaction costs like points, prepayment penalties, appraisal fees, etc.

But it can still be the best investment you have available...especially if you have any 12% or higher mortgages. If you were planning to exchange up anyway...and use your cash horde as additional down payment along with your old property's equity...there are no **incremental** transaction costs to paying down the mortgage on that property now.

But if you were going to **keep** your current properties, using your cash horde to pay down mortgages now would require you to pay refinance transaction costs to get the money **out** later to use it as down payment money. In that case, the return on the pay down is the interest you **save** between now and refinance time **less** the transaction costs. In other words, the sooner you'll be refinancing to get the money back, the less sense paying down a mortgage makes.

Tax reasons to pay down

The Tax Reform Act of 1986 gives you several **additional** reasons to pay down loans. By paying down mortgages on investment property, you increase your **passive** income. If you have rental property losses which would otherwise have to be carried forward, that would enable you to use them **now** instead.

Also, even on personal debt other than home mortgages, you may bump up against the phase-in of nondeductibility (35% in '87). Paying down those loans reduces the need to carry deductions forward there, too.

Finally, if you are one of those who ignores my advice to never take back mortgages, paying down business debt will lessen the impact of the new installment sale law's proportionate disallowance rules on you. [*Editor's note: the proportionate disallowance rule has since been repealed.*]

Conclusion

I know it's tough to find good income property deals out there these days. That's why I've been writing about leper properties (April '87, See Chapter 45.), conventionalization of FHA apartment loans (June '87), the Contrarian Strategy (Nov. '86, See Chapter 43.) and numerous clean-up-your-management-act articles. I think there are attractive deals available out there today. But that it takes much more effort and moxie to find them than usual because of the Tax Reform Act of 1986's one, two punch of lower income property values and anti-installment sale rules.

I am concerned that some of you will be so eager to do deals that you will talk yourself into jusifying purchases at 1985 prices on the grounds that double-digit appreciation rates will return. Or that you will start believing sellers who say their operating expenses total 30% of gross income.

Hold your fire until you can see the whites of their positive cash flow. JTR

37
"Sit Back and Wait?"

November 1988

According to a study for Equitable Real Estate Management by Real Estate Research Corporation,

"Prospects for individual investors are poor in 1989, and small players are advised to sit back and wait."

That reminds me of a press release a big syndicator put out in the early eighties saying the days when small investors could invest on their own in real estate were over...only investment through syndicators would work henceforth.

I note that Real Estate Research Corporation is not known for its interest in "small players." Also that the same study says there is a "decreased number of available properties" for its big clients. Might their advice to us small players be translated as, "Go away, kid. You bother me." JTR

38
Get a Real Estate License

March 1988

In 1980, when I decided to buy my first California house, I got a California real estate license. Getting a commission on the purchase of that one house was the **only** reason I got that license. After I bought it, I refused to pay the renewal fees, take required continuing education courses, etc. and the license lapsed.

Too much money to ignore

Does that seem like a lot of trouble for one commission? It was $4,000, which was 25% of my down payment. All I did to prepare for the license exam was read a book. Total time to read the book and take the test probably did not exceed 8 hours. So I got paid $500 an hour.

In my early years in New Jersey, I always got a commission for selling investment properties to myself. And, in the typical case, the commission represented 15% of the down payment. That's a significant edge in a business where making money is no snap.

The commission

The main reason to get a license is to get a commission on the properties you buy. Typically, you get 1/4 of the total commission, which, in turn, is 6% or 7% of the purchase price. On the next page is a chart showing the percentages of down payment 1/4 of a 6% commission represents in some common financing structures.

Income properties

I recommend that you get a real estate license if you buy one- to four-family properties. I do **not** recommend it if you buy **income properties**. The reason is the hardest part of **income** property investing is **finding** good deals. If you tell the sellers you encounter in your property search that you want a commission on the purchase, you become **second best** on their list of buyers. Coming in second in the race for the best deals can dramatically lower your return.

Financing	Commission	Down %	Comm. as % of down
3% FHA	1.5%	3%	50%
0% VA	1.5%	0%	∞%
5% PMI	1.5%	5%	30%
10% PMI	1.5%	10%	15%
20% Conv.	1.5%	20%	7.5%

And real estate **agents** will drop you like a hot rock if they find out **you** want a commission in the deal. Agents don't bring me **all** the deals I buy. But they bring me enough that it would hurt too much to lose them. So as an income property buyer, I proudly tell agents that I do **not** have a real estate license.

Fiduciary responsibility

If you get a commission, you have to treat the **seller's** interests as you would your own. In other words, you **cannot** get a good deal. If the seller could probably do better selling to someone else, you have a duty to **tell** the seller that.

I still think small property buyers should get a license. You don't need to buy properties for less than market value to get a decent return on investment. And if you find an opportunity to buy a property for less than market value, make it clear from the start that you do **not** want a commission on that deal and that you are **not** the seller's agent. In writing.

Insider knowledge

Laymen think the great advantage of being a real estate salesperson is insider knowledge. They think that agents are the first to hear of good properties and buy them up before the public hears about them.

There's a kernal of truth to that. But generally, it's **not** true.

For starters, most real estate agents do not own real estate other than their home. Many cannot **afford** to buy investment property. Others wouldn't do it if they could. They are commission-oriented.

On the other hand, most real estate offices **do** have one or two agents who invest on the side. And those agents do indeed try to use their insider position to the maximum. As it happens, I did not buy any of my own company's listings when I was a real estate agent. Being an insider in **one** real estate company does **not** make you a **county**-wide, or **multiple listing service**-wide insider. And one company's listings are too few to matter. So the value of insider status is negligible on average.

General insider knowledge

Working as a full-time real estate agent can get you insider knowledge in a **general** sense. General insider knowledge includes such things as knowing people like escrow officers, loan officers, attorneys, surveyors, insurance agents, etc.; local settlement procedures; tax assessor procedures. General insider knowledge can't hurt. But neither is it valuable enough that you would work as a real estate agent just to get it.

Commission, si; insider knowledge, no

If you buy small residential properties, get a real estate license and get a commission when you buy. On **larger** acquisitions, you are probably better off **not** getting a commission. The commission is the only reason to get the license. The insider knowledge that laymen assume agents benefit from is vastly overrated. JTR

39
Less is More Under the
Tax Reform Act of 1986

How to deal with the Tax Reform Act of 1986 (TRA '86) continues to be one of the main preoccupations of real estate investors these days. For good reason.

Small is beautiful

TRA '86 turns the flow of tax benefits upside down. It used to be the **highest** income people who benefitted. Now it's the **lowest**. And they benefit in many ways.

Good deals for small investors

- **$25,000** passive loss limit exemption.
- **Old installment sale rules** apply if sale price $150,000 or less.
- **First-year expensing** limit of $10,000 per year.
- **Home** purchase mortgage **interest** and property **taxes** fully deductible.
- **Home refinance** mortgage fully deductible in most cases.

- **Second home** interest and property taxes deductible in most cases.
- $40,000 exemption from the **alternative minimum tax**.

So shrink your property

The good deals which lower income (adjusted gross not counting real estate below $100,000) investors get make the properties such investors buy **more valuable** per dollar of net income. In other words, such properties sell at **lower capitalization rates** (net operating income divided by sale price) than larger properties...which means the sellers of smaller properties get **higher** prices.

With a 100-unit building, for example, tax-favored little guys are **not** your market. So chop the complex up.

Convert to condo

You could convert to condo. I know the condominium conversion market is **dead** in most markets. But that's the sell-'em-for-50%-more-than-rental-apartment condominium market. If the apartment complex were worth $2.5 million **before** tax reform, you'd only have to get **$25,000** a unit as condos to erase the effect of TRA '86 (which caused about a 15% to 25% drop in the value of income property). Actually, condo conversion will create substantial incremental **transaction costs** so you'd have to sell for $27,000 a unit or some such.

But that ain't bad. Buyer puts 20% down or $5,400 and gets a $27,000 - $5,400 = $21,600 mortgage at 11%. Monthly principal and interest payments are $205.70 on a 30-year mortgage. Add another $80 a month for taxes and insurance and the former tenant is now an **owner** for $285.70 a month. Furthermore, while he could deduct **no** part of his rent as a tenant. He can **now** deduct his property taxes and interest, which is **most** of his monthly payment. And he gets price appreciation. Why would anyone rent?

invest in rental housing, Congress probably inadvertently set in motion forces which will push the homeownership percentage to record heights. It's now at 63.8%, down from a peak of 65.6% in 1980 according to the Census Bureau.

Tax *that,* Congress!

It's not an investment consideration, so I probably shouldn't even think about it. But one of the things that appeals to me about the massive condo conversion solution to the TRA '86 is the look it would put on Congress' faces. They beat up on us because we are less numerous than homeowners. What's to stop us from retaliating by converting our numerous tenants to condo owners. The apartment building that Congress was going to squeeze would then disappear from the face of the earth. And in its place are a

The more I think about it, the more it seems to me that there should be widespread condo conversion to cheap apartments all across the nation. The nation's apartment owners could recoup the value they lost in TRA '86. And it might even **add** value above and beyond what the properties were worth **before** TRA '86. The key is to forget the much higher prices that condo conversion **used** to bring. Rather sell for the same $20,000 to $40,000 per unit prices that apartments recently brought **as** rental apartments.

You're now taxed at **ordinary** rates anyway, so you no longer need to worry about losing your long-term capital gains exclusion as a result of being declared a dealer…which was probable in past condo conversions. By reducing, to an unprecedented degree, the incentives to

hundred homeowners. Tax **that**, you lilly-livered, boot-licking, blow-dried, "members of the most exclusive club in the world."

Subdivide to smaller rental properties

You may be able to just subdivide so that you end up with smaller investment properties.

For example, if your 100-unit apartment complex consists of 25 fourplexes, you may be able to subdivide the property and sell to 25 different buyers. In fact, you could do this over a period of years selling enough each year that the gain from the sale would equal your **carried forward losses** on the property you still owned (See "The Ham Slice Method of PIG Use" in the January, 1987 **Real Estate Investor's Monthly**). That'd give you tax-free gain without the need to structure tax-free exchanges. Furthermore, your basis in any new property you bought would **not** be reduced by the gain you avoided tax on...as it **would** in an exchange.

Should you buy smaller properties?

Income property investors typically started out with single-family houses or duplexes. Then they moved up and never looked back.

It may be time to look back. To put it as starkly as possible, how much better off would you be today if the investment real estate you owned on May 1, 1986 (just before the Senate Finance Committee approved TRA '86) had been in the form of **single-family** rental houses instead of **income** property?

Speaking for myself, my net worth would be about 50% greater today if I owned all San Francisco area **houses** instead of Texas **apartment buildings**. Part of the difference is due to **overbuilding** in Texas. The rest is due to TRA '86 adversely affecting income property, but not houses. Run the numbers on your **own** portfolio.

Political risk

I have longed warned you against political risk. I specified that I meant the risk of your apartments becoming **rent controlled** or your raw land being **down-zoned**. Now add a third, equally dangerous category...the risk of radical change in the **tax laws** that pertain to your properties in a way that affects them adversely.

There is little or no political risk in single-family homes. Because there is strength in numbers.

So, yes, I know many of you are income property owners. And going back to single-family homes seems an unthinkable "retreat" from the success you strove so long to achieve. But radical changes in your investment environment warrant radical changes in your thinking. I am not ready to get out of income property myself yet. But I ain't brain dead, either. If Congress plans to drain dry America's income property owners with adverse tax laws, the only sane thing to do is "emigrate from Income Property Land."

Don't be too hasty. Smaller properties generally have higher transaction costs per million dollars invested, lower cap rates, and more expensive management. They have long had the advantages of greater liquidity and less rent control risk than income property. All that's changed is that they now have **another** big advantage...little risk of adverse tax laws. JTR

40 Thoughts on Investment Strategy 1987

May 1987

From time to time, I analyze various aspects of real estate investment strategy in articles. This article, however, will set forth the overall strategy I currently recommend. In order to achieve such big picture breadth, it will necessarily be short on depth.

Upgrading versus buy and hold

Upgrading means paying fair market value for properties that have some **unrealized potential**, making the changes necessary to realize that potential, then repeating the process with the next property. There are many ways to upgrade other than cosmetic renovation. Real estate investors often refer to the kinds of properties I'm talking about as "situations."

Buy and hold is what it sounds like. You pay fair market value for any decent property, then you hold it for its income, tax benefits, and appreciation.

I recommend upgrading. Successful upgrading always pays a higher return than buy-and-hold. In today's market, buy-and-hold may actually produce a **negative** return in most markets.

Upgrading is a deliberate program of calculated risk. Buy-and-hold was a conservative, income-oriented approach in the sixties. In the seventies and eighties, buy-and-hold became a speculative approach would required high appreciation rates to produce an acceptable return. Speculators don't need advice. A dartboard will do.

Holding period

An upgrader ought to upgrade as fast as he can then move on to the next upgrading opportunity. So the holding period is the length of time it takes to upgrade. That can vary from next to nothing...as in a "flip" (reselling a property at a profit between the time you agree to buy it and closing)...to a career...as in the build out of the Irvine Ranch.

The important thing is to move on when the upgrading potential of the property has been exhausted. To linger longer converts you to being a buy-and-holder with its suboptimal ramifications for your return.

In the past, I have recommended a two-year holding period on the theory that most upgrades can be completed in that much time. But to my chagrin, I have found that my readers consistently remember my two-year holding recommendation but rarely remember that it only applies to upgraders. I abandon the two-year recommendation now partly to prevent being quoted that way out of the upgrading context. I hesitate to admit that longer holding periods may apply in a few situations for fear that the majority of readers will seize on it to justify long, return-depressing, holding periods. A case of 95% of the people claiming to fall into a category that applies only to 5% of the people. If your upgrade takes longer than two years, you better make sure you're not coasting.

Urban versus rural

You should only invest in major metropolitan areas with diversified economies. Money has been made in small towns and rural areas. But they are unacceptably dangerous. They offer a decidedly unattractive combination: low entry barriers and high exit barriers.

Entry and exit barriers

Low **entry** barriers mean it's easy for others to go into competition with you. In real estate, that means build a similar building. Podunk usually has few building restrictions. So if Podunk's one industry booms, competitive buildings pop up quickly thereby limiting your ability to profit from the boom.

High **exit** barriers means it's hard to go **out** of business in **bad** times. An example of a Podunk business with **low** exit barriers would be rental cars. You just drive them out of Podunk to a place where they're needed. You can't do that with buildings.

So rural areas offer the **worst** of both worlds...rapid buildup of competition in good times and few, if any, alternatives in bad times. You can lose...but it's hard to win big.

In diversified major metropolitan areas, if one industry goes sour, you can rent your space to another industry or its workers or switch to another use.

Management is also easier in major metropolitan areas because you have many alternative vendors. Small, outlying towns suffer from island-like disadvantages of few vendors and high transportation costs for items not available locally.

Property type

Upgrading opportunities are generally greatest in management-intensive property types...namely, residential, retail, and office. Industrial is rarely management intensive. Retail and office can go either way depending on the lease terms and tenants. Hotels are so management intensive they are not real estate investments.

You should confine your investing to general purpose, multi-tenant properties. Special purpose property like fast food restaurants requires special expertise and perhaps even a franchise to be viable. Single tenant properties (other than residential) can make sense but are much more risky than multi-tenant properties with few offsetting advantages.

Raw land is highly speculative. **Farm** land is as much special purpose property as a factory. **Building** land is subject to large, overnight drops in value as a result of downzoning, building moratoria, and so forth. It has negative cash flow (property taxes and sometimes interest) and can rarely be leveraged other than by seller financing...which I oppose when you are the seller.

You should only mess with raw land by way of options or contingent purchase agreements...and then only when you can see a way to upgrade the property by upzoning or some such during the option period. In other words, only when you can "flip" it.

Political risk

Political risk is the risk that the government will confiscate part of your property value and not compensate you for it. That's supposed to be unconstitutional. But the courts allow it. It happens in two main ways: rent control and downzoning.

You must avoid those two things. They each cause dramatic, instantaneous drops in property value. Rent control typically causes a steady decline in property value after the initial drop. You avoid rent control by:

- Buying only **non**-residential
- Buying residential buildings with **three or fewer** units (usually exempt)
- Buying **multi**family (four or more units) only in states with state laws that make it difficult to enact rent control (See Chapter 101), namely (Updated 12-90):

AZ	LA	NC	SD
CO	MI	NH	TX
FL	MN	OK	UT
GA	MO	OR	VA
ID	MS	SC	WA

If you buy multifamily property in states which **can** get rent control, avoid **liberal** communities. You can tell by looking at the results of the '84 presidential election. Communities that gave more than 40% of their vote to Mondale are more likely to enact rent control in the future. Avoid also multifamily property in communities with affluent high-rise apartment buildings (the tenants are highly skilled politically) and communities with lots of college students (liberal and activist).

You avoid the political risk in raw land by not ever owning it. **Control** it instead...as I described above. ᴊᴛʀ

41
Clauses for When You Sell Property

December 1986

Here are clauses you should try to get and clauses you should try to avoid when you sign an agreement to sell real estate. (You should **exchange**, not sell, in the vast majority of cases. This article covers only the **sale** portion of the exchange agreement.)

No blank-check clauses

A blank-check clause is one where you agree to pay something that is outside of your control. Do **not** sign such a clause. An example:

"Seller agrees to repair any termite damage at seller's expense."

Either **let the buyer get out** of the agreement if the termite inspector finds damage or put a low **ceiling** on how much you'll pay for or give yourself the **option** of either **paying** for the damage or **cancelling** the contract. This clause is especially important in California where termite inspectors seem to require replacement of the **majority** of bathroom floors no matter how new or how recently the floor was previously replaced. When the work required by the termite guy is unnecessary...and the lender will allow it...you might offer the buyer the choice of having the work done or getting **half** the cost estimate in cash.

Sell your loan impound account

If you pay taxes or insurance or mortgage insurance or all of the above to the lender, **sell** the balance in the account to the buyer. This is standard practice in the industry. I include it here to make sure you don't forget it.

Closing day proration

Try to say that **you** will be considered the owner on closing day for the purpose of prorating the rental property's income and expenses...unless the property has negative net operating income.

About the only kind of property which would have negative operating income would be a one-family or two-family house with a vacancy. You want the income and expenses because the income is **greater** therefore, you pick up extra money.

On smaller properties, the one day's net income would pay for one dinner to celebrate the sale. On a larger property with, say, a net operating income of $100,000 a year, the prorated credit to you for closing day income net of expenses would be $100,000 ÷ 365 = $273.97.

If the buyer is really asleep, get him to let **you** have the **income** on closing day and let **him** be the owner on closing day for **expense** purposes. You might agree to be liable for any lawsuits on that day as a bargaining chip to get the income but not the expenses.

Mortgage pay off

If you are paying a mortgage off, **wire** the money to the lender. That way you avoid being charged three to five days extra interest for the time the pay off check is in the mail to the old lender.

One day's interest on a $100,000 10% mortgage is $100,000 x 10% = $10,000 ÷ 365 = $27.40. On a million dollar 10% mortgage, $274.

Check with the title or escrow company and the lender in advance for wiring instructions. **Hand carry** the pay off check if the old lender is local. But do not assume that you can pay off the loan at **any** branch. Lenders frequently say the interest meter does not stop until the check arrives at their mortgage payment central processing office...even when you took it to another office of the same company and got a receipt.

Warranties

Warrant only **past events** of which you have **certain** knowledge and which the buyer cannot verify for himself before purchase. Attorneys generally write purchase offers so that the seller warrants everything under the sun. That's one of the reasons they have their deal killer reputation. Do **not** agree to those warranties.

Warranty only things like:

"Seller warrants that he has not received verbal or written notice from the government that the subject property is in violation of pertinent building codes or zoning laws."

"Seller warrants that the attached rent roll accurately reflects the occupancy and rent collections for the month of December 1986."

Refuse to agree to warranties like:

"Seller warrants that subject property is not in violation of pertinent zoning laws."

Tell the buyer to read the zoning laws himself.

"Seller warrants the attached income statement accurately reflects the income and expenses for 1986."

Income and expenses can get subjective. Show the buyer the **books** and your **receipts**. Give him written **permission** to get expense information from your creditors like utilities and insurance agent. Tell him to **estimate** expenses like repairs and supplies which vary according to how the building is managed.

Watch out for the word "all"

One buyer I negotiated with was an attorney. He kept wanting me to certify that I had shown him "all" the books, and told him about "all" the expenses, and so forth.

I said, "Look, I have shown you everything to the best of my knowledge. But I will not put myself in a position where forgetting to include one of thousands of transactions will make me guilty of fraud. Tell me specifically what you think is missing and I'll do my best to cover the subject."

Possession

Do not let the buyer take possession before closing. If you do, I can almost guarantee he'll come to closing with a list of demands based on the inspection "by microscope" he made after he moved in. Better you should pay his motel and furniture storage bill if necessary.

Prohibit recording agreement

Prohibit the buyer from recording the purchase agreement. If he does, it can foul up your title and put him in a position to subject you to nuisance extortion.

Check the buyer out

Entering into an agreement to sell real estate is really an extension of credit. The amount extended is how much it would cost you if the buyer backed out at the last minute.

So check the guy out. And put a clause in the agreement giving you permission to do that. You want to talk to the last several people he bought from and ask them if they'd sell to him again.

I know that's an unusual suggestion. But the fact that few have figured out the need for it does not diminish the need.

Miscellaneous

- Do not agree to share forfeited deposits with broker
- Sale is subject to rights of tenants in possession.
- Time is of the essence.
- No oral agreements.
- Binding on heirs.
- Purchase agreement assignable by seller but not by buyer.
- Seller gets all proceeds of condemnation occurring before closing.

If no broker, say so

If you are selling without a real estate broker, make the buyer warrant that to the best of his knowledge, no broker is involved in the sale.

If you are a real estate agent, say so. If you have a real estate license, you are required to tell the buyer that in writing in every state I know of.

If commission due

If a real estate broker is due a commission in the deal, get the broker and the buyer to warrant that to the best of their knowledge, no other broker is involved.

The commission clause should make payment of the commission contingent on the deal closing.

Put a tight deadline on all contingencies

All contingencies should expire on tight deadlines. Inspection-type contingencies should die in two to ten days. Don't lose sight of the difference between days and "working" days. Give enough time for mortgage contingencies.

Specify which party pays which costs

Specify which party pays which costs. When the paying party is you, specify the amount or at least set a dollar limit. You are looking for trouble if you agree to pay the "customary" cost or "reasonable" cost of something. JTR

42

For the Investor Who Has Everything: A New Goal

October 1986

You say you're a millionaire. You already own the home you want, the car you want, and you can afford to send your kids to college. So what's left?

When I got out of the army, my first goal was to **make a living**. After I achieved that, I wanted to **increase** my income and net worth. When I had filled all the hours I wanted to work with profitable activities, I switched to activities that made **more per hour**.

Now I'm in a new phase...a phase which many of **you** might be ready for. Additional money really does not change my life anymore. Because I already have **enough** money to cover the mortgage payment, the boys' preschool tuition, and the credit card bills. At this point, additional income just goes to the tax man and into our bank account. So instead of trying to increase my income per hour, I try to increase my **satisfaction per hour**.

If it ain't fun, don't do it

More specifically, I ask myself, "What did I do today?" Then I ask, "Did I **enjoy** doing it?"

Inevitably, the answer is yes to some activities and no to others. So my present goal is to **get rid of** the activities I do **not** enjoy...regardless of their income-producing potential.

Examples of activities I do not enjoy and wish to reduce or eliminate:

- Dealing with problem tenants.
- Paying bills (the administrative, not the financial burden).
- Dealing with problem employees.
- Auditing accounts.

What to do

In my opinion, the solution to these problems is **not** what most people think, i.e. to **insulate** yourself from them by hiring employees to take care of them. That rarely eliminates the problem. And new employees bring **additional** vexations...like increasing the number of problem employees you have to deal with, bills you have to pay, and accounts you have to audit.

When possible, I **subcontract** out the activities I don't enjoy. In theory, you can subcontract out everything. Beginners often make that mistake. But in reality, only **some** activities can be subcontracted out satisfactorily. Property management is one activity which I generally do **not** believe can be subcontracted out with satisfactory results. Another is telephone answering service. Examples of activities which **can** be subcontracted satisfactorily include steam cleaning carpet, plumbing, leasing nonresidential space, and pitched roof installation.

When subcontracting is not feasible, I **reduce or eliminate** the activity. For example, you can deal with **fewer** problem tenants by holding your **rents below market**...or by switching to a property type with fewer tenants per million dollars of value like **industrial** or **retail**. Those two property types also rarely have employees. And because the tenants pay most of the expenses in industrial and retail, you have fewer bills to pay and fewer audits to do. ЛТR

PART FOUR

THE CONTRARIAN STRATEGY

43

Everybody's a
#%&@! Contrarian

Ah, the contrarian strategy. See what everbody else is doing and do the opposite.

It's simple. It sounds like a plausible way to achieve a better than average return. A way to pick up property at bargain prices because nobody else wants it.

Does it work?

Sometimes.

Is now an excellent opportunity to use the contrarian strategy in real estate?

Not yet.

Reasons to shun real estate

At present, real estate investment sports a bunch of turn offs:

- Low inflation in most areas
- High vacancy rates
- Worst tax law ever
- Insurance crisis
- High foreclosure rates
- Falling property values in many cases

- Increased bankruptcies
- Toxic chemical liability

OK. Those are the reasons why builders and investors **ought** to be getting out of the market.

But **are** they?

Darned few of them so far.

Everyone believes everyone else is getting out

Having read about the turn offs I listed above, the vast majority of real estate investors have concluded that everyone else is getting out of real estate. A Real Estate Research Corporation report ("Emerging Trends in Real Estate: 1987" $8, Equitable Real Estate Investment Management, Inc., 787 7th Ave., NY, NY 10019) said that a survey of developers and others indicated that they expected new construction of income property to be down sharply next year...but, "that many respondents apparently expect **others** to absorb the reductions." [emphasis added]

Office mania

In spite of massive over-building in virtually every office market, 68% of those surveyed by RERC said they expect to be developing, buying, or lending on new office buildings next year. Seems to me that anyone who knows a would-be office building developer has an obligation to try to get a legal guardian appointed for them. Friends don't let friends develop office buildings in 1987.

In June, I reported a *U.S. Housing Markets* comment that in some Sunbelt markets that there were so many "contrarian" developers that the contrarian strategy wasn't working.

But there's a big difference between reading reasons why people **ought** to get out and concluding that they **did** get out.

Get-In-Under-The-Wire Syndrome

One of the reasons the contrarian millennium has not arrived is Get-In-Under-The-Wire Syndrome. Tax reform proposals since 1984 have threatened to make real estate investments less attractive. But each proposal had a future effective date. Those dates became wires to get in under. And they kept getting postponed.

"No need to run the numbers on this one," fifty thousand developers thought. "Getting in under the wire will be such a great deal when the tax law changes you don't have to concern yourself with minor matters like vacancy rates."

Get-In-Under-The-Wire Syndrome applies to more than just tax reform and tax exempt bonds. In overbuilt Walnut Creek, California, they are still **starting** new office buildings. Why, I asked. Because voters passed an initiative restricting office construction. Buildings that were started by a particular time get in...you guessed it...under the wire.

There was even a surge of real estate syndication sales in the second and third quarters of this year...**after** the new tax bill was virtually law. Why? To get in under the wire for 19-year ACRS and the five-year phase-in. In view of the fact that the passive loss limits and alternative minimum tax nearly wipe out the benefits of 19-year ACRS and the phase-

in, I must conclude that you don't need much of a wire to inspire an attack of Get-In-Under-The-Wire Syndrome.

Contrarian strategy does not work until prices fall

Today's contrarians seem to forget **why** the contrarian strategy works when it works. The departure from the market of the majority of the former buyers causes prices to fall. When the prices fall **farther** than the underlying problems warrant, the properties become bargains.

To put it another way, the problems in today's market **do** warrant a drop a values. But if prices only drop as much as the problems call for, there are no bargains. It's only when the market **over**reacts that bargains appear.

That has not happened yet. Indeed, the market has hardly reacted at all. Stories in *The Wall Street Journal* and Marcus & Millichap's *Resource* newsletter reported price drops of 6% or so. But that is not enough to take things beyond the **appropriate** reaction to the **over**reaction stage. **Under**reaction is what the market has done to date. If real estate were stocks, it would still be time to sell short in most markets.

Contrast with 1975

I said in a recent article that failure to remember the lessons of 1975 was one of the causes of the present overbuilding. Maybe the **opposite** is true. Maybe too many investors remember how many bailed out of real estate in 1975...and how those who bought in '75 made a killing. (I bought a 12-unit in '75 for $102,500 and exchanged out of it in '78 for $132,000.)

But this ain't 1975. In 1975, real estate's name was mud. People laughed at you if you admitted you had invested in real estate. Talk was the real estate investment trust debacle was going to bring down most of the major banks in the country. An article in the Summer '76 *Real Estate Review* (which is written well in advance) was titled, "The Reasons Behind the Real Estate Crash" and made reference to the "recent real estate debacle." Other articles in that issue talked about "troubled real estate," "workouts," and "Real Estate Owned" (foreclosed real estate).

Realtors® printed "Real Estate Is Alive in '75" bumper stickers. I have yet to see a "Real Estate Still Ticks in '86" bumper sticker. The number of real estate agents plummeted in '75.

There is some talk these days about workouts and troubled real estate. But the only time I've seen the word "crash" lately was when Tony Downs wrote about the "Silent Crash in Office Building Prices" (See the October issue of **REIM.**) And Down's point in that article was similar to the point I'm making in this article...namely that the market is still **under-**reacting to its problems.

Not yet

We have not yet reached the point at which the contrarian strategy makes sense in most markets. Things are bad. That's for sure. But few players seem to be leaving the game. Everybody figures everyone **else** will leave.

The contrarian point has arrived when virtually **everyone** tells you you're crazy for investing in real estate. It has been said that a **recession** is when your **neighbor** is unemployed and a **depression** is when **you** are unemployed. By the same token, the contrarian strategy works when **you** are scared to death that **you** are making a mistake to invest now...**not** when you think everybody **else** is scared to death.JTR

44
Where Real
Contrarians Invest

January 1989

Quick, name a severely depressed market where you can get great bargains in real estate. Most people would say Houston.

Wrong.

Houston properties are available on terms that give **breakeven** or **negative** cash flow...which is no bargain. But Anchorage properties can be bought at prices which yield high cash-on-cash returns. Would ya believe 70% cash-on-cash per year?

That's what one of my readers said he got on a recent deal. He bought 9 bays (7 vacant) in a 12-bay industrial condo for $280,000. Down payment was $30,000, mortgage (from a government-related mortgage agency) of $250,000 at 9%, and he spent an additional $10,000 on improvements. He leased up in six weeks and grosses $5,800 per month. After expenses and mortgage payments, he gets to keep about $28,000 per year.

Who, you may wonder would lease a 1,200-square foot-bay in depressed Anchorage? Businesses who **used** to rent 5,000 square foot bays. Anchorage is depressed. But it's not totally depopulated.

You can buy top-of-the-line, 800-square-foot residential condos with garages there for about $30,000 (formerly $84,500)...and rent them out for $675 to $700 per month.

Another Anchorage reader tells of a recent $250,000, 8-unit bought with 10% down and an 11% mortgage. Rents are $625 per month per unit. That suggests an annual cash flow of about $6,600 or 26% of the $25,000 down payment.

The rule of thumb on a single-family rental unit is 100 times monthly gross rent. If you can buy for less than that, it's probably a decent deal. California and Northeastern houses often sell for **200** times monthly gross. The Anchorage condos are at $30,000 ÷ $675 = **44** times monthly gross.

As with the rest of the Oil Patch, the seller is usually a **lending institution** or some government agency that bails out lenders. Non-owner-occupant financing is hard to come by in Anchorage.

Caution: Connie Yoshimura of Fortune Properties (907-562-7653) says Anchorage used to have 250,000 people and it **still** has the residential and non-residential space to house 250,000. For example, there are several thousand vacant condos which are for sale, but not yet on the rental market. In a market as small as Anchorage (219,000 and falling population), that overhang is scary. On the other hand, you're buying for a third of replacement cost or less.

Alaska's economy is narrowly based on oil, fishing, timber, tourism. It's not for the faint of heart.JTR

45
The Selective Leper Strategy

April 1987

When the Tax Reform Act of 1986 (TRA) appeared, I said you would henceforth have to buy cheap. Cheap enough to get about a 10% cash on cash return.

No one disagreed. Except the sellers.

Not that they're able to sell at **higher** prices. They generally can't. Rather they are holding their properties off the market because

"Now's not a good time to sell."

Actually, now is as good a time as any to sell. But income property values have sagged because of TRA...and sellers refuse to admit it.

What to do

So much for the psychology of sellers. What about **you**? You've got money in your jeans and you want to buy some income property. Should you pay a pre-TRA price in order to do a deal...any deal?

Nope.

I think you'd better consider the selective leper strategy.

Real estate lepers

Just as there are people with communicable diseases who are shunned, so are there parcels of real estate which are generally shunned. Does the fact that a piece of real estate is shunned mean that it is a good investment? No.

Some real estate lepers are good investments. Most are **not**.

Selectivity is what's lacking in the contrarian strategy. Sometimes...perhaps most of the time...the "Street" is right.

Low price

These days, many retail stores have a table on which are piled extremely cheap books or records or whatever the store sells. If you take the time to go through them, you occasionally find a bargain. But most of what's in the extremely cheap pile is worth its price.

One way to approach acquisitions today is to look only at the very lowest priced properties. The "Dogs." The "junk." The properties in the beginning of a Multiple Listing Service (MLS) book in which the properties are listed in ascending order by price...although you won't find many income properties in the typical MLS book.

I'm talking about the kind of properties that, if you inquire about them, the agent will say,

"Those garbage listings!?"

or words to that effect.

Again, most of the lowest priced properties **are** garbage. But once in a while, there's one there with potential.

Long time on market

Another leper indicator is the fact that the property has been on the market a long time. In MLS books, the original listing date is often shown. In nonMLS property, how long a property has been on the market is find-outable...if not easily found out.

Virtually all long-time-on-market properties are overpriced. Do **not** buy them...at least not for their asking prices or near them. What you are looking for is the occasional property which everybody **thinks** is overpriced...but isn't.

An alternative approach would be to systematically make **low ball** (meaning **at** market value in this case) offers on all overpriced, long-time-on-market property. The goal being to turn up the rare property which was actually buyable **at** market value...but which everyone assumed was **not** because of its asking price and the normal asking-to-sale-price ratio in the area.

Not on market

I long ago abandoned the notion that I could limit my property-acquisition searches to properties which were on the market. I always systematically contact all owners of the type and size property I'm looking for.

I bought my Corsicana, Texas property as a result of calling an officer of the Dallas Apartment Association. He happened to be the property manager of the building and knew the owner was thinking of selling.

And I bought my Fort Worth property by sending a form letter to dozens of owners listed in the apartment association directory. No one else looked at either property.

Some not-on-market properties are really extreme, long-time-on-market cases where the owner still wants to sell but got tired of running ads or let the listing expire.

Out-of-date owner

Not-on-market properties are often owned by investors who have not been in the market for a long time. I've noticed that real estate investors tend to believe that conditions that prevailed when last they were in the market are still prevalent. If they were last in the market in a positive cash flow time, they will expect to sell at a price which will give **you** positive cash flow.

This is a case of buying **below** market value. Be careful ethically in such acquisitions. For example, many real estate investors have real estate licenses and like to get commissions when they "sell" themselves a property. Nothing wrong with that. I got commissions on most of my early acqiusitions. (I am no longer licensed.)

But when you get a commission on a deal, you are the seller's agent...even if you are also the buyer. As the seller's agent, you have a duty to advise the seller of the fair market value of the property. If you buy for **less** than market value...and get a commission for doing so...you'd better have a waiver letter or letter of indemnity signed by the seller...and possibly his or her heirs-to-be.

Non-agents also need to be careful about buying below market from an unsophisticated seller. It may violate state unconscionable act laws.

Toxic chemicals

The latest property disease which causes buyers to shun real estate is toxic chemicals...most commonly asbestos. In many cases, the market is probably overreacting. That creates an opportunity. But you'd better know your stuff.

Asbestos and other chemical problems are finite. They can be corrected at some cost. The key to profiting from such deals is knowing how to accurately estimate the clean-up cost...and how to get the job done. Then, if you can buy cheap enough to make a substantial profit on the resale of the cleaned-up building, buy. Don't overlook **carrying costs** during the clean up period.

Long-time owners

An investor who bought a building for $1,000,000 two years ago is unlikely to sell it to you for $850,000...even if $850,000 is the current fair market value. But if that same building is owned by a guy who bought it for $400,000 seven years ago, he may well sell it for $850,000. "I made $450,000 on the place," he can brag.

There is no rational difference between the two situations. But real estate investors often behave irrationally. So you may want to systematically seek out long-time owners. Atlanta Real Estate Investors Association president, Bill Manley, said he has noticed that sellers tend to want their **original equity** out in **cash** when they sell. But they'll often take their **gain** in the form of a **note** (before the installment sale changes in the TRA, anyway). That's the same mentality that'll sell "cheap" by recent standards because "I'm making a profit."

Other leper situations

- **Title problems** like I wrote about in the October '86 issue of **Real Estate Investor's Monthly** ("Case Study: Title Problem = Profit") can create profitable lepers.

- **Bad tenants** are common in rental houses. Often, the owner becomes a desperate "don't wanter" and the tenants are so bad that all prospective buyers become "don't wanters," too. An experienced investor recognizes the finite nature of the situation and buys at a substantial discount. One could systematically search for such properties by asking real estate agents if they have or know of any listings that are hard to show or dirty...or both because of bad tenants.

- **Trashed-out, smelly, filthy buildings** can turn off every other buyer leaving a bargain.

- Undersized and other **unbuildable lots** can be profit opportunties if you can get a variance or acquire enough adjacent property cheap.

- **Bad location** can even be fixed by **moving** the building. Again, the expense of moving a building is finite. But most people assume it's either impossible or would cost too much. Decent structures can be obtained cheap or even for free in cases where the alternative for the owner was to pay for demolition.

- **Lack of utilities** (water, sewer, electric) can make rural land leper-like. But in some cases, the utilities can be obtained for less than the discount their lack causes.

- **Slide** hazards make lepers of some California properties. In selected cases, either moving the building to a non-slide site or eliminating the slide hazard could increase the property value profitably.

Contrarian versus selective leper

The contrarian approach of buying what others shun is too broad. Better you should look at what others shun...and buy only the rare gems you can find in that leper colony. And do that only when you have the skill and resources to "cure" the "leprosy" in question.ⒿⓉⓇ

46
Workout

February 1988

It's beyond hope, my life is ruined," said Mark Chelling "Twelve of my limited partners are suing me. The bank is foreclosing. They won't renegotiate. The property's been running negative cashflow for three years. The reserves have been exhausted. Forget asking the limiteds for more cash. And I don't have the money to make up the losses...wouldn't do it if I could. To top it all off, we are all going to have a whopping tax bill."

"And your wife has filed for divorce," added Craig Lehmkuhl.

"How'd you know that?"

"I didn't. But it's par for the course you're describing. You may be wrong about the situation being beyond hope, though."

"How?"

"Lemme look at the property and the books and I'll get back to you tomorrow. One more thing. You're not personally liable on the mortgage are you?"

"No, but what difference does it make with the lawsuits and the tax liability?"

"It makes all the difference in the world. There's a good chance I may be able to get you out of this mess. You'll make little or no money. But you may be able to get rid of the property, the lawsuits, and the tax liability."

"Offshore Money"

After a whirlwind inspection of the syndicate's apartment complex and its books, Lehmkuhl is back in his office (415-934-1322). On the desk lies a well-worn copy of Lehmkuhl's main tool... The Bankruptcy Code. Lehmkuhl's not bankrupt. Never has been and never plans to be. To him, the bankruptcy law is a clinical tool.

He calls Chelling. "Mark, Good news. I think I might be able to work something out."

"No need."

"Really! What happened?"

"I've been talking to this mortgage broker. He's got offshore money. They're willing to lend on deals like this."

"And you gotta put up front money, right?"

"Well mortgage brokers don't work for free!"

"I know. And I also know that they don't have offshore money. It's a scam. Who're you gonna call next, a loan shark?

Look, if the broker's legitimate, he can give you names of satisfied customers. Ask him for the names and phone numbers of the last two or three borrowers he got 'offshore' money for."

Two days later, Chelling calls Lehmkuhl. *"No references. He says they're confidential. I called the Department of Real Estate and they say he's not licensed. OK. You were right about the guy. So what's your deal?"*

Chapter 11

"You sell me your interest in the partnership...not the real estate...for $5,000. I will then either renegotiate the loan so I can live with it. Or I'll put the partnership, not you, into Chapter 11. That stops the foreclosure. Since the property hasn't gone back to the lender, there's no excess loans over basis tax liability. And I have some ideas that might get the limited partners to settle their suits against you."

"No way. Bankruptcy's out of the question. I have a reputation..."

"Mark, you don't have to deal with me. But this partnership is bankrupt, dead, kaput, whether it's me or somebody else who files the papers. Face it."

"That's the only way?"

"Unless the lender will renegotiate."

"Nah. Already tried that."

Renegotiation

After signing an option to acquire the partnership, Lehmkuhl makes an appointment with the loan officer, Steve Linder.

"The collateral's got a net operating income of $143,000. If you cap that at ten, it's worth $1,430,000. There's also $225,000 worth of deferred maintenance. We need you to cut the loan amount to $1,400,000. And back off the balloon to '98. We promise to fix the deferred maintenance. When we're done, we'll raise the rents and the place will be worth $1.8 million...maybe $2 million if we're lucky."

"No way. That loan's on our books at $2,147,000. We might to willing to accrue some interest. But there's no way

we'll forgive, what, $700,000 of principal. What consideration do we get for the renegotiation? No way."

"If we can't get the loan changed to $1,400,000, our only alternative is Chapter 11. The bankruptcy judge will almost certainly **order** you to agree to what I'm asking you to do. One of the basic principles of the bankruptcy code is that the amount of a secured loan cannot exceed the **current** value of the collateral. Bankruptcy is expensive and time consuming."

"No way. We'll take it back. It appraised at $2,975,000 in '84. We'll get all or most of our money out. We don't have to give it away. No way."

Two weeks later...on the eve of the sheriff's sale, Lehmkuhl gets a call from the banker's superior. *"I understand you're interested in changing the terms on the Oak Meadow property?"*

"That's right."

"Well, I've taken over that account from Mr. Linder. I think we might be able to work something out."

The workout game

Craig Lehmkuhl is real. And he does this sort of thing for a living. The story above is fictitious, however. It's based on Lehmkuhl's general description of how deals go in his specialty... workouts of insolvent syndications. He did not tell me any details of any specific negotiations.

Lehmkuhl cautions that workouts and Chapter 11 are no quick-study technique that beginners should try based on what they read in an article. I agree.

But I think my subscribers ought to know some of the details and flavor of workouts...if only to know how much they **don't** know. And the principles which practitioners of the workout game have learned can often be applied by a broad audience to analogous situations. Finally, some subscribers may be involved in a workout situation in some way and would benefit from calling Lehmkuhl.

"Cram down"

Lehmkuhl's primary tool is the "**cram down**" provision of the bankruptcy law [Bankruptcy Reform Act of 1978 §1129 (b)(2)(A)(i)(II)]. It is the lender's main incentive to renegotiate before bankruptcy is filed. If filing is necessary, the Bankruptcy Court, uses the "cram down" provision to force creditors to accept reality.

Reality is one of the things Lehmkuhl brings to the deal. The troubled borrower is typically panicky. The lender is loathe to take a loss.

Like accident victims who have been told they must have an amputation, they are in the denial phase when Lehmkuhl arrives. His skill is convincing all concerned to agree to the "amputation"...and performing it skillfully. His compensation is the profit that results if the property can be turned around successfully.

His allies are a team of real estate, tax, and bankruptcy lawyers. And he has studied the daylights out of the pertinent laws himself .

Chapter 11 seeks to optimize the ongoing value of the assets and to fairly allocate interests (albeit reduced) in the assets to the creditors.

Cash

Reportedly, you can get **nothing down** deals in workouts. But Lehmkuhl says the 100% leverage is illusory. "By the time you get done with the legal fees, negotiating time, and deferred maintenance, you've put down a regular down payment even on an ostensibly nothing down workout."

Money talks and "creative finance" walks in the real world of million-dollar workouts. Until contractors, employees, and suppliers work for free, properties with deferred maintenance and/or high vacancy rates will require large cash transfusions. If you want to play the workout game, you'd better come up with cash in the 25% down range.

"Where the action is"

Workouts are where the action is in real estate in 1988 and the foreseeable future. Fifteen years ago, it was REITs. Then, condo conversion, tax-oriented syndications, and now, cleaning up the wreckage of tax-oriented syndications. That's not to say we should **all** do workouts. Most real estate investors have never been where the action was. Yet they have done quite well. JTR

47
Beware of Pretty Faces And Gamblers

Pretty faces attract us all. So does the thrill of gambling. Most of us recognize the emotional nature of these two forces and resist their pull when we need to. The problem in real estate investing is that nobody told us that it, too, has pretty faces and gamblers to avoid.

The pretty faces in real estate are on **buildings,** not people. And they're not called "pretty faces." They're called "pride-of-ownership" or "quality" properties. But the attraction and the danger in falling for them is no less than when it's pretty **people.**

Most of us recognize gambling when it is in the form of a lottery ticket or race track or casino. We know its unfavorable odds and its addictive power. But gambling can appear in real estate investment's clothing. In which case we are not so quick to recognize it.

Pride–of–ownership properties

I keep hearing that pride-of-ownership properties are the only ones selling these days. These are gorgeous buildings that sell for prices that are too high in relation to their net operating income. The equivalent of one Baa-rated bond selling for more than another Baa-rated bond…where both have the same interest rate…because the second bond had a **prettier** engraving job.

I wrote a whole article about the pride-of-ownership market in the August, '86 issue of **Real Estate Investor's Monthly,** so I won't go into detail here. A Realtor® recently told me that both syndicators and individuals will still "kill" to get these buildings. They will pay whatever it takes. Damn the cap rates, full speed ahead. (The cap or capitalization rate of a property is its net operating income divided by its value.)

Stay away from this stuff. A building's gorgeousness is only relevant in so far as it is reflected in higher net operating income.

Never make a pretty building your buy

William Nickerson, author of *How I Turned $1,000 Into $5,000,000 in Real Estate in My Spare Time,* said to buy the **worst property** in a good neighborhood.

Bill "Tycoon" Greene, much of whose other advice I disagree with, said to only buy properties that make you say, "**Yuk!**"

Look for economics, not aesthetics. The profit must be built into the deal when you buy it...either in the form of a positive cash flow based on the net operating income as of closing. Or in the form of an economic, value-increasing opportunity which you recognize prior to agreeing to purchase the property. By "economic" value-increasing opportunity, I mean that the **cost** of making the value go up will be much less than the amount of the value **increase**.

Stay out of real estate's "casinos" and "lotteries"

Millions of people gamble in casinos. Tens of millions gamble on lotteries. This, in spite of the fact that the odds are well known to be undeniably and substantially against the gamblers. People play to buy the **chance** of winning big. "You can't win if you don't play," goes the lottery ad.

Gambler's Syndrome is not confined to casinos and lotteries. There are gamblers in the stock market and in real estate. Furthermore, the number of gamblers in real estate goes up and down. After a boom gets under way, the number of gamblers goes **up**.

The late '70s boom, the tv real estate gurus, and the regional mid-'80s booms have convinced millions that real estate offers the gambler's dream of big winnings for little or no effort. The equity portion of the "securitization of real estate" is, in part, a "casinoization" of real estate.

Place your bets

Gamblers don't want to get their hands dirty with **management**. They just want to place a bet and get a result.

Used to be you could not do that in real estate. You **had** to get your hands dirty. Then Wall Street got in the act. REITs and limited partnerships "allowed the little guy to participate in big time real estate investing," to "diversify his portfolio" more than he could buying property the old-fashioned way.

That's the way those bookies in three-piece suits describe it, anyway. But, at bottom, there's not a heck of a lot of difference between "Thank you, Paine Webber, and "Thanks, Fast Eddy"...between a quote board and a tote board.

If the army of gamblers who have joined us real estate investors would wear identifying uniforms with "GAMBLER" in big letters, we investors would recognize when we are bidding against them...and promptly excuse ourselves from that particular auction.

But they do **not** wear identifying uniforms. And as a result, a lot of investors have unwittingly become gamblers. That happens when you are interested in properties that you suddenly can only buy for prices much higher than the properties' net operating income can justify.

Triple lemons and double digits

When the price you pay is low enough to let you have a significant positive cash flow or to upgrade profitably, you are **investing**. But when the sale price of that very same property gets bid up dramatically, it becomes a pure **gamble** which will only pay off in the unlikely event of double-digit appreciation...not unlike the odds on a slot machine or lottery ticket.

The vast majority of real estate investors see themselves as people who take **calculated risks**. They do **not** see themselves as gamblers. And they could eloquently denounce betting money on games of chance in which the probability of success was less than 50%.

But those same investors often do not understand that their familiar world of real estate can be transformed from an investment to a gamble with no more "announcement" than a price rise.

Don't bid against them

Do not bid against the **love-struck**, "quality" building buyers. Do not bid against the **gamblers** who overpay so much that real estate's payout rate drops to slot machine frequency.

If you're not getting a cap rate of 10% or more…or not buying a building with high-probability upgrade potential… you're gambling. To find those things, you generally have to avoid the most sought-after properties.

"Keep Wall Street, your securitized landmarks!

Give me your ugly, your redlined,

Your down-zoned yearning for higher density,

The unrealized potential of your myopic management.

Sell these, the appreciationless, market-rejected to me,

I lift my HP-12C beside the closing room door."

Apologies to Emma Lazarus. JTR

48
A Self-Postponing Prophecy

You've all heard of self-**fulfilling** prophecies. But did you know that there is also such a thing as a self-**postponing** prophecy? And that it is one of the most powerful forces in real estate investment?

The prophecy

Real estate's self-postponing prophecy is the statement that,

"Real estate is cyclical."

The cycle is caused by investors getting into and out of real estate in huge numbers. They get **in** because they believe real estate is **not** cyclical. By getting in, they bid up prices and thereby drive down yields. In the late seventies, I had many a cocktail-party argument with people who believed real estate was a **permanent** sure thing because of the certainty of population growth, inflation, and so forth.

And people get **out** because they think real estate is **not** cyclical. In the mid-seventies, people abandoned real estate in droves because they were convinced it

was a **permanent** loser...what with all the headlines about REITs going bust and taking the banks with them.

In other words, the cycle is caused by the coming **in** and going **out** of mobs who believe real estate is **not** cyclical...that the **current** situation is **permanent**. But when people believe that real estate **is** cyclical, they do **not** get out. They **wait** for the cycle to turn up. Thus believing, "Real estate is cyclical," causes investors to **stay in**...thereby **postponing** the bottoming out and turning up that is the cycle.

Signs of belief that bad returns are permanent

Things will turn **up** when the consensus says we are in a **permanent down** market. Are there any signs of belief that the downturn is permanent? A few. I saw one prominent one the other day in the real estate section of the December 21st *San Francisco Examiner*.

Jay Kaplan used to be the head guy at Consolidated Capital, one of the biggest syndicators. He now writes a weekly column for the *Examiner*. In his first column, he wrote,

"We are headed for a time of near-perpetual oversupply."

Attaboy, Jay. You tell 'em. Encore! Let's get this guy a **nationally** syndicated newspaper column.

Do I **agree** with him? Of course not. I believe real estate is cyclical and always will be. But we gotta keep that between me and the subscribers to **Real Estate Investor's Monthly**. As far as the **rest** of the world is concerned, we want them to believe Kaplan.

The more talk like Kaplan's that appears in the media, the sooner our cycle will return.

Other signs of belief that the down turn is permanent

I've seen a few other signs that the bad market is permanent. Some mortgage lenders refuse to lend in Texas, Louisiana, Oklahoma, and Florida's Dade or Broward Counties (See page 7 of the November **Real Estate Investor's Monthly**). Those lenders apparently believe that the bad market there is permanent. Otherwise, they would not abandon those markets to their competitors.

Another sign is the recent tendency of those commenting on the **office** market to say that high vacancies will continue until the '90s.

That's not permanence. But the farther out the recovery is depicted, the closer the market gets to concluding that the bad market is permanent.

A permanence index

Pollsters monitor consumer confidence and the president's job rating. Would that we had a "permanence" index for real estate investors. It would measure the percentage of real estate investors who thought current conditions, good or bad, were permanent.

The higher the percentage believing the current market is permanent, the sooner the cycle will reverse direction.

Until there **is** such an index (which itself would tend to postpone the upswing), you and I are going to have to jury-rig our own. Please keep an eye out for comments that the bad market is permanent and pass them on to me.

And if your market has the **opposite** comments...i.e., that the current good times will never end, lower thy loan-to-value ratio.JTR

49
Pride of Ownership And Your Strategy

August 1986

Pride of ownership is a widespread and widely misunderstood motivation in real estate investment. Herewith, an attempt to show where it belongs in your strategy.

Gorgeous, prestige properties

Pride of ownership is a phrase from the income property **brokerage** business. It means the property in question is gorgeous and located in a prestige location. As a result, there are investors who will pay a **premium** for it. And lenders who prefer such buildings.

Logic would call for no such thing. Logic would say that any extraordinary gorgeousness and prestige would be reflected in the **rents**. And that any buyer would pay the **same** price per dollar of **net** income as the buyer of an ugly, property in a non-prestige location. But it doesn't work that way.

An "income stream?"

When I took the CCIM (Certified Commercial Investment Member of the Realtors ® National Marketing Institute) course in the early '70s, the instructors kept saying, "The investor is buying an income stream." In the case of a pride of ownership buyer, an income stream is only **part** of what he's buying.

Pride of ownership buyers are buying **bragging rights**. The right to show off by saying, "Fred, do you mind if we stop by one of my properties on the way back from the deli? I need to give my manager something." Then you take envious Fred to Gorgeous Manor on Ritzy Drive. Fred is impressed. He'd be less impressed if you showed him the **income statement** for Gorgeous Manor. But then Fred will never ask to see that. That'd be gauche. Besides, Fred's probably not a real estate guy. He wouldn't recognize a low return on equity.

How much does pride cost?

Let's say there are two properties: Gorgeous Manor Apartments and Average Arms Apartments.

Gorgeous Manor is beautiful. Architecturally appealling. Lushly landscaped with mature trees and a golf course type lawn. It's located in a prestige, single-family neighborhood.

Average Arms is OK. Your basic apartment building. With your basic apartment landscaping of shrubs along the walls. The neighborhood is OK. Nothing to write home about.

But both Gorgeous Manor and Average Arms have the **same** net operating income...$100,000 a year. Investment theory would say the properties must be worth the same, then. But they're **not**.

Gorgeous Manor will sell for more. A buyer for the Average Arms might want a 10% capitalization rate (net operating income divided by property value). But a buyer for Gorgeous Manor will probably settle for a cap rate of 9%. That'd mean the buyer of Average Arms would pay $100,000/10% = $1,000,000 and the buyer of Gorgeous Manor would pay $100,000/9% = $1,110,000 (rounded).

Assuming they both put 25% down and got 11% 30-year mortgages, their before-tax cash flow (btcf) on cash return is

	Gorgeous	Average
NOI	$100,000	$100,000
mtge	$85,709	$95,137
btcf	$14,291	$4,863
down	$250,000	$277,500
c on c	6%	2%

So, in this case, the pride of ownership buyer is paying $14,291 - $4,863 = $9,428.00 per year purely for bragging rights. In other words, the side trip on the way back from the deli cost Mr. Pride-of-ownership $9,428 if it's the only one he took that year. To get the **cost per brag**, divide the annual lost cash flow by the number of brags per year. If you showed the property to **four** friends or relatives in a year, that's $9,428 ÷ 4 = **$2,357 per brag**.

What a Rolls Royce is to transportation

A pride-of-ownership building is to real estate investing what a Rolls Royce is to transportation. If your goal is to bring home your groceries, a Rolls is mostly a waste of money. You can bring them home quite well in a Chevy. The incremental price you pay for a Rolls is for the right to **show off** during the trip.

By the same token, if your goal is to earn a return on your equity, a pride-of-ownership building is a waste of money. You can earn a return in the Average Arms. The incremental price you pay for Gorgeous Manor is for the right to show off during the holding period.

But what about the "advantages" of a "quality" building?

I said pride of ownership is a brokerage term. Pride of ownership investors do not call themselves that. That say they buy, "quality" properties.

Tell them they're nuts (which is what I'm doing), and they'll say you are overlooking the **advantages** of "quality" properties.

"Quality" properties stay full, they'll tell you.

Baloney. **All** buildings stay full when the asking rent is **fair market value or lower**. If there is any evidence of "quality" buildings having higher occupancy rates, it is simply because the "quality" property was **below** market before the downturn. And **during** the downturn it was either **still** below market or at market. Whereas the non-"quality" properties were **at** market **before** the downturn. Then, when they did not lower rents fast enough **during** the down turn, their vacancy rate **increased**.

The same mentality that inspires owners to buy "quality" buildings at low cap rates inspires them to keep rents below market in order to have 100% occupancy. So any tendency of "quality" buildings to have higher occupancy rates during downturns and otherwise is simply an additional manifestation of the poor investment practices of the owner.

Ah, but the resale value...

The wonderful thing about a "quality" property is you can sell it at a premium. Indeed. But since you **bought** it at a premium, how are you better off? You're **not**. Selling at a premium is **only** a good deal when you can buy at **less** than a premium. To make that point crystal clear, consider how much profit you make if your holding period is **one day**.

Are **appreciation rates** higher in "quality" buildings? No. That's mathematically impossible. To say that appreciation rates are higher you are, in effect, saying that the **cap rates** on such buildings **fall continuously**. In order for that to be true, it must have started only recently. Because the cap rates on "quality" buildings are only about 1% below the cap rates on other buildings. That spread would have to increase to 2%, then 3% and so forth for "quality" buildings to go up in value faster than others. Try doing the numbers above with a **7%** cap rate. You'll get a **huge negative cash flow**. Even if anyone were **willing** to absorb such losses, few have the financial **ability** to do so. Especially if they cannot deduct the losses as the new tax law would require.

Higher class of tenants

"Quality" buildings have a better class of tenants. True. But how does that improve your bottom line?

The lowest class tenants do cause more management headaches. But their managers and owners expect a **higher return** to compensate them for such hassles. For the same reason ghetto grocery store owners charge more for their groceries than suburban grocery store owners. Hassles scare off the competition. That, in turn, allows the hardy few who remain to reap extra profits. Same law of economics applies to apartments, offices, etc.

And I suspect there is no discernible-in-the-bottom-line difference between **middle** class and **upper** class tenants. If there **is** a difference, the higher class tenants are probably the less desirable. As I noted in my book, *How to Manage Residential Property for Maximum Cash Flow and Resale Value*, higher class tenants are more prone to get rent control and similar laws passed. They know how to get things done. They have attorneys, accountants, friends in high places, etc.

Want evidence? Beverly Hills and Palm Springs have rent control. Detroit does not.

I prefer the middle class tenants.

I'll grant liquidity

The only legitimate investment advantage I'll grant pride-of-ownership buildings is **liquidity**. At times, when the income property market is down, average buildings are hard to sell. Pride-of-ownership buildings seem to **sell in any market**.

Their would-be owners lust after the building in question for years. "Let me know if you ever decide to sell, Ward." Little things like a down market can't dim the torch those would-be owners carry. They're affluent, cash-rich investors who harbor what under other circumstances is called pent-up demand. Realtors ® call their pride-of-ownership investors instantly when one of these gems comes on the market. I suspect the **holding periods** for pride-of-ownership properties are **much longer** than for non-pride-of-ownership buildings. So when an investor finally gets his long-awaited chance, he jumps.

Sell them, don't buy them

I have no objection to your **selling** pride-of-ownership buildings. Just don't ever **buy** one of the darned things. From an investment standpoint, they are simply **poor performers** to buy. In the example above, you'd get a better return on a money market checking account.

But if you can **convert** the Average Arms into Gorgeous Arms, then you've done something.

In the example above, converting would earn you a $110,000 premium. Of course, you'd have to spend part of that money to pull off the conversion. And there's no guarantee that converting the Average Arms to Gorgeous Arms would not cost you as much or more than the premium you'd earn. If it was easy, everybody would be doing it.

In order to buy non-pride-of-ownership buildings and convert them profitably to pride-of-ownership buildings, you'd need to be **highly selective**. The "before" property would have to have certain essentials like **excellent location, quality construction,** and **large rooms.** And what it needed changed would have to be relatively cheap.

More to life than return on equity

In my old age (40), I have discovered that there is more to life than return on equity. If you've run out of useful things to spend money on, maybe you **ought** to buy a Rolls...and show off on the trip to the Safeway. And why not add Gorgeous Manor to your "empire?" It's a harmless, if expensive, vice. It beats playing the horses, drinking to excess, and such.

And if showing off is how you get your kicks...hey, it's your money.

But spare me the investment rationalizations. Pride-of-ownership buildings are **lousy** investments. They yield less than average-looking properties ...less, even, than risk-free, hassle-free investments like federally-insured certificates of deposit. Contrary to popular belief, "quality" properties do **not** have any occupancy rate, management, or resale financial advantages which offset their lower yield. They **do** have a slight liquidity advantage over less attractive properties. But cd's beat pride-of-ownership properties all to heck on the liquidity score, too. ЛПR

PART FIVE

THE VULTURE STRATEGY

50

Should You Use the "Vulture" Strategy?

March 1986

here's trouble right here in Houston City. Trouble with a capital "T." And in Denver and Dallas and Silicon Valley and a bunch of other places.

Is one man's trouble another man's opportunity? Is it **your** opportunity?

Be careful.

A distress property that was not a bargain

At first, it was the highest priced property of its kind in the world.

Then it became a distress property. The owner' employees tried to turn it around. But they were making no progress. If you could have negotiated with the owners immediately after it became distressed, you could have picked it up for a fraction of its cost. A classic opportunity to use the "vulture" strategy, right? Think again. The property I have in mind was the Titanic.

There's distress and there's distress

There are two main categories of distress in real estate:

- **Market** distress
- **Management** distress.

The theory some vultures work on is that the current owner is a management idiot. That **you** are a management genius. And that once you get rid of the idiot and start managing the place **properly**, it will turn around.

If that theory is **correct**, and the damage done by the idiot can be **economically repaired**, the vulture strategy **can** work.

Unfortunately, many a would-be vulture has mistakenly diagnosed **management** distress when **market** distress was actually the problem. Market distress is to a building what a huge iceberg is to a ship at sea. You don't **manage** market distress. You simply try to **avoid** it. And if you can't avoid it, you try to **survive** it with staying power. In ships, staying power comes from watertight compartments, pumps, and life boats. In income property, it comes from on thing...cash. Enough cash to cover the negative cash flow until the market turns around.

Bargain price?

Distress property can generally be picked up for little or no money down and at a price much lower than the property was worth in the recent past. A bargain, right?

Maybe not.

Distress properties have **negative cash flow**. That's what distresses their owners. So you really don't **know** what your final purchase price and down payment are until the negative cash flow stops. If you buy an apartment building for $20,000 a unit, nothing down...then lose $3,000 a unit a year for two years...you actually paid $26,000 a unit and 30% down. If it takes **three** years, $29,000 a unit and 45% down. Still sound like a bargain? And what if it takes **four** years or **five** to cross breakeven?

I'll remind you that the current slump in apartment and office performance started **two or three years ago**. And they are **still** building apartment buildings and office buildings in most overbuilt markets. If you had vultured into the Houston market, for example, back in '83, would you have predicted things would still be as bad as they are? More importantly, would you have had the staying power to survive those negative cash flow years plus however many more there are to come?

Reserve funds

So-called "vulture funds" have large cash reserves for paying negative cash flow while waiting for the market to turn around. Although the reserves only go **into the property** a little bit each month, the money has to be raised **up front**. So from the viewpoint of the limited partners, the reserve is essentially the same as a down payment.

Individual vultures had better set aside a cash reserve, too. A nothing down deal that requires a large cash reserve is not much different than a **something** down deal.

"Turnaround" management

Many in business would have you believe that turnaround management is different from run-of-the-mill good management. That turnaround managers are a special breed. They are not. Good management is good management. In good times and bad. What poorly managed buildings need is good management, not "turnaround" management.

Bad times simply **reveal** managers who were bad all along. Typically, they were lulled into complacency by positive cash flow. Then when vacancies climb, and cash flow turns negative, they are slow to change their ways because their old methods seemed to work before.

That's why new "turnaround" managers can come in and quickly improve a property's performance in some cases. But turnaround managers cannot improve the performance of a well-managed property that suffers from **market** distress.

Vulture funds

I am against group investing in general. That goes double for the vulture funds that have sprung up lately.

I suspect these funds stem more from the syndicator's need to pay his overhead and $10,000 a month home mortgage payment than from faith in vulture opportunities. Syndication companies take on a life of their own. They have employees and rent to pay, self images to uphold. For an individual investor, sitting out a bad market is a normal periodic occurrence. For a syndicator, it is **starvation**.

So how do syndicator raise money during a bad market? Vulture funds.

Management distress, si; market distress, no

Forget vulturing into **market** distressed properties. That is **speculating**, not investing. The word investment implies a degree of probability which is not present when you speculate on market trends. You cannot forecast how much more building there will be. Especially when tax reform is a large part of that equation.

Nor can you forecast the next **recession**. The last was in '82. Recessions occur about every three to five years. Imagine how much **more** distressed the market would be now if we did not have a booming economy. Which may well be the case in the next year or so.

Precautions for management distress vulturing

Vulturing into management distress properties can work. But you can get burned there, too. First, remember that the existence of obvious management distress does not mean there is not **also** market distress. In fact, market distress usually **causes** management distress.

An owner cannot fill his vacancies, so he lowers his tenant screening standards, That's bad management. You can raise the standards back up to where they should be. But that will not cure the **market** distress that inspired the previous owner to lower his standards. You'll simply go back to the same high vacancy rate and good tenants that he had to begin with.

Also, you must accurately estimate and provide for the cost of **deferred maintenance** and the **vacancy loss** as you make the transition from a building full of bad tenants to near empty building to a building full of good tenants.

Clean-out vacancies

That will occur even in a **good** market. Because one good tenant will not move into a building with 99 bad tenants and one vacancy. You must get rid of the majority of the **bad** tenants before the first **good** tenants will venture in.

The diagram below shows what I mean. Point number 1 is where you begin to throw out the bad tenants. Point number 2 is where the first good tenant is willing to move in. And point number three is where the building has been refilled; only now with good tenants.

Vacancy during turnaroud

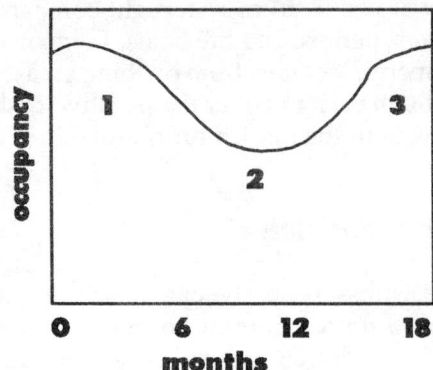

Both deferred maintenance and clean-out vacancies require lots of cash staying power.

Low prices and down payments alone are not enough to make a real estate investment profitable. A successful vulture will also need above-average **skill** and **staying power** (cash). And to the extent that he's speculating on the **market** turning around, he will need above-average **luck**.ЛТR

51
Back-Door Vulture Strategy

Scott Hendersen is an apartment broker with The Alliance Realty Group in Dallas. He is in the trenches in the apartment market there. Here are some of his observations and my interpretations of some of the facts he reported to me.

Regulators and unhealthy lenders and refuse to acknowledge reality

The savings and loans own many income properties as a result of foreclosures. Healthy (typically out-of-Texas) S&Ls will generally sell for current market value even though that makes them take a loss. But the unhealthy S&Ls will rarely take the hit and sell for current market value. Here's an example of a deal that was done by an unhealthy S&L:

1985 price for the building with 10% down. Debt service is whatever your net operating income (NOI) is for the first three years, 9% interest only for the next two years, then 5 years self-amortizing at 9% ending with a balloon.

Is that a good deal? A vulture opportunity?

An optimist's option

Nope. That's an option. A panglossian optimist's option. The 10% "down payment" is the option price.

If the property appreciates from its current value ($10,000 to $20,000 a unit) up to the 1985 price you've agreed to pay for it ($25,000 to $40,000 a unit), you **begin** to acquire some equity for your 10% and your management effort. That will only require appreciation rates in the **20% per year** range...in a market where the appreciation rates have been **negative** recently.

Owners with equity will sell for current market

The only owners who will sell for current market value are those who have equity above their investment at the current market value. That typically is the **original lender** on properties with ten-years or older mortgages...nobody on newer mortgages. Wraparounds are collapsing back to the seller **before** the seller who sold it to the recent owner.

S&Ls would rather keep than admit loss

Many zombie savings and loans are totally controlled by federal regulators and are independent in name only. Regulators refuse to shut them down and thereby staunch their continuing losses because accounting conventions force them to 'fess up to the losses in the value of the loan and "Real Estate Owned" portfolios in a shut down...but allow them to maintain the fiction of **book value** as long as they **refrain** from shutting down the S&L. But since the value of the loan and income property portfolios **continues** to deteriorate, **not** shutting down the money-losing S&Ls borders on criminal neglect.

Who will ultimately pay for that neglect? The *de facto* owner of these properties is the FSLIC and Congress passed a resolution that the full faith and credit of the U.S. government stands behind the FSLIC. And we taxpayers are the U.S. government.

To buy *property,* buy selected second *mortgages* instead

Hendersen says some investors who want to buy **property** are instead buying second **mortgages** which have early balloons. The loan-to-current-value ratios are such that the second mortgage holder has some equity, but the owner does **not**. That means the current owner will **neither** be able to refinance or sell when the balloon comes due.

Make sure the sum of the underlying loans plus what you pay for the mortgage you buy is no more than 75% of current market value.

These mortgages sell at a sufficient discount that they provide a reasonable return even if the owner makes the balloon payment.

Makes sense to shut some buildings down

If the rental income from a building is less than its **variable operating expenses,** the building should be shut down. You still have to pay the **insurance** and property **taxes.** But the property taxes should be reduced dramatically because the building... impressive though it may be...is worthless.

But by shutting it down, you at least save the **other** operating expenses like payroll, utilities, repairs, and so forth. If the rental income is less than the expenses you avoid by shutting down, you are actually **better off** financially if you shut it down.

The mortgage payments are irrelevant. You are even better able to pay **them** if the building's shut down because at least you are avoiding the losses from operating the building. Hendersen says that some office buildings in Houston are indeed shut down because they cannot cover their variable operating expenses.

Back door vultures

It sounds mean-spirited to buy a mortgage in the hope you can foreclose. But it's simply a way to get a property for its current market value. You shouldn't have to pay **more** than market value to be conisdered a nice guy. So while the much heralded vulture strategy does not yet work, the **back-door** vulture strategy just might. JTR

52

Should You Use the Deep Pockets Strategy?

December 1986

There's a notion in real estate that if your pockets are deep enough, **you can't lose.**

Nothing is that easy.

Real estate, like any other business, must be managed efficiently. And since real estate is capital-intensive, its owners must remain mindful of the opportunity cost of tying up their money in the property in question...or in their "pockets" ...rather than in some other capital-intensive investment like other property or second mortgages or whatever.

The Deep-Pockets-Conquers-All theory implies that you can turn your brain off in real estate...if you have enough reserves. No need to manage efficiently. And earning a good return will take care of itself.

Deep pockets = lousy leverage

Everything is relative. To a rental house owner with monthly carrying costs of $750, a $15,000 savings account constitutes "deep pockets." To an office building owner with monthly carrying costs of $7,500, that same $15,000 savings account is just a brief stay of execution.

Leverage magnifies return. And real estate is one of very few investments where the overall return on the investment is consistently higher than the cost of borrowing...and therefore one of very few investments where an investor can profitably use leverage. Anything you do that **reduces** your **loan-to-value ratio** will also **depress** your **return.**

Maintaining deep pockets reduces your loan-to-value ratio and, therefore, your return.

Example

For example, let's say you have $1,000,000. Normally, a real estate investor would invest that as a 20% to 25% down payment and buy $4,000,000 or $5,000,000 worth of property with it.

Beginners think they'd use much higher leverage and buy $10,000,000 or $20,000,000 worth of real estate if they had $1,000,000 cash. In reality, neither the sellers nor the lenders are likely to permit 90% to 95% loan-to-value ratios on large income properties. And few millionaire buyers would take such risks.

A believer in the deep pockets approach, on the other hand, would have to leave much of that $1,000,000 in his "pocket." Otherwise, he'd be following the "empty pockets" strategy…which is what most real estate investors do.

22 months of mortgage staying porwer

If he left $400,000 in his "pocket" and used the remaining $600,000 as a down payment, he'd buy a property worth about $600,000 ÷ 22.5% = $2,700,000. Debt service payments on that $2,100,000 mortgage would be about $18,500 a month (10%, 30 years).

So the $400,000 in "deep pockets" reserve would enable the owner to carry the mortgage for about 22 months with no help from net operating income. With the severe vacancy rates, rent reductions, or substantial rent concessions that characterize depressed markets, you'd have little net operating income.

But look at Mr. Deep Pockets' loan-to-value ratio. The total value of his assets is $2,700,000 in real estate + $400,000 in liquid assets = $3,100,000. His total loans are $2,100,000. So his loan-to-value ratio is $2,100,000 ÷ $3,100,000 = 68%.

More important, $400,000 of his assets are **liquid**. That means they are earning far less than they would in real estate. Money market, accounts, for example, are earning only 5.5% (October national average).

If that $400,000 were in **real estate**, it would presumably be earning an overall return of 20% or more. The difference in the money market and real estate returns is 20% - 5.5% = 14.5% or 14.5% x $400,000 = $58,000 a year in this example. Deep pockets are nice. But so's $58,000.

You need to survive the cycle

Real estate is a **cyclical business**. It is also generally a **profitable** business. But

in order to be around to **collect** the profit, you must **survive** the cycle.

The need to survive the cycle is the kernal of sense in the deep pockets theory.

If your investment's cash flow, tax benefits, and appreciation add up to a good return during the first five years after you bought it, you are a successful real estate investor…but **only** if you are **still** the **owner** at the end of that period.

In many cases, the **five-year** performance is good. But the **first three years** were **terrible** and only saved by a stellar fourth and fifth year. That's the nature of real estate investing.

If you were unable to hold on to the property during the tough first three years, the profit of the last two years may end up in the pocket of someone who did nothing more than have enough money to make the payments when you no longer could. Deep pockets.

The trick to using leverage to magnify real estate investment is to use as much **leverage as possible**…but **not** so much that you **lose** the property.

Two investors

Let's say Willie and Joe are investors starting with equal amounts of cash. Willie puts **all** his cash into a property as a 20% down payment. Joe, on the other hand, holds back a bunch and buys a smaller property on the deep pockets theory.

A severe downturn hits the market. Willie tries to hold on. But with his higher mortgage payments, it's too much for him. He's forced to sell to Joe for little more than his mortgage balance. Thereby losing nearly all of his investment.

Then the market turns around. Property values go up. And Joe profits enormously from his bargain purchase of Willie's property.

Willie's a lousy investor and Joe is a shrewd investor. Right?

Not really. Joe was just more conservative. Had the downturn been less severe, Willie would have been able to hold on. And, because he was more highly leveraged than Joe and therefore owned more property, **Willie** would have been the investment performance leader.

The deep pockets theory is nothing but 20/20 hindsight

You pays your money and you takes your choice. The deep pockets approach...which is nothing but a **low** loan-to-asset value appraoch...is **smart** if times get tough. But it's **dumb** if times do **not** get so tough. So the deep pockets theory is nothing but the 20/20 hindsight of those looking at what happened in hard times.

The deep pockets approach to real estate investing is no more correct than a stopped clock. The optimum strategy is deep pockets or low loan-to-value ratio when net operating income and/or appreciation rates are **low** and the opposite when they are **high**.

The deep pockets approach will prevent you from ever **losing** a property as a result of a downturn. But it will cause you to show a poor overall return over the long run. A return similar to what you'd get investing in second mortgages ...only with the additional disadvantages of lawsuit liability, property management duties, and higher purchase and sale costs.JTR

PART SIX

APPRECIATION, INFLATION AND YOUR INVESTMENT ASSUMPTIONS

53

Where Appreciation Comes From

February 1987

In some markets, appreciation is the biggest of the three returns from real estate...cash flow and tax savings being the other two.

But most real estate investors still misunderstand appreciation. Herewith a clarification.

Income stream

Whether they understand it or not, real estate investors buy income property for the after-tax cash flow it generates. Therefore, virtually all appreciation comes from improvements in after-tax cash flow. The after-tax cash flow of a building increases if any of the following occur:

- rent increase
- operating expense decrease
- interest rate decrease
- improvement in income tax laws

Appreciation also occurs as a result of speculative mania.

Speculative mania

Speculative mania occurs when investors start believing that appreciation no longer depends on the four things listed above. That real estate in a particular area will go up because of some unknown force.

Speculative mania is a self-fulfilling prophecy...sometimes called the "Greater Fool Theory." It is also a self-inflicted Ponzi Scheme in which the late comers get wiped out.

Investing in a hot area where property values are climbing independent of rents, interest rates, or tax laws is like betting that a pop fly will **continue** to climb on the grounds that it climbed during its first few seconds. It's like concluding that because a baseball went from three feet above the ground when it was hit to 100 feet above the ground two seconds later that, "Boy that baseball really knows how to fly."

What goes up...

Baseballs don't know how to fly. They simply abide by the laws of physics which include Newton's Third Law of Motion and the Law of Gravity.

By the same token, income properties don't know how to appreciate. They simply abide by the laws of economics which include the Law of Supply and Demand and the laws of mathematics. The fact that a property went up in value 20% in a year does not mean that going up 20% per year is a characteristic of that property...any more than the fact that a hit baseball climbed 100 feet in two seconds means that baseball will **continue** to climb another 100 feet every time two seconds pass.

Profit and danger

You can make a lot of money from speculative mania. Just as you can make a lot of money from investing in a Ponzi Scheme. The trick is you gotta get out before it ends.

When it ends, property values should return to the levels indicated by the laws of economics. That is, to where the after-tax cash flow return is appropriate given the risk and hassle level of real estate.

Sometimes the market **overreacts** to the collapse of speculative mania and thereby creates bargains. Then you can buy properties in which the after-tax cash flow is **greater** than what is appropriate given the risk and hassles of real estate.

The biggest danger is that you invest in a speculative mania market on a highly leveraged basis...and do not get out in time. A lot of that occurred in the late seventies. Then appreciation rates were in double digits and investors were leveraging higher and higher.

The "Silent Crash of '81"

One of the least understood events in real estate is the fact that the Economic Recovery Tax Act (ERTA) of 1981 (15-year ACRS) concealed a drop in income property values. Real estate was hurting when that law was passed.

Based on arithmetic, the law should have instantly raised income property values by about 20% between '81 and '82.

But there was no such jump. Instead, the soft terms which sellers were having to give in '80 and '81 because of high interest rates gave way to more normal terms as syndicators and high income individuals began bidding against each other for the right to shelter other income.

If income property values had been **at** the equilibrium point in '81 instead of levitated **above** equilibrium by speculative mania...they would have shot **up** after the August 13, 1981 enactment of ERTA. The pop fly did not fall because the field was suddenly raised up to the apex of the ball's flight. But most investors simply saw the fact that values did **not** fall after the '70s speculative mania as further evidence that real estate values never fall.

Inflation

Inflation is an increase in the Consumer Price Index. CPI increases do not cause appreciation any more than thermometers cause heat waves. Price increases only cause real (adjusted for inflation) increases in building value when they increase **real** net operating income. In other words, if both rent and operating expenses increase equally, your net operating income will increase... but only by an amount precisely equal to inflation. As a result, if you owned the building **free and clear**, your building **value** would go up. But your **buying power** would stay the same. In **real** terms, there would be no increase in value from price increases.

But if you are **leveraged**, the picture changes dramatically. Although there is no increase in real building value as a result of inflation...there is a real decrease in the value of the **mortgage**. So inflation does not change the **real** value of your property. But, by decreasing the **real** value of the amount you **owe**, inflation causes a **real** increase in your equity. These figures demonstrate:

	At start	After 10% inflation	Adjusted for inflation
Value	$100,000	$110,000	$100,000
Mortgage	$80,000	$80,000	$72,000
Equity	$20,000	$30,000	$28,000

In this example, you can see that the real (adjusted for inflation) equity increased by $8,000. But it was **not appreciation** of the building value that caused it...but **de**preciation in the value of the **mortgage**.

Single-family houses

Single-family homes work about the same as income property except you substitute **salary** for rent and living expenses for operating expenses. Increases in salaries cause increases in home values. So do decreases in living expenses like Prop 13's lowering of California property taxes.

Home prices certainly respond to interest rates and tax law changes. And home prices are every bit as susceptible to speculative mania as income property prices. Witness the late '70s.

Know the difference between speculative mania and real appreciation. Enjoy the mania when it occurs. But never **invest** in it. JTR

54
Do High-Priced Properties Appreciate Faster?

Where would you rather have invested in 1982: Anaheim-Santa Ana, the highest priced area in the U.S. then...or Louisville, the lowest? Let me put it in dollar terms. Would you rather own an Anaheim house that was so sought after that people were willing to pay $133,000 in 1982 dollars for it; or one of those poor, pitiful Louisville houses that people would only pay $46,000 for?

If you are a real estate investor who's trying to make the maximum return, Louisville was by far the best investment in 1982.

Area	1982	1985	Appreciation Rate (annual)
Anaheim	$133,000	$136,200	0.8%
Louisville	$46,000	$50,600	3.0%

If you had bought a million dollars worth of Louisville houses in '82, by '85 you'd have made $68,534 more than if you bought a million dollars worth of Anaheim houses.

On hot days, cliche-prone people comment that it's not the heat, it's the humidity, that gets you. When it comes to real estate investing, it's not the price, it's the appreciation rate that makes you money.

High face amount or high coupon?

Bonds have a face amount... typically $100,000...and a coupon rate of interest. Bond buyers buy the bonds which offer the highest yield or coupon for the risk level they are willing to accept. If a bond issuer put out bonds with a face value of, say, $200,000 instead of the usual $100,000... and you told your broker to buy the $200,000 bonds on the theory they are more likely to appreciate because of their higher price...the broker would conclude you needed your head examined. And rightly so. You buy a bond based on its **risk/reward** characteristics. The **face value** of the bonds are irrelevant (except possibly for diversification if you don't have much money to invest).

AREA Highest prices	1986	1987	Appreciation Rate
Hillsborough	$425,000	$550,000	29.41%
Marina	$425,000	$475,000	11.76%
St. Fran. Wood	$400,000	$475,000	18.75%
Presidio Hts.	$350,000	$425,000	21.43%
Blackhawk	$289,000	$360,000	24.57%
Lowest prices			
South San Jose	$79,000	$115,000	45.57%
Santa Rosa	$80,000	$125,000	56.25%
Rohnert Park	$85,000	$100,000	17.65%
Petaluma	$85,000	$105,000	23.53%
Santa Clara	$90,000	$102,000	13.33%

Source: Coldwell Banker, *San Frencisco Chronicle*

In real estate, the appreciation and capitalization (net operating income divided by price of property) rates are the equivalent of the bond coupon rate. Buying real estate on the basis of price makes no more sense than buying bonds on the basis of price. You buy the best risk/reward combination you can find.

San Francisco Area

The March 28th *San Francisco Chronicle* had an article headlined "Prices Of Cheap Homes Going Through The Roof." Actually, the statistics in the article showed a mixed bag, not that cheap homes appreciated faster. But the mixed bag is enough to prove my point. The '86-'87 prices and appreciation rates for the five highest and lowest priced neighborhoods in the San Francisco area shown here.

You can play this game with statistics from anywhere in the country. The bottom line is appreciation rates move in fits and starts with today's champ being tomorrow's loser and vice versa. But properties at the high end are not more likely to turn in championship appreciation rates than properties at the low end.

Choose by cap rates

If a high-priced area is no more likely to have a high appreciation rate than a low-priced area, then you should invest where you get the best cap rates. Almost invariably, that's in the lower-priced neighborhoods. On page 99 of the February '88 issue, I reported that higher-priced areas generally had the lowest rents in relation to the price of the property.

That means you can get **positive cash flow or breakeven** in the low-priced areas. But you have to suffer **negative cash flow** in the high-priced areas. If the appreciation rates are the same, why suffer?

And in their *1988 Apartment Market Study*, Seattle income property brokers reported that the higher the **rents** in an apartment complex, the lower the **cap rate**. Meaning that the prettier a building was, the higher the price the investors were willing to pay in relation to the building's rents. That, in turn, means that the prettier the building, the poorer the **return** its owner gets.

That's like buying a bond based on the attractiveness of its engraving rather than its yield and credit rating. Or like buying IBM stock instead of Walmart because IBM has a more prestigious clientele.

It's **ratios**, not **prices**, that matter. The very definition of return on investment is a ratio. Put your money where that ratio is **highest** in relation to the risk involved.
JTR

55
Do Higher-Priced Homes Appreciate Faster?

March 1989

In a 4/88 article with a title similar to this item I said the answer was, "No" and provided supporting data. Now a March '89 report ("High Home Prices—A Worldwide Problem" by Anthony Downs and issued by Salomon Brothers, Inc.) says higher-priced homes **do** appreciate faster.

Among other things, the report says owners of higher-priced homes exhibit more hostility to growth than owners of lower-priced homes. That hostility manifests itself in the form of restrictions against new construction. Such restrictions on supply, without diminution of demand, drive up prices of existing homes.

That's logical. But the data in Downs' report is less conclusive. For one thing, it only covers one year, 1987. And even then, it contains numerous examples of lower-priced cities appreciating faster than higher-priced cities.

Very high-priced New York and Boston appreciated only about 1% in 1987. While lower-priced Grand Rapids went up 8.7%; Buffalo, 17.7%; Detroit, 14%; and Orlando, 11.5%. Also, the oil areas, which happen to be in lower-priced regions, insert a lot of negative appreciation rates into those price groups.

It's also logical to say that higher-priced homes are less likely to appreciate as much as cheaper homes on the grounds that the higher you go, the fewer people there are who can qualify for the necessary mortgage and the more reason exists for businesses and individuals to move to lower-priced areas. Highest-priced Orange County, CA may become the Boston of 1990. Anaheim appreciated at .8%/year from '82 to '85. JTR

56

Can You Assume Inflation When Deflation is so Widespread?

October 1986

Ever since the early '70s, you and I have been assuming that our rents would **increase** annually. And that those rent increases would, in turn, increase both our cash flow and building value.

Are those assumptions still valid? If they are **not**, what should you do about it?

Not always up

Real estate values do not always go up. Back in the seventies it **seemed** that they did. Or at least they never went **down**. They were flat at worst. And periods of no price increases were considered anomalies.

But those days are gone. Recently, we've been reading about actual value drops.

- Salt Lake's Triad Center office complex drops 50% in value.
- Existing home prices drop in Birmingham, Milwaukee, Orlando, Phoenix, San Antonio, Tampa, and Tulsa in '85.

- Office rents drop 41% after concessions and inflation are taken into account.
- Condos discounted 10% to 20% in Atlanta, 40% in South Florida
- Biggest farm land price drop since Depression in '85.
- Fort Worth apartment building worth $25,000 a unit in '83 worth $17,500 to $20,000 a unit in '86.
- Salomon Brothers' Kenneth Rosen says apartments have to drop 16% and office buildings 11% in value to offset Tax Reform Act of 1986.

Today's inflation rate

The Consumer Price Index for July of '86 was 328.0 (1967 = 100). That's only **1.6%** higher than the 12 months before.

Real estate investors whose properties are on leases with CPI escalation clauses will hardly get rich on that. Ditto apartment owners with CPI rent control.

Of course some investors in strong markets have neither long-term leases nor rent control. So they have been able

Will inflation like this make you rich?

Median Existing Home

$90,000
$80,000
$70,000
$60,000
$50,000
$40,000
$30,000
$20,000
$10,000
$0

A S O N D J F M A M J J A

Source: NAR   1985   1986

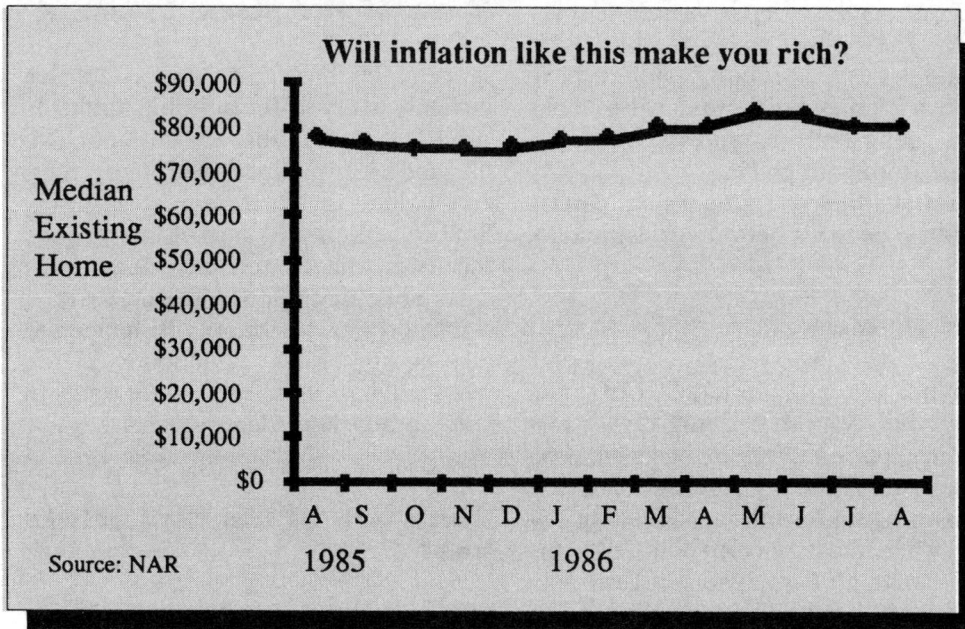

to raise rents more than the national CPI increase. And their property values have gone up accordingly. So they can ignore the national inflation rate and the troubles in other markets, right?

"But I'm in God's Country."

People in strong markets like the Northeast and Orange County, California read about soft rents and prices elsewhere and think, "That'll never happen here. This is God's Country."

Then they launch into what I call the Chamber of Commerce speech. "But you don't understand. We're the high tech capital of the universe. We've got 16 colleges and universities. We've got in-migration. We're the third fastest growing county in the nation. Blah blah."

Need I remind you that Houston once had one of the best Chamber of Commerce speeches in the world. Oil capital of the nation. Home of the Johnson Space Center.

Want hard evidence? Houston was the only major city which boomed right through the 1975 recession while the rest of the nation suffered.

If Houston wasn't immune to a downturn in its economy, why should Quincy or Santa Ana be immune?

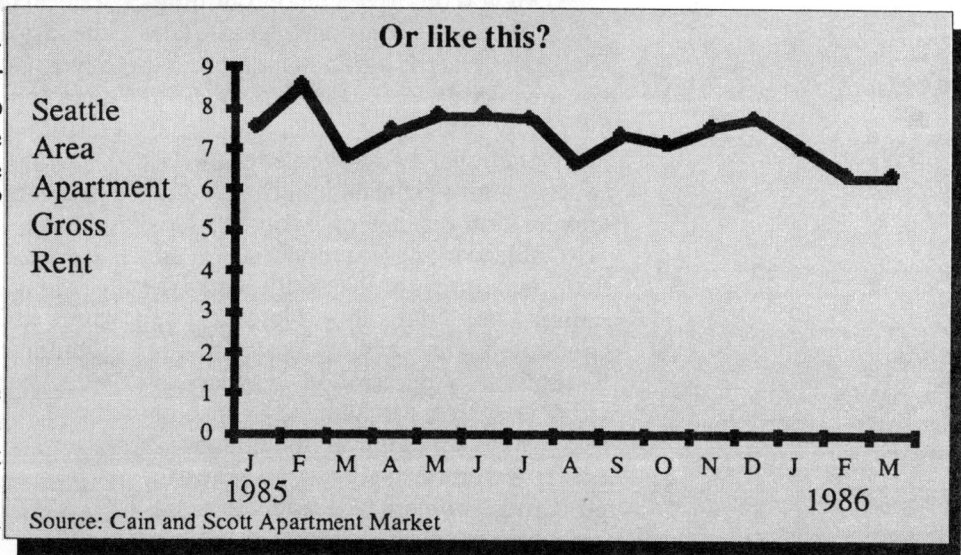

Or like this?

Seattle Area Apartment Gross Rent

9
8
7
6
5
4
3
2
1
0

J F M A M J J A S O N D J F M
1985   1986

Source: Cain and Scott Apartment Market

More speculative

The recent drop in the national inflation rate to near zero...and reports of deflation in many areas and property types...mean that counting on inflation to make you rich is more speculative than it used to be. Roughly speaking, it's hard for a particular community to buck national trends for long.

For example, if Orange County real estate appreciates at 10% per year at a time when salaries and other real estate values are appreciating at only 1.6% per year, then Orange County becomes relatively less attractive with each passing day. In other words, the higher prices go in Orange County, the better commuting from neighboring Riverside County looks. The higher prices go in the Boston area, the better accepting a job offer in Research Triangle, North Carolina looks to a young college professor with job offers from both places.

Extraordinary appreciation carries within it the seeds of its own destruction.

What to do

When the inflation rate is 1.6%, you sure don't want to use any higher rate when preparing an offer to buy a building on long-term leases with **CPI escalation clauses**. Ditto for rent-controlled buildings where the **rent control** is tied to the CPI (although I am against investing in rent-controlled buildings at all).

When you buy free market buildings which are **not** on long-term leases, take another look at the inflation assumptions you are making. Are you sill using 3% to 5%? How come?

The national inflation rate for the last twelve months or the national home price appreciation rate are probably the most justifiable working assumptions. The fact that your area has outpaced the rest of the nation lately does **not** warrant your counting on that extraordinary situation to continue. Appreciation is caused by either an increase in demand or speculative mania. An increase in demand will cause builders to build competitive properties...which will eventually depress prices. And it will cause competing areas to look relatively more attractive, which will also depress prices. Speculative mania is nothing but a self-inflicted Ponzi scheme.

Minus appreciation rates

In overbuilt markets or markets dependent upon commodity prices (oil, agriculture, and mining areas), you should probably assume **negative** appreciation rates!

"But," you say, "you'd have to have **huge** cash flow to overcome a negative appreciation rate. You'd have to buy such a property **very** cheap to earn a decent return."

No kidding.

More of the same to come

But facts are facts. It is a fact that virtually every **office** building market in America has no prospects for appreciation and every prospect of dropping rents and values in the foreseeable future. Sunbelt **apartment** markets aren't quite that bad...but few, if any, show clear signs of having gone on the upswing.

Nobody knows what will happen to commodity prices. So nobody knows what will happen to **real estate** prices in commodity-dependent markets.

Don't live in the real estate past

Don't play the real estate investing game like the generals who keep fighting the last war. Or like the Depression survivors who kept thinking that the Depression would come back...and, as a result were afraid to invest.

Don't be one of those whose mind is open in his twenties...then closes to change. And who spends the rest of his life repeating what **used** to work...in spite of clearly different conditions. Double-digit inflation may come back. But I wouldn't bet my net worth on it.JTR

57
Inflation Affects Real Estate Differently Today

A lot of investors who are hurting today figure it's only a matter of time before inflation returns to its "normal" double-digit rates...and real estate returns to its golden days. I think not.

No one knows whether double-digit inflation will return. But if it does, it will return to a different world than we had in the '70s.

Effect on rents

Rent increases help investors. But rent increases make **rent control** a more compelling issue to tenants. Apartment owners who fall under rent control as a result will suffer dramatic loss of property value overnight...typically about 20%...followed by a gradual decline to zero value.

Investors who own **one- to three-family** dwellings or **non-residential** properties are rarely be covered by rent control and therefore would clearly benefit.

Effect on expenses

As long as operating expenses went up no faster than rents, inflation would raise net operating income...because rents are two to three times greater than operating expenses. In the mid-'70s, however, operating expenses went up **faster** than rents. In that case, net operating income falls.

Effect on cash flow

Before-tax cash flow is net operating income minus mortgage payments. If you have a **fixed-rate** mortgage, inflation will not only increase your cash flow, it will increase it in **real** terms... that is, even after you adjust for inflation you'll be better off.

If you have an **adjustable rate mortgage** (ARM), however, your cash flow would probably not improve in real terms. And more likely would go **down**. I have consistently recommended against ARMs. They are financial Russian Roulette if you cannot afford the worst case. And if you **can** afford the worst case, you could have bought a **bigger** building if you had bought a building with a fixed-rate loan…which would have had a lower interest rate than the ARM's worst case.

Don't forget that a fixed-rate mortgage becomes an ARM, in effect, if and when it has a **balloon** payment. Because, at that point, you have to get a new mortgage at then-market rates. A balloon payment instantaneously converts a fixed-rate mortgage to an ARM with no cap.

ARM becomes fixed

On the other hand, a run-up in interest rates causes an ARM to metamorphose into a fixed-rate mortgage…and typi-

erty, fixed-rate loan lasts only until balloon day.

The ideal loan…30-year, fixed-rate, and assumable…is generally only available on **FHA** and **VA** homes.

Effect on interest rates

The main difference between inflation now and in the '70s is its relationship with long-term mortgage rates. Inflation bounced between 3.3% and 9.1% from 1970 through 1978. But mortgage interest rates remained stable in a 7.5% to 9.7% range throughout.

Then inflation got nasty in '79 rising to 11.3% for the year. The Federal Re-

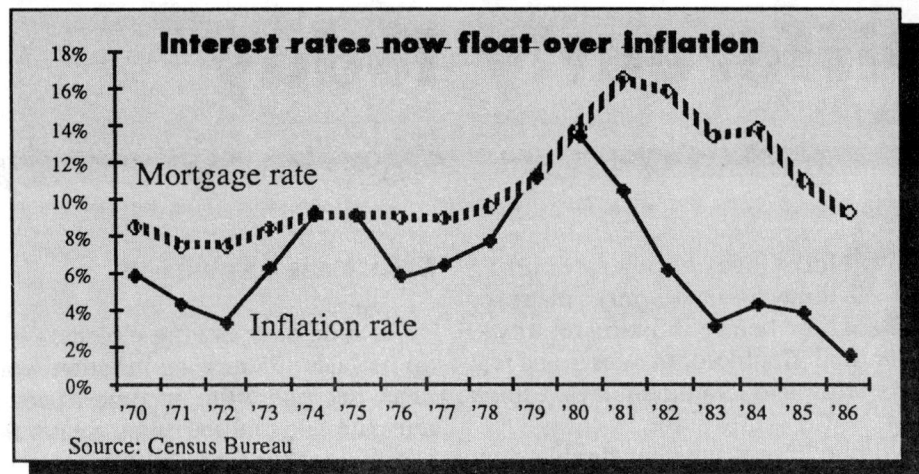

Interest rates now float over inflation

Mortgage rate

Inflation rate

'70 '71 '72 '73 '74 '75 '76 '77 '78 '79 '80 '81 '82 '83 '84 '85 '86

Source: Census Bureau

cally an **assumable** one at that. For example, the ARM may start at 8.5% and allow increases of up to 1% every six months, with a lifetime ceiling of 5% total increase. That means the rate could rise to 13.5% within two and a half years. But **then** it would be **fixed**.

Homes versus income property

In the one- and two-family market where 30-year, fixed-rate loans are readily available, a fixed-rate is all the investor needs to protect his cash flow from an increase in interest rates. But in the **income property** market, most "30-year" loans are actually 5- to 15-year loans with 30-year amortization schedules until the balloon payment date. The cash flow protection of an income prop-

serve raised the discount rate dramatically in October of that year and mortgage rates jumped to 11.16%.

Since then, mortgage rates have been as high as 16.55%. Annual inflation was **never** that high. And mortgage rates only dipped below 10% recently when inflation approached zero. In other words, mortgage interest rates used to be about 9% no matter what happened to inflation. But in the '80s, mortgage rates have maintained about a 9% **spread** above inflation and tracked inflation up and down. So any run-up in inflation would probably be matched by a parallel run-up in mortgage rates. And that is not good at all for real estate investors.

Interest rates & value

An increase in mortgage interest rates causes a corresponding drop in the values of all real estate. The only exception is real estate which has a **fixed-rate, assumable** mortgage. If the mortgage in question is an ARM, the value of the property will fall **until** the maximum rate is reached...at which point the ARM becomes, in effect, a fixed-rate loan.

could be **so** high that real estate investors would be **worse** off than with present inflation.

As described above, cash flow will benefit from inflation for those with fixed-rate loans...until balloon day. ARM borrowers will see cash flow hurt or stable in

The Effect of High Inflation on Properties With Various Mortgages		
Loan type	Cash flow protected from higher interest rates?	Loan portion of property value protected from higher interest rates?
30-year, fixed-rate, assumable	Yes	Yes
Fixed-rate, assumable, balloon	Yes, until balloon	Yes, until balloon
Fixed-rate, not assumable	Yes	No
ARM, assumable	Not until ceiling is reached	Not until ceiling is reached
ARM, not assumable	Not until ceiling is reached	No

Assumable mortgages do **not** protect the **entire** value of the property...only the portion represented by the loan. The value of the **equity** will still fall when interest rates rise...because the return on alternative investments like bonds and mortgages will go up...and real estate equity must earn a premium over those alternatives because of its added risk and hassle. The higher the return the buyer wants, the lower the sale price must be.

The *net effect*

It's easy to identify the forces at work on real estate. Easy even to predict the forces that **will** be at work if conditions change. What's hard is forecasting the **magnitude** and **timing** of those forces. Inflation's effect on rents, net operating income, and construction costs will tend to **increase** the values of existing properties. But inflation's effect on interest rates will tend to **decrease** the values of existing properties.

I cannot get any more precise than to say that a second bout of double-digit inflation will not be as good for real estate investors as the first one was in the seventies...because higher interest rates will take back most or all of any gains. It's possible that mortgage interest rates

real terms...until ceiling day...when their cash flow will behave like a fixed-rate borrower's.

Investors with assumable loans which are below the market rates that will prevail during high inflation will be partly protected from the value-depressing effects of higher interest rates...up to their loan-to-value ratio.JTR

58

What if Values Don't Always Go Up?

September 1988

Recent articles in *Money* (September), *Fortune* (9/12), and the *San Francisco Examiner* (9/12) noted that appreciation rates were **negative** in a number of markets. I've been saying that real estate prices go up **and** down for years. But I always had to add that you don't **see** actual negative appreciation rates in the reported figures. Rather the value drops were **hidden** in such things as below-market interest rate seller financing and withdrawal of properties from the market.

Now you can see it

That explanation is no longer necessary. Negative appreciation rates are now visible in the actual reported figures. For example, Federal Home Loan Bank Board average home sale price figures for the 2nd quarter of '88 show drops ranging from minus 1.3% in Detroit to minus 21.8% in Honolulu.

The negatives are not just in Detroit, Honolulu, and the Oil Patch. California's Silicon Valley was the booming envy of the world a few short years ago. More recently, it's been one of the nation's see-through building capitals. And value-

depressing federal government actions like the Tax Reform Act of 1986 affect every rental property in the nation.

Profound change

The emergence of clearly visible negative appreciation rates should profoundly change perceptions of real estate as an investment. Now, everyone has read stories of people selling properties for less than they paid for them and of collapsing property values in Texas and other markets.

For those whose only real estate skill was buying a "good" property in a "good" location and waiting for appreciation, this new two-dimensional world is uninhabitable. Most of those who stay will probably take too long to get around to changing the way they do things. The main purpose of this article is to make sure you change before you get burned.

Your assumptions

We virtually all have appreciation rate expectations and assumptions built into our strategy...whether we are conscious of them or not (See "Are You Aware of Your Investment Assumptions?" in the October '86 issue, Chapter 67). Given the prevalence of negative appreciation rates these days, you'd better adjust your appreciation assumptions **downward**. Zero appreciation strikes me as a good working assumption for deals you do in the near future.

I've also said you should get an overall return in real estate of about a 24% (appreciation, tax savings, cash flow, amortization) to buy real estate these days. If you assume even a moderate appreciation rate...and you use leverage... it's easy to get 24% from appreciation alone. For example, the combination of 5% appreciation and 20% down gives a 25% return on investment.

More built-in profit

But if you get an appreciation rate like Detroit's -1.3%, that 25% return turns to -6.5%. Then you need a 30.5% return on your investment from cash flow, tax benefits, and amortization to end up at 24% net.

Is that so hard to do that you should forget about real estate? No. Lately, I've been writing about techniques that enable you to achieve very high returns. In brief, they include:

- the value increasing techniques in my book *How to Increase the Value of Real Estate*;
- "leper" property techniques like bad foundations, title problems, buildings that are to be demolished; and
- techniques in which you buy ordinary properties on **extra**ordinary terms...like contacting hundreds of owners by direct mail, focusing on sellers who sell cheap like foreclosure auctions, heirs, and non-real estate businessmen.

In general, my point is that relatively steady appreciation has made us lazy. We've been **floating** down the real estate river on appreciation-powered inner tubes...rather than rowing. The message of the negative appreciation rates is that if you want to continue to prosper in real estate, you'd better learn how to **row**.

Real estate still offers extraordinary opportunities. Better opportunities than alternative investments. It must. If the yields available in real estate ever fell below second mortgage yields, people would stop investing in real estate... which would...in turn...drive the yields back up.

But real estate's extraordinary opportunities will profit only those experienced investors who **retool**... and newcomers who were not spoiled by the old, easy appreciation days. These days, you must build substantial profit into your acquisitions **on closing day** by using one or more of the kinds of techniques mentioned above. Do **not** rely on market-wide appreciation for all or even most of your return.⏀

59
The Siren Song of Speculation

October 1988

Today, most real estate deals are overpriced. If you pay the going rate for a property, it'll run negative cash flow or breakeven at best. That limits your ability to buy very many properties. And it turns you into a **speculator** who relies on unpredictable, uncontrollable market-wide appreciation for an adequate return.

You should **not** pay the going rate. You should get superior deals. Most people consider real estate agents to be the main place to go when they want to buy real estate. Does that hold true for investors who insist on high yields?

They represent seller

It's hard to reconcile the notion of getting a really good purchase through an agent when agents legally represent the **seller**. They have a duty to treat the seller's affairs as they would their own. Even when an agent does not buy his own listing, he has a duty to alert the seller to a price:

"so grossly inadequate that it is clear to any broker in the locality that the prop-erty is underpriced." (Gaudio *Real Estate Brokerage Law* §272)

If you ask an agent to help you get an extraordinary deal, you're asking him to violate his duty to his client. But I'm telling you that you **must** do an extraordinary deal because the **ordinary** deals are **overpriced** by investment standards. So, in theory, an agent who represents the seller is of no use to an investor who seeks a deal that makes investment sense in a generally overpriced market.

Hidden potential

There are, however, three ways agents fit my advice. One category of deals that make sense is deals with **hidden potential**. Like below-market rents. Or excess land that could be split off. Or upzoning. Or any of the other techniques described in my book, *How to Increase the Value of Real Estate*.

Should agents know about those? In my opinion, they should. I made one of my listing clients some extra money when I was agent by recommending that she divide a side-by-side, two-family into two legally, but not physically, separate houses. But agents who see such hidden potential are rare. So rare that a court would probably not hold them to that standard.

So you should look at agent's listings in order to buy the occasional hidden-potential deal.

Leper properties

Agents also get leper properties sometimes. These are problem listings they can't sell. For example, it may be a rental house with tenants who refuse to allow the place to be shown. Or a property with a title problem. Or a bad foundation.

You could selectively buy such properties on terms that makes sense. In fact, I suspect it would make sense to send quarterly post cards to the sales managers of all the local real estate offices saying something to the effect of,

"I buy dog listings. Does your firm have a problem listing? Call me. I am not an agent. Your commission is fully protected."

The third way to buy decent deals from agents is when the agent is grossly unqualified to sell the particular property in question. For example, house agents occasionally get **income property** or **raw land** listings. Since those require special skills, there is a good chance a house agent will underestimate the value.

Agents' goal

Real estate agents get paid for doing deals. Not for doing good deals. Oh, they'll tell you they'd starve if they didn't do well by their clients. But in fact, the agents who get buyers and sellers to closing, not high yielding investments, are the ones who eat.

Selectivity vs. speed

A competent investor wants the **rare** deal. He recognizes that to get it he must consider dozens of properties...maybe hundreds.

Agents, on the other hand, want the **quick** deal. They seek the buyers who are easiest to please. If you really want a house agent to work for you, tell him that you are staying in a motel...at your own expense...with four kids...that you have all cash...and that at this point you'll take anything with a roof. The agent will drop everything to work with you.

When no customers can hear them, many agents brag that they "never show more than three houses to any one buyer." Given that, what do you think they'll do when an investor comes in and says, "I'm a *Real Estate Investor's Monthly* subscriber. So I know that I have to consider 50 to 200 properties to find a deal that makes sense."

Siren song of speculation

Some agents will show you the door. Others will nod and take your name and you'll never hear from them again. And others will try to **convert** you to being easier to sell. They will sing the siren song of speculation. I recently saw a classic version of it in a newsletter put out by a commercial brokerage. It made the usual Chamber of Commerce speech about why the local market was the center of the universe and poised for a great leap forward then said in pertinent part,

*"Many investors attempt to maximize their profits by trying to purchase 'bargain properties.' Certainly these properties exist, but frequently they are very difficult to locate on a regular basis. While the investor is looking for a bargain valuable time is lost, especially during an upward cycle. Even if a bargain is eventually located and purchased, the same profit could have more easily been made by looking into several fairly priced properties and by purchasing the best available at the **beginning** of the up cycle. Of course, if the bargain property is **not** located, then the investor **loses** because all properties have now become more expensive.*

*"1988 is the **right time** to purchase apartments. In a few short years all properties purchased in 1988 will look like bargains!"* [emphasis in original]

Does that pull on your heart strings? Make some sense to you? I thought so. That's why I call it a siren song.

Lash yourself to the mast of investment rationality, friend. This is a blatant pitch for speculation. "Property values are going up," it says in no uncertain terms. But of course no one knows what appreciation rates will be. And as with any rosy depiction of the future you get from a seller, you can always smoke them out by saying,

*"If you're so sure property values are going up, how 'bout we make your commission **contingent** on them going up? Instead of 6% now, you get 6% plus prime in five years if the property value increases at a rate of 4% per year or more."*

I did that once to a Realtor® on a radio talk show. He sheepishly mumbled something about Realtors® needing cash now because they had "bills to pay." Yeah, and so will you **investors** have bills to pay if you go around buying income properties with 7.5% cap rates.

If a company selling **securities** ever put out a prospectus which contained nothing but the sort of shameless optimism investment real estate agents constantly spout, they'd go directly to jail without passing Go or collecting a 25% front-end load.

It should not come as a surprise that the siren song above is so compelling. Singing that song is part of what investment real estate agents do for a living. They're good at it. (I did not sing the siren song of speculation when I was an agent. I refused to show properties or otherwise work with **buyers** at all. I only worked on selling my own listings.)

Gambling or investing

If I wrote a casino gambling newsletter instead of a real estate newsletter, it would focus only on games where you could win an advantage...like black jack or certain progressive drop-poker slot machines which have a high probability of paying off before you run out of money to bet.

The agent's line that while looking for bargains, you lose out on the money you could have made in market-wide appreciation is like saying you should forget about learning how to count cards in black jack because while you're studying that, people are winning lots of money pulling slot machine levers.

Agents try to talk you into speculative deals because that's what they've got on their shelves. Not because it's best for you.

There's an old saying in trial law:

"If the law is in your favor, pound on the law. If the facts are in your favor, pound on the facts. And if neither is in your favor, pound on the table."

If investment real estate agents had a similar slogan, it might be:

"If the cash flow is in your favor, pound on the cash flow. If the recent appreciation rates are in your favor, pound on the appreciation rates. And if neither is in your favor, pound on the notion that real estate is a long term investment."

Remember where investment agents are coming from. And where you're going. JTR

60
Why Prices Soar

A Rhode Island subscriber sent me a clipping about a survey done on why house prices soared in California, sagged in Boston, and went nowhere in Milwaukee last Spring. The results of the survey had been reported in the Nov./Dec. 1988 *New England Economic Review* which is published by the Federal Reserve Bank of Boston.

The authors of the article surveyed May 1988 home buyers and sellers in Boston (a post-boom market), Anaheim and San Francisco (boom markets), and Milwaukee (the control market—no boom in the last five years).

My interpretation of the survey results is that home prices are driven by **mob psychology**...although, comically, each member of the mob claims he or she is motivated by sober economic analysis.

When asked if they thought buying a home in their area involved "little or no risk," the effect of recent appreciation rates on buyers' minds was clear.

Said "yes" to "Little or no risk"

Anaheim	63.3%
San Francisco	55.7%
Boston	37.1%
Milwaukee	29.5%

That partly explains why California is so overpriced from an investment standpoint. Californians think appreciation rates are darned near FDIC insured.

When asked what the average annual appreciation rate would be over the next ten years, buyers said:

Annual appreciation rate next 10 years

Anaheim	14.3%
San Francisco	14.8%
Boston	8.7%
Milwaukee	7.3%

Now I'm not one who claims to be able to predict the future...like the home buyers who filled out this survey. For all I know, their predictions may come true. I will only note that there has **never**, in the history of the universe, been a ten-year run of appreciation rates as high as the **lowest** (Milwaukee) expectations, let alone the ten years of 14.8% rates they expect in San Francisco.

The survey asked buyers and sellers why they thought home prices went up at the rate they did **in their area.** "Rather than citing any concrete evidence, people retreat into cliches and images," the authors found. Indeed, the most often cited reason was **interest rates**...which absolutely **cannot** explain why one region appreciates faster than another...because interest rates are the **same** nationwide.

The authors cited a similar 1987 survey of stock market investors. When the market **soared** to unprecedented price-earning ratios, stock market investors thought **fundamentals** were the reason. But when the market **crashed**, investors attributed it to market **psychology**.

In spite of their insistence that fundamentals caused the price changes in the four real estate markets, not a single one of the 886 respondents to the survey cited any quantitative evidence relevant to the future supply or demand for housing.

The local media seem to influence prices in the **upward** direction by reporting welcome news to a receptive audience. But that same audience seems to discount media reports suggesting future price sags.

The media get swept up in the mob psychology, too. For example, California papers breathlessly reported sales above asking price (and I repeated those reports in my July '88 issue). But would you believe that 3.3% of the sales in **Milwaukee**...which had an appreciation rate of -.3% last year...sold **above** asking price? The incidence of above-asking-price sales in Anaheim and San Francisco was higher...6.3% and 9.8% respectively. But reading the papers in each area would have left you with the impression that the incidence of above-asking-price sales was about 50% in California and 0% in Milwaukee.

Homebuyers and investors are betting most of their life savings on "hearsay, cliches, and casual observations," to use a phrase from the Boston article. The buyers' future appreciation rate assumptions are simply rose-colored projections of past rate highs. JTR

61
The Holy Graph

T he graph below is the fundamental driving force for the vast majority of real estate investors today. Stock, bond, and commodity prices may fluctuate randomly. But real estate seems to march steadily upward.

Baloney.

Cooking the books?

Consider the source of this graph. The National Association of Realtors®. It would **not** be in their interest for people to perceive that real estate values go up and down like pork bellies.

Am I accusing NAR® of cooking the books? No. But I will accuse them of **under**cooking them.

As an indicator of real estate price **appreciation**, this graph leaves out a lot.

They don't build 'em like they used to

Stocks, bonds, and commodities are fungible, interchangeable, standardized. An ounce of 1970 gold is the same as a 1989 ounce.

But real estate is just the opposite. Every parcel is unique. So the word "home" in the NAR® phrase "median-priced existing home" is misleading if it conjures up an image of a standardized commodity.

The home that sold for $23,000 in 1970 is not the same home that sold for $89,300 in 1988. For example, in 1970 only 10.7 million houses had central air-conditioning. In 1988, about 40 million did.

This effect is more pronounced in reports of **new** home prices. But it also shows up in the existing home price statistics because of resale of formerly new homes as well as renovation.

So the median home price graph is partly a chart of the increased **quality** of homes. The $23,000, 1970 home will probably **not** sell for $89,300 in 1989 unless it has been upgraded.

Government rules

The percentage of a new home's price attributable to various government requirements has increased substantially in the last thirty years. One Southern

California developer reported he now pays 600% more for government approvals than he did just six years ago. That reduces the supply of new homes which allows the prices of existing homes to rise faster than they would have.

That's an **artificial** cause of increased values. That's not to say that it doesn't count. However, **artificial** causes of appreciation aren't the same as **market** causes.

Government requirements for building a home are getting ridiculous. So it would not be surprising if the growth rate

crystal, you are likely to decide that you'd better put **champagne** rather than beer in the glass and raise the price even more. In houses, that manifests itself in the form of higher priced finish and more appliances.

Diversified portfolio

The NAR® graph does not depict the median-price increases enjoyed by a **particular** investor or home owner. Rather it depicts the median-price in-

Median Price Of Existing Single-Family Homes

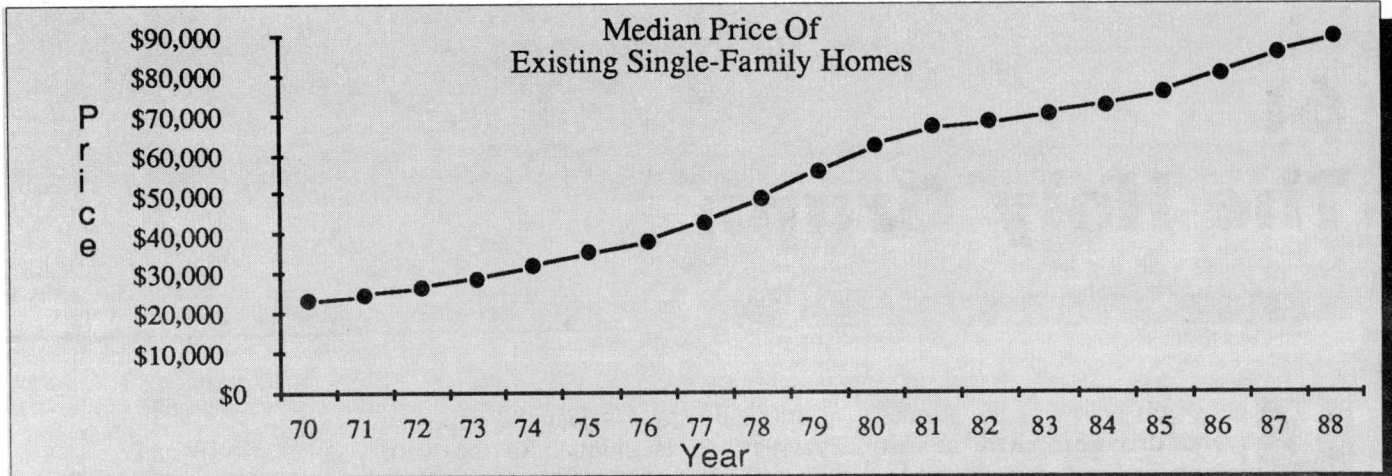

of such restrictions dropped...even to zero. That would **reduce** the rate of increase in the median home price. Because it's not the **existence** of expensive government requirements that increases the median price...it's the **growth** of such restrictions.

There are even glimmers of a **reversal** of the growth of government building restrictions. Some states forbid anti-mobilehome zoning. Supreme Court decisions like *First English Church* (6/87 issue) and *Nollan* (7/87) and the lower court decision to force a New York City suburb to accept low-income housing, try to reverse the ever more restrictive trend.

Finally, government requirements not only raise the price of the house by the amount they cost **directly**. They also push the house up into a different market segment. It's as if you were selling beer in plastic cups and the government insisted that you sell it in crystal glasses instead. Given the amount the total price would have to go up to cover the price of the

creases on **millions** of homes sold in every area of the U.S. A graph of a the median home prices in a **smaller** area like just Texas or Massachusetts would show more fluctuation. A graph of a single neighborhood, even more.

Funny financing

When market interest rates go **up**, the value of all capital assets goes **down**...including real estate. So how come the NAR® graph shows only a **slowing** in high interest rate periods like 1981 and 1982 when market interest rates went over 16%?

NAR®'s median home prices are **nominal** prices. They ignore the discount inherent in below-market interest rate financing.

The discount in below-market interest rate financing should be subtracted from the nominal sale price to arrive at the **true** sale price. A graph of the true sale prices would show value **declines** where NAR® shows mere slowings.

Bond price graphs are jagged and random. But they would be less so if the people who created them ignored the **market** price at which the bonds sell and used the **face value** of many of the bonds instead, during times of rising interest rates. In the bond market, that would instantly be denounced as outrageously inconsistent and misleading. But that's roughly what happens in home price reporting with nary a peep of protest.

Non-Realtor® deals

In order for a home sale to end up in the NAR® figures, it's seller must have paid a **commission**…typically six percent. If the seller's equity is **less** than six percent of the value of the home, he cannot **afford** to sell through a Realtor®.

Many of the homes which have less than six percent equity are in markets which have turned down. By excluding non-Realtor® sales, the NAR® figures systematically exclude a high percentage of the homes which have fallen in value.

They also exclude involuntary deals like foreclosure auctions. Foreclosures also disproportionately include those homes which have declined in value.

Time to sell

Implicit in the figures on stock, bond, and commodity prices is a standard time to sell. The 1970 price of gold and the 1989 price of gold both mean the price at which your gold could be sold **immediately**.

But in home price figures, there is no such standard time to sell. The average time to sell in a high-interest-rate market like 1981 might be 120 days. In a hot market like 1977, it might be 12 days.

Time is money. On a rental house with $250 per month negative cash flow, an extra 108 days of time to sell reduces the net proceeds by 108 ÷ 30 = 3.6 months x $250 = $900. If the house is **vacant**, the negative cash flow can exceed $1,000 per month.

Withdrawn

Bad markets are also manifested by multiple listing books swelling up to twice their normal size, far more expired listings, and far fewer sales. Would-be sellers who are unhappy with the current market value of their property, refuse to sell.

The effect is like what the OPEC cartel seeks when it imposes production quotas on its members. Prices are artificially elevated for a time.

This happens in the stock, bond, and commodity markets as well. Studies have shown that investors in those markets are more likely to sell when they have made a **profit** than when they have suffered a loss.

But the behavior is much more pronounced in real estate because the market values are not published in the financial pages of the newspaper. If a guy buys gold at $450 and it drops to $300, he feels like a fool and looks like one to those who know of his investment. Selling adds little embarrassment.

But in real estate, one can only speculate as to whether there is a value drop and how much…in the absence of an actual sale price. By not selling a property which has dropped in value, a seller can largely avoid feeling like a fool or suffering the embarrassment of having his friends think him one.

By pointing out that massive withdrawals of property from the market during value drop times are **artificial**, I do not mean to imply that they do not count. As with artificial value props resulting from government restrictions, they **do** matter. If you can count on your fellow real estate investors always protecting **your** property value in down markets by taking **their** property off the market, that makes real estate values more stable than other investments.

But the question is, "**Can** you always count on them?" And the answer is, **no**. If the going gets rough enough, the "cartel" collapses. OPEC and the current Denver real estate market are examples of that.

Other property types

The NAR® figures are of home prices. But since they are about the only real estate price figures available, investors in other property types tend to view them as surrogate indicators of all property prices.

That's not valid. Homes have the least political risk of any property type. Raw land values, for example, have frequently been slashed by zoning changes, the California Coastal Commission, etc. They don't pull that stuff with homes.

Apartment building values are often cut or suppressed by rent control. Many industrial property values are now nosediving because of toxic contamination. All income property had its values cut about 15% to 25% by the Tax Reform Act of 1986, which, if anything, made homes **more** attractive by eliminating the deductibility ef interest other than home mortgage interest.

In addition to political risk, there is **overbuilding** risk. That appears to be greatest in the office and retail sectors where the number of people who want to **own** such prestigious buildings exceeds the number of people who want to **rent** them.

In what **might** be suspected as a bit of cooking the books, NAR® reports condo and co-op prices **separately** from "home" prices. Condo appreciation rates have lagged well behind detached single-family home prices in virtually every region in virtually every quarter (See "Condo Investment Return Well Behind Houses" in the 5/88 issue).

Dot to dot

Graphs like the home price graph are usually actually based on **points**. They graph as a line because the people who prepare the graph connect the dots to make the graph neater. But in making it neater, they make it more misleading. The line implies a smoothness that doesn't exist in the real world the graph supposedly depicts.

There are many instantaneous events like court decisions, plant closings, Prop 13 passage, etc. which affect property values. For example, when the Tax Reform Act of 1986 came out of the Senate Finance Committee in May of 1986, values of affected properties dropped instantaneously. For example, a $1,000,000 income property might have dropped to $800,000. A graph which accurately picked up the $1,000,000 and $800,000 points would nevertheless mislead if it connected them with a line sloping downward. Because such a line suggests that **between** the two points buyers willing to pay $900,000. They were not. It wouldn't even do to draw a vertical, fell-off-a-cliff line connecting the $1,000,000 and $800,000. What actually happened was more like Startrek's Captain Kirk saying, "Beam me down, Scotty."

The sum of its parts

Interest rates, unemployment, tax laws, lumber prices, etc. all affect home prices. Graphs of those variables are jagged and random.

How come the various things that **make up** home values all produce jagged, random patterns when graphed...but home prices themselves...which are mere sums of those parts...move so smoothly in one direction?

In fact, home values and the values of other property types move in the same jagged, random patterns as everything else. Inside that smooth, ever upward NAR® existing-home-price graph is a jagged, random appreciation rate truth waiting to get out. The difference between that jagged, random truth and the NAR® graph is the cumulative effect of all the stuff left out of the NAR® figures.

Making money in real estate just ain't as easy as that NAR® graph makes it look. JTR

62
Real Estate in the Depression

In view of the recent stock market behavior, I thought it would be interesting to see what happened to real estate in the Great Depression. So I went to the library and read *Time* magazines and *Sunday New York Times* Real Estate sections from 1933 through 1935. Mind you, I'm not **predicting** a depression. I don't think anyone can do that. But I **do** know that a lot of people are worried.

Not the end of the world

When people under 50 express fear of a Depression they speak as if the world came to an end during the last one. It did **not**.

The Depression was finite. Not **everybody** was unemployed. Twelve million people were...out of a population of about 125 million. Rents did not drop to zero. They dropped **38%** from the 1925 peak to the 1935 bottom.

Many parallels to today

Depressions are much less likely these days because of the many government safety nets, right? If you cherish that thought, don't read 1930s papers. They sound disconcertingly like today's Sunbelt stories.

- 2/3/33 *Times* reported real estate owners appealing their property taxes in record numbers.
- Manhattan foreclosures up from 942 in first 8 months of '32 to 1,235 in same period in '33.
- 7/23/33 representative of the Bronx Landlords Protective Association: "no market price or value can be placed upon [a property], notwithstanding its real and intrinsic value" because of the lack of comparable sales.
- Isidor Berger, General Manager of the Greater New York Taxpayers Association, complained about, "the granting of rent **concessions**."
- Calls to stick together and not reduce rents.
- Complaints about high fees charged by receivers who were running foreclosed property.
- Much discussion of the need for better property management and tenant relations.

As the Depression worsened, journalists and real estate executives strained to see the light at the end of the tunnel…and repeatedly saw nonexistent lights.

While writing this article about the way it was in the '30s depression I came across a story in the February 12, 1933 *Times* in which a writer of **that** day wrote about the way it was in the Panic of 1837.

Residential rent index during the Depression

[A line graph titled "Residential rent index during the Depression". The vertical axis ranges from 0 to 90 in increments of 10. The horizontal axis shows years from '20 to '40. The line starts around 65 in '20, rises to a peak of about 83 around '24-'25, declines gradually through the late '20s, drops sharply in the early '30s to a low around 52 in '33-'34, then recovers slightly to about 58 by '40. Source: Census Bureau 1967 = 100]

Government help

Businessmen and consumers alike clamored for government help back then. I surmise that '30s businessmen were naive about the **dis**advantages of government involvement because they had never experienced it.

What's worse, help wasn't the only thing the government had in mind. Here's a '34 FDR speech,

"The toes of some people are being stepped on and are going to be stepped on. Those toes belong to those who seek to retain…riches…by some short cut which is harmful to the greater good."

That's a scary, demagogic, appeal to the politics of envy with an implicit threat of government confiscation. Various Depression era laws prevented or restricted foreclosure, thereby, confiscating lenders' property.

On the other hand, the government was an important source of mortgage money by the late thirties and that helped end the depressionl.

Partial depression *now*

We **already** have a depression in many markets. For example, Texas apartments have fallen 40% to 60% in value in the last three years. Office buildings worse.

Action to take

• Appeal your property tax assessment
• Renegotiate your loans
• Cut your rents so that they stay even with falling market levels
• Forget concessions
• Learn how to use government programs
• Remember, basic management and tenant relations principles do not change in hard times.

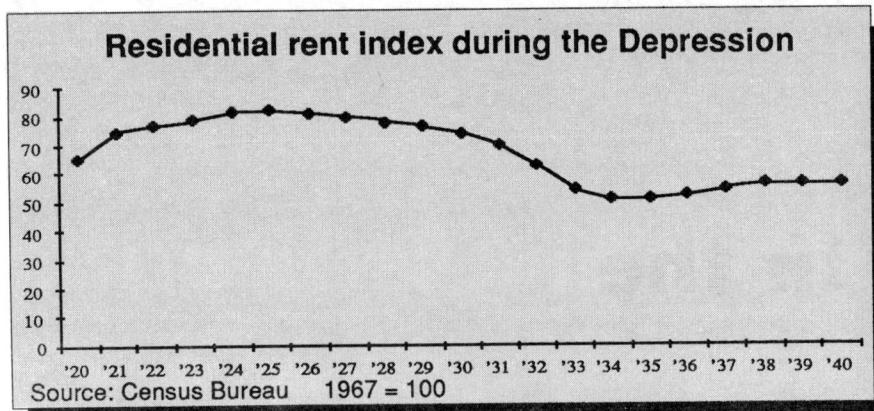

Real estate investors who own properties leased **long-term** to **high credit** tenants would not notice a depression. Nor would **rent-controlled New York City landlords** because their rents are already way below market. Landlords in cities with less severe rent contral laws might suffer some but not as much as those at market rents.

Once again, I am **not** predicting a depression. Just thought you would find what happened in the thirties interesting. JTR

63
The Stock Market Plunge & Real Estate

October 1987

The scare which the October 19th stock market plunge threw into the world economy will probably hasten the overdue recession. In a recession, the rental market value of your properties typically goes down. The main mistake to avoid is being **too slow to lower your rents**. (See "Small Rent Decrease Raises Income Dramatically" in the May '87 issue of **Real Estate Investor's Monthly**.)

Also, you should get your **property tax assessment reduced** during a recession. I've noticed strong resistance to further property tax assessments in Texas even though such reductions are warranted. So you should approach tax appeals with much more determination than normally. You are entitled to the reductions by law and you'll never be **more** entitled to them than during a recession.

In all other respects, what's good management during **boom** times is good management during **recessions**.

The lowering of rental market values results in a corresponding lowering of property values in income properties. If your overall debt-coverage ratio (overall net income from properties and other sources divided by overall debt service payments) is low (1.1 or lower), you may wish to try to **increase** that ratio by refinancing to debt with lower interest rates or lower amortization payments...or by selling property before the recession hits.

Avoid balloon payments falling due during the recession. With property market values lower, it becomes harder to refinance or sell. Refinance or renegotiate **before** then, if you can, to postpone or eliminate balloons. JTR

64
What Free-and-Clear, Zero-Bracket Examples Reveal

May 1986

Leverage and tax-savings are so important in real estate investing that you rarely see anything written about **free-and-clear** ownership or the **zero- bracket**. I'm going to deviate from that pattern in this article.

I'm not **advocating** free-and-clear ownership in this article. Although I wouldn't rule it out. The purpose of this article is to reveal some important things that you may have lost sight of as a result of always thinking of real estate in leveraged, tax saving terms.

The *three* real estate returns

I and others have often said that there are **four** returns from investment real estate:

- Appreciation
- Cash flow
- Tax shelter
- Amortization

A more accurate list would be:

- Appreciation
- Net operating income
- Tax savings

Cash flow is **not** a real estate return. It is net operating income less debt service. Real estate produces net operating income, not cash flow. Cash flow is part real estate and part financing. The same property might have many different cash flows depending on how it is financed.

Amortization is not a real estate return either. Rather, it is simply one of the things you typically spend your net operating income on.

Tax shelter is a very imprecise word. A great many people think negative cash flow is tax shelter. A notion which drives me up a wall. Tax **savings** is a **precise** phrase.

A free-and-clear house

Let's say you buy a $100,000 rental house...free-and-clear. Here are your first-year returns:

Rent Income	$9,000
Less:	
Real estate taxes	$2,400
Insurance	$375
Vacancy loss (5%)	$450
Repairs (5%)	$450
Net Op. Income	$5,325
Plus:	
Appreciation (4.7%)	$4,700
Total 1st-Yr. Return	$10,025

That's a 10.025% return on your $100,000 investment.

A $1,000,000 apartment building

The median operating **expense ratio** for garden apartments in 1984 (most recent) was 44.6% according to the Institute of Real Estate Management. The only statistical study of apartment building **prices** I know of is done by Cain & Scott, Inc. in Seattle (206-285-7100). Their 1985 study shows a median gross rent multiplier of 7.0.

A $1,000,000 building with a gross rent multiplier of 7.0 would have gross annual income of $1,000,000 ÷ 7.0 = $142,857. If 44.6% of that goes to expenses, the net operating income is 100% minus 44.6% = 55.4% x $142,857 = $79,143.

The appreciation would just be ten times its rental house counterpart or $47,000. Note that the apartment building will **not** shelter any taxes. In fact, it will cause you to pay **more** taxes than you'd pay if you did not own it. That's not bad, of course. Rule #1 of Reed's Rules for Understanding Income Taxes says that "**Income is good**" (see Chapter 6 of *Aggressive Tax Avoidance for Real Estate Investors*, $23.95 plus tax and shipping).

Your overall return would be:

Appreciation	$47,000
Net Op. Income	$79,143
Total 1st-Yr. Return	$126,143

Comparing rental houses and income properties

I have long said that **rental houses** are lousy investments. That you should buy **income properties instead**. The numbers above show the difference. On appreciation and depreciation, the properties are identical. But there is a big difference on **net operating income**. The apartment building has a $79,143 ÷ $1,000,000 = 7.9143% capitalization rate. And the rental house, $5,325 ÷ $100,000 = 5.325%.

Some may quibble with my income and expense assumptions. Others believe that rental houses **appreciate faster** than apartment buildings. (I know of no data to support that widespread belief.) The only rental house advantages I will agree to is that they are **more liquid** than apartment buildings and less exposed to the risk of coming under **rent control** laws.

I suspect that **apartment buildings** have slightly **better depreciation** deductions because they typically have higher improvement rations (% of value allocated to depreciable improvements) and because they often have coin-operated vending machines which are eligible for **first-year expensing** or the **investment tax credit**. But I stand by the basic statement that income properties generally have higher capitalization rates than rental houses.

Real estate versus alternative investments

Another question the free-and-clear analysis helps us answer is should you be in real estate at all? Real estate provides overall after-tax returns in the 10% to 12.6% range. That assumes no tax on appreciation because you exchange rather than sell. Can you get before-tax returns of 10% to 12.6% elsewhere? It's possible. But difficult.

According to the May *Money* magazine, the national average interest rate on five-year CDs is 8.14%, the national average tax-free fund rate is 4.9%, and eight-year single A rated bonds are paying 8.6%.

So real estate is still better than a bond...although rental houses are only **marginally** better for a zero-bracket individual. A few years ago, though, bonds were in the 13% to 16% range...and real estate was in the doldrums. So real estate is **usually** the best investment...but **not always.**

In general, real estate will provide **higher** returns than bonds. But there are times in the business cycle when that's not true.

Should you use leverage?

Finally, free-and-clear analysis helps you decide **whether** to leverage or not. You only borrow to invest when the overall return on the investment **exceeds** the interest rate on the borrowing.

Can you borrow for less than 10% to 12.6%? Maybe. The narrower the spread between your overall return and the interest rate on the money you borrow, the less benefit you get from leverage.

In recent years, mortgage loan interest rates have been in the 13% to 16% range. Was the overall return on even an income property enough to clear that? It's questionable. But it's clear that a zero-bracket individual would **not** have been smart to leverage a real estate investment with institutional financing in recent years.

The return from real estate

In this article, I've shown you the overall returns you can get from real estate. 10% to 12.6% in my examples. That's hardly what you'd expect given real estate's vaunted reputation as the greatest investment.

True, I've left out leverage and tax savings. But keep in mind that leverage only magnifies return in a positive direction when the interest rate on the debt is **less than** the return on the asset being financed. When I started in real estate in 1969, debt cost 7.5% and capitalization rates were in the 10% to 15% range. Appreciation was meager...but **in addition to** cash-on-cash returns of 10% on a free-and-clear building. My first duplex rented for $230 a month total and had operating expenses of about $100 a month. That's an annual net operating

income of 12 x $130 = $1,560 on a building I paid $14,000 for. An 11% cap rate or return ($1,560 ÷ $14,000 = 11%), not counting appreciation.

But those days are ancient history. Now we're looking at cap rates of 5% to 8% in the examples above...and mortgage interest rates of 9.5% to 11%.

The break even point

The break even loan-to-value ratio is the cap rate divided by the loan interest rate. For the single-family rental house above, that'd be 5.325% ÷ 10% = 53.25%. That is, a single-family rental house will have **positive** cash flow if its loan-to-value ratio is below 53.25% (in this example), and **negative** cash flow if it is **above** 53.25%. In the typical deal, it is **well** above 53.25%. Highly leverage deals have **high** negative cash flows.

The break even loan-to-value ratio on the apartment building would be 7.9143% ÷ 10% = 79.143%. So an apartment building bought with 25% down would typically show a small positive cash flow. Only when you put down **less** than 21% would you go negative.

Your tax bracket

I have said on many occasions that real estate in the eighties has taken on the characteristic of a **tax-exempt bond.** That is, people in low brackets have no business owning real estate as an investment. The rental house investment above makes less sense than a GNMA bond for a zero-bracket individual. Leverage won't change that. Because the entire return from the property will be consumed by debt service and transaction costs.

High bracket individuals are another matter. For them, the 10.125% return they get from the house is tax-free income. And a much higher yield than they could get on tax-exempt bonds. Plus, **excess** deductions will shelter non-real estate income which increases their yield still further. Because the **high** bracket individual's overall after-tax return is **higher** than the after-tax cost of borrowing, he **can and should** benefit from leverage.

Conclusion

Real estate is not magical. It does **not** produce wonderfully high returns for everyone who owns it. **Leverage** is not magical. It does **not** improve returns for everyone who uses it. **Tax savings** are not magical. They are finite and benefit only those with high taxable incomes.

All real estate investors will earn higher returns in **income properties** than in single-family rental houses. **Low-bracket** investors probably cannot even earn a **positive** return on highly leveraged single-family rental houses. **High-bracket** investors can and should use leverage. Their overall after-tax return is almost certainly above their after-tax return is almost certainly above their after-tax cost of borrowing. **Low-bracket** investors should either buy **non**-real estate investments or **income** properties. Furthermore, low-bracket investors ought **not** assume that leverage will improve their return. They must do the numbers because their overall after-tax return is very close to their after-tax cost of borrowing. Unless that after-tax return is **higher** than the loan interest rate, leverage will **reduce** their return. JTR

65
The Borrowing Buyer Who Always Sells

February 1987

In the last chapter of my book, *Aggressive Tax Avoidance for Real Estate Investors*, I suggest that readers who want to pay zero income taxes become "borrowing builders who never sell." That is, you build properties and live off refinancing proceeds and depreciation-sheltered rent. Your income would not only be **tax-free**, there would be **no debate** about its being tax-free. In other words, it's not even an aggressive strategy. The refinancing proceeds which exceed your living expenses are reinvested

Recently, I met, by phone, a variation on the borrowing builder who never sells. Bill Manley is a borrowing buyer who always sells...some of his properties.

Bill Manley's technique

Bill, who is president of the Georgia Real Estate Investors Association and gives occasional seminars on this technique (404-948-0585), buys single-family houses. Some, he keeps forever. Others, he sells immediately. Here's an example to illustrate.

Bill owns a "keeper" house on Elm Street. It's worth $70,000 and has a $25,000 first mortgage. He finds another house to buy on Main Street. The seller wants $50,000 but hasn't been able to get it. It's free and clear. The seller is willing to take back a mortgage for $30,000.

Bill agrees to buy the house for $50,000...but persuades the seller to put the $30,000 mortgage on the **Elm** Street house instead of the Main Street house he's selling.

Bill gets the $20,000 down payment from cash on hand or a line of credit. Then he immediately puts the Main Street house **up for sale** for $45,000 acting as his own real estate agent. At that price, it typically sells quickly...as it must to minimize carrying costs. In some cases, Bill arranges to resell the property simultaneously with the purchase.

Bill receives $45,000 at closing. He pays off the $20,000 credit line which was only outstanding for a month or so. He nets $25,000.

Income taxes? On **what**? He **lost** $5,000 on the deal.

Non-bank refinancing

In effect, he has refinanced his Elm Street property...and paid transaction costs of $5,000. He also paid **additional** transaction costs in the form of the **effort** he put forth to buy and sell the Main Street property.

Loan-to-value ratio

The loan-to-value ratio the seller of the Main Street property originally had in mind was $30,000 ÷ $50,000 = 60%. The loan-to-value ratio the seller ended up with is ($25,000 + $30,000 = $55,000) ÷ $70,000 = 79%. A 60% loan is less risky and therefore more valuable if sold for cash that a 79% loan. Bill argues that as long as you stay below 80% of value, there is little or no difference in the resale value of the loan.

I believe that a buyer using this technique ought **not** do so in a **bait-and-switch** fashion which gets the seller to accept the 60% loan on his **own** property, then switches him to the 79% loan on the other property. Bill starts by offering a "note secured by other real estate" which should eliminate the possibility of a bait-and-switch accusation.

A number of real estate gurus use what is arguably a bait-and-switch scheme and call it "substitution of collateral." The phrase substitution of collateral refers to a legitimate technique in which an **already existing** mortgage is cancelled in return for a new mortgage on another property. If the "substitution" occurs only in the seller's mind...and then only after the buyer has encouraged the seller to agree to a loan on the property being sold...bait-and-switch is the more accurate name.

Resale value of mortgage

In addition to the loan-to-value ratio, there is also a question as to the seller's ability to appraise the Elm Street property, the creditworthiness of the buyer/borrower, and the adequacy of the loan documents.

A seller would typically be easier to fool than an institutional lender regarding the value of a property. Most sellers do little or no credit checking. And the typical seller loan (Bill's technique or not) documents are grossly inadequate even though an attorney drew them up. Especially if the **buyer** drew them up.

One in 35 sellers

Bill says about one in 35 sellers will go for this deal. The seller needs to own the property free and clear or nearly so. And they need to have had the property on the market for a long time in order to be ripe for the unusual, mortgage-on-another-property terms.

To get the loan at all

Bill is essentially living off the **equity buildup** in his keeper properties. The properties he buys and sells are just convoluted refinancings of the keeper properties.

There is little **financial** advantage to Bill's buy/sell approach over just refinancing the keeper properties through a bank. But Bill says there is a **qualitative** advantage. He figures he would not be able to borrow **at all** from institutional lenders because he has no steady source of salary income. He says his credit record is clean. But single-family lenders have their approval formulas and a guy who lives off refinancing proceeds makes their formulas go "tilt." So he refinances through **sellers** in order to get the loan at all...as well as to get a better deal, i.e. no due-on-sale clause, possibility of future discount payoff.

Staying out of trouble

In some deals, the cash value (cash received by seller plus cash resale value of the note taken) is much lower than the cash that could be had from a sale at a more realistic price to a buyer who would get his **own** financing... and thereby pay **all cash** to the seller.

A real estate agent getting a commission on the deal...as the buyer or as a third party agent...has a clear duty to explain to the seller both the cash value and the risk aspects of this technique. But

I also feel a **non**-agent buyer has a duty to **refrain** from doing such deals even with full disclosure to the seller.

The only exception I make is for "consenting adults." By that I mean a seller who is or should be as **sophisticated** as you. That is, they have an **earned** net worth of at least $50,000...which is greater than or equal to **your** net worth. **Or** that the seller is a **professional**, not clerk, in a field related to mortgage lending. Like a real estate attorney, loan officer, or title officer. Or they are **advised** by such a professional.

Bill's deal and other seller-financed deals **can** be done without violating my unconscionability standard. Often, however, the seller would have gotten a much higher cash equivalent deal by cutting the price instead of taking seller financing.

Equity buildup is the key

Keep in mind that this way of making a living will **not** work unless you have appreciation in rents and/or equity. There is no money made by the technique itself. The money is **made** by the equity buildup. The technique simply converts the equity build-up to cash...tax-free. Bamboozling sellers is not required. JTR

66
How Trump
Lost a Billion

According to *Forbes* magazine (5/14/90), Donald Trump's net worth dropped from $1.7 billion in 1989 to $.5 billion this year. How did the world's most famous real estate investor do that?

By doing what the vast majority of real estate investors do: buying breakeven or negative-cash-flow property on the theory that it will appreciate. Unfortunately for him, it didn't. In fact, his properties went **down** in value.

Forbes notes that "the steady appreciation in prime properties seems to have come to a halt." I told readers that such properties do **not** appreciate more in "Do high-priced properties appreciate faster?" in the 4/88 issue. And I've warned that appreciation rates on all properties are totally unpredictable in many articles, e.g., "Calculated Risks" in the 2/90 and 3/90 issues (See Chapters 81, 82).

Forbes prefaces one sentence in the article with the words, "Even granting his magic touch in upgrading properties..." If Trump **has** such a magic touch, he ought to use it...then get **rid** of the properties after he upgrades them.

Upgrading real estate is a profitable activity for those who know how to do it. **Holding** real estate, as Trump has learned to his sadness, is a speculative and risky activity.

Forbes says Trump has assets of $3.7 billion, debt of $3.2 billion, and **negative cash flow** of $38 million a year. If you divide those numbers by 10,000, Trump looks like a guy who owns a $370,000 rental house with a $320,000 mortgage and $3,800 a year in negative cash flow. Those are about the same numbers you'd expect Joe Average investor to have. Can it be that Donald Trump is just Joe Average magnified ten thousand times?

Trump denies that he's less than a multibillionaire. But in its 5/14/90 article, *Business Week* says, "Trump typically places lofty valuations on his properties."

Oh, really. Under certain circumstances, that's a **felony**. When Geraldine Ferraro's husband, John Zaccaro exaggerated his net worth by $16.64 million, he was convicted of "scheming to defraud." JTR

67

Are You Aware of Your Investment Assumptions?

October 1986

If you invest in real estate, you make assumptions. Assumption is the mother of all screw-ups. So you'd better be aware of the assumptions you are making.

Higher return than seconds

One assumption that you make when you invest in real estate is that you will earn a **higher after-tax return** than you would earn on discounted second mortgages. How do I know that? Because owning real estate is far more risky and far more time-consuming than investing in mortgages. Therefore it must be more rewarding financially. If it's **not**, get out of real estate and go into investing in mortgages.

The return on **first** mortgages these days is about 10%. Seconds must go for about 13%. Discounted seconds would go for a bit more...maybe 15%.

How much higher?

We know the return from owning real estate should be higher than the return from mortgages. But how much higher? I'd guess about 50% higher. 150% x 15% = 22.5%.

So by investing in real estate, you are impliciting saying, "I expect to earn an overall return of at least 22.5% on this investment." Note that I said "**overall**" return, not cash on cash. The overall return comes from:

- Cash flow
- Appreciation
- Tax savings.

A little algebra for you

That minimum return assumption can be stated as a crude algebraic formula:

$$R = C + A + S$$

where R = overall % return, C = cash flow % return, A = appreciation % return, and S = tax savings % return.

And we can restate it as:

$$22.5\% = C + A + S$$

Buying at breakeven

In recent years, real estate investors bought income property on terms that would **break even** before taxes. That is, their cash on cash return % was zero. Adding that to the equations we get

$$22.5\% = 0 + A + S \text{ or}$$
$$22.5\% = A + S$$

In other words, an investor who buys real estate on terms that produce break even cash flow is assuming that his appreciation and tax savings alone will add up to 22.5%.

Tax savings?

What about the tax savings part of that equation? Properties you buy after the President signed the new tax law into effect come under the new **passive loss** limits. If your adjusted gross income not counting real estate is less than $100,000, and you have not already used up your $25,000 loss exemption with other property, you will indeed get some tax savings from an income property.

Let's say the property costs you $500,000, is residential, and has an 85% improvement ratio. That gives you 85% x $500,000 = $425,000 of depreciable improvements. And let's say you are in the maximum marginal tax bracket which will be 33%. The annual depreciation deduction will be $425,000 ÷ 27.5 years = $15,455. At the 33% bracket that will save you $15,455 x 33% = $5,100 a year on your taxes. If you put down 20% or $100,000, your tax savings as a percentage of your investment is 5.1%. Let's add that to the equation.

$$22.5\% = A + 5.1\%$$
$$A = 22.5\% - 5.1\% = 17.4\%$$

Appreciation assumption must be 3.48%

Since you are leveraged 5 to 1 ($5 worth of property for every $1 of down payment), the proeprty needs to appreciate by 17.4% ÷ 5 = 3.48% per year in order for you to achieve a 17.4% appreciation component on your investment return.

Here are the dollar figures. Appreciation at 3.48% would be 3.48% x $500,000 = $17,400. Added to the $5,100 in tax savings gives you a total return of $22,500 which is a 22.5% return on your $100,000 down payment.

Will the appreciation rate be 3.48%? I don't know. But if it is **not**, you made a lousy investment.

What if tax savings are zero?

Now suppose your adjusted gross income not counting real estate losses is **more** than $150,000. In that case, you wil get **no** tax savings. So by buying income property on a break even basis in that tax situation, you are making the following appreciation assumption.

$$22.5\% = A + 0 \text{ or}$$
$$22.5\% = A$$

That means you are assuming the appreciation rate is 22.% ÷ 5 = 4.5% per year. And again, if it is **not**, you made a lousy investment.

It's a numbers game

Investment is not some magical black box. Whether conscious or not, you are making mathematical investment assumptions when you structure deals. You'd better be aware of the assumptions implicit in your deals. They may surprise you.∎

PART SEVEN

MOBILEHOME PARKS, CONDOS, AND OTHER INVESTMENTS

68
Mobilehome Parks
As Investments

September 1986

Mobilehome parks are one of the more common forms of real estate investment. But they are rarely written about. That's too bad. Because they can be worthwhile investments.

Cash cows?

Some investors believe mobilehome parks are cash cows. That is, they generate much higher before-tax positive cash flow than apartment buildings. Not true.

The notion that a particular property type is a cash cow is nonsensical on its face. **All** types of income proprty are cash cows if they are **unleveraged**. And all types lose their positive cash flow when you leverage them up to about 75% or 80%.

From time to time, one type may **temporarily** have a higher capitalization rate (net operating income divided by market value). But profit begets competition. If mobilehome parks produce higher returns than other types of properties, investors will switch. The more investors bidding for mobilehome parks, the higher the prices they sell for. The higher the prices, the higher the mortgage amounts and the higher the mortgage payments. Bye bye cash flow.

Lower expenses?

Apartment investors may expect to find lower expenses in mobilehome parks. After all, you own **pads, not buildings**. The **tenants** own the mobilehome coaches.

Forget it. I was amazed to see the number and size of the expenses on typical mobilehome park income statements. As with apartments, you have a resident manager salary, common area electric, insurance, property tax, pool maintenance, landscaping, phone, dumpster, water, sewer, licenses, repairs, etc. About all you **avoid** is roof, appliance, and miscellaneous structure repairs like glass and stairways.

How about the operating expense ratio? Surely the operating expenses must take a lower percentage of income than in an apartment building. Nope. Because although you have fewer categories of expenses and some, like hazard insurance, are lower...so are the **rents** lower.

California mobilehome park owner, Leigh Robinson (author of the apartment management book, *Landlording*), says his average rent is about $150 a month.

Tenant differences

Mobilehome park tenants are different from apartment tenants. Yes, many are senior citizens. But there are plenty of family parks, too. The main difference is that the tenants **own** the homes themselves.

That has both good and bad effects. One **good** effect is that mobilehome park tenants behave like owners. The collection of rent is analogous to a city's collection of property taxes. That is, virtually everyone pays.

Eviction

For an **apartment** tenant, being kicked out means loading the U-Haul and moving a couple blocks. For a **mobilehome park** tenant, being kicked out means finding a place for the **house** and incurring the expense and hassle of moving it there. And mobilehomes aren't mobile anymore. So the house acts as a sort of $20,000 "security deposit" and encourages good behavior. Also the eviction preocedures are far more difficult for the park owner...generally requiring an attorney. On the other hand, if the home is financed, you can demand that the lender pay the rent to avoid eviction...as if you were a first mortgage holder and the lender had a second.

The down side of tenants owning their homes is that they are more militant. They stay much longer than apartment tenants...and therefore view such things as rent increases as something that will affect the rest of their lives...not just the next year or so.

Mobilehome park tenants are much better organized than apartment tenants. As a result, they are more dangerous opponents on such issues as rent control, condo conversion (yes, you can condo convert a mobilehome park), and conversion of the park to another use.

The propensity of municipal governments to control mobilehome park rents is one of the **biggest disadvantages** of this type of investment. If you decide to invest in mobilehome parks, I urge you to do so **only** in states where local rent control laws are either **prohibited**, or effectively prohibited by state laws. Examples include such states as Washington, Oregon, and Texas.

Partly as a defense against rent control, **long-term leases** (2 to 10 years) are more common in mobilehome parks. Long-term leases control rents themselves ...and blunt tenant union effectiveness by dividing the tenants into those whose leases expire soon and those whose don't.

Rural aspects

A significant percentage of mobilehome parks are in **rural** areas...or areas that **were** rural when the parks were built. As a result, mobilehome park investors coming from apartments or office buildings may be surprised to find that they have to deal with such facilities as **septic tanks** and **wells**.

If the park you're considering has no public water or sewer, educate yourself by getting Les Scher's book, *How to Find and Buy Your Place in the Country* (Collier Books, 866 Third Avenue, NY, NY 10022).

Tax aspects

At first glance, you might think mobilehome parks have nothing to depreciate. Not true. You can and should depreciate landscaping, pavement, underground pipes (of which mobilehome parks have more than apartment buildings), pool, clubhouse (more common than in apartment buildings), the laundry building and equipment, septic system or sewage treatment plant, well, fencing, common area lighting, etc.

In addition, the manager's quarters...either a mobilehome or a permanent structure...are usually owned by the park owner. And some parks also have a number of mobilehomes which are owned by the park (with tenants who misbehave accordingly).

Exchanging

Mobilehomes owned by the park owner are **personal property** for tax purposes. They are depreciated using the **200%** declining-balance method over **ten** years under the new tax law. That, of course, is much better than the 27.5-year straight line which will apply to apartment buildings under the new law.

But be careful if you **exchange** into or out of a mobilehome park. Personal property like mobilehomes is **not like kind** to real property like apartments or office buildings. That doesn't mean you **cannot** do such exchanges. Just that you must be **careful** to balance the personal versus personal and the real versus the real property to avoid having a partially-taxed exchange.

Attractive under new tax law

The **improvement ratio** (depreciable property value divided by total property value) probably averages about **50-60%** in mobilehome parks. That compares to 70% to 90% in other types of income property. So mobilehome parks will be **less** affected by the new tax law than other types of income property. And they would make a nice passive *income* complement to other types of income property with passive *losses* during the next several years.

A better investment?

Are mobilehome parks a better investment than other income properties? No. They're probably **worse** where rent control is a possibility. And their income will not all be sheltered by depreciation the way a regular income property's cash flow would be. **But** if you can insulate yourself from rent control worries...and you can shelter the taxable income mobilehome parks throw off (as a result of relatively little depreciation),

mobilehome parks are as good an investment vehicle as other types of income properties.

For further information, check the Western Mobilehome Association, 1121 L Street, Suite 400, Sacramento, CA 95814 or *The Mobilehome Parks Report* at 916-971-0489. JTR

69

Investment Dangers And Opportunities in Homeowners Associations

March 1987

I have heard of legal difficulties like title problems and lawsuits at a number of homeowners associations. It occurred to me that homeowners associations may be **more** prone to such problems than straight fee ownership. That, in turn, has investment and insurance ramifications.

The theory

Seems to me homeowners associations are more likely to be **sued** than a single homeowner... and more likely to **lose** the suit. More likely to be sued because suing a single homeowner is man-to-man combat. Whereas suing an association is suing an impersonal corporation. Besides, they have insurance...and any increase in premiums will be spread over all the members of the association.

I suspect homeowners associations are more likely to **lose** such suits because:

- They are more likely to be guilty.
- They are less likely to care about the outcome.
- Juries are less sympathetic to associations than individuals.

More likely to be guilty

When a **homeowner** sees a hazard on his property, he will likely correct it. But when a homeowner sees a hazard on property owned by the homeowners **association** of which he is a member, he will likely assume somebody **else** will take care of it...or figure it's the association's problem, not his. And if a member of the association brings the hazard to the attention of an association officer, that officer is more likely to neglect it because he is typically unpaid for his services...and covered by liability insurance.

Less likely to care about outcome

When a homeowner is sued, he is typically very concerned about the outcome of the litigation. The judgment could **exceed** his liability insurance coverage. Or the policy may **exclude** the particular loss.

So the homeowner will select his attorney carefully...or complain loudly if the insurance company's selection appears incompetent. The homeowner and his family will also assist in gathering evidence and testifying.

But when the **association** is sued, who will worry about the outcome? The volunteer officers? And who will gather evidence and testify? Both activities are pains in the neck. When your financial well being is at stake, you work hard to protect it. But an officer/member of, say, a 140-member homeowners association …with a $2,000,000 liability policy…has a hard time getting motivated to gather affidavits from witnesses or subject himself to cross examination at a trial…in order to protect his 1/140th interest in a possible excess (greater than $2,000,000) judgment.

Corporate continuity

If you buy a house, you cannot be sued for a **prior** incident which occurred as a result of the negligence of a previous owner. But if you buy into a homeowner's **association**, you are buying into a corporation which can subject you to liability for incidents which occurred **before** you bought in.

Juries

Jury members can identify with a homeowner. But juries have much more difficulty identifying with the Whispering Oaks Homeowners Association, Incorporated…especially if Whispering Oaks is upscale.

Loss assessment insurance

One thing you can do about this is get loss assessment insurance. It covers you if the homeowners association is sued and the court judgment or settlement exceeds the limit of the association's liability insurance. Loss assessment insurance is relatively cheap…25¢ a $1,000 on my homeowners insurance policy. And if your association is **large**, a low individual limit will protect you from a large, excess association loss.

For example, in a 200-member homeowners group, $25,000 of loss assessment coverage on your property would protect you from an excess loss of $25,000 x 200 = $5,000,000. In other words, if your association had a **two** million dollar policy and got hit with a **seven** million dollar judgment, you and your fellow members would each be assessed roughly $25,000 (it might vary by size of each property). You would probably be covered if you had loss assessment coverage (loss assessment policies have exclusions, too). But your neighbors would have to get the $25,000 out of their **pockets**.

Smaller associations more dangerous

The smaller the association, the more dangerous. Because **your share** of it increases. But you still have the no-one's-in-charge problem.

Non-lawsuit problems

Real estate is heir to many ills. Construction defects, soil conditions, buried toxic wastes, title problems, and so forth. If you own a home with no homeowners association…and your neighbor 150 yards away has such a problem…it's **his** problem, not yours. But if that same neighbor is a member of your homeowners association, it's probably **your** problem, too.

I know of one condo development where three units slid down a hill. Because of that, resale values of **all** the units in that development were depressed for years. Another association property had a **title** problem relating to one part of the common area. As a result, none of the would-be buyers for that development could get title insurance…which, in turn, killed financing and, therefore, resale values.

Problems unique to homeowners associations

A homeowners association in Marin County, California decided it did not need to put aside reserves for capital expenditures. They figured they'd pay as needed. But required financial reports indicated that their reserves were too low by $7,000 a unit...which, in turn, caused lenders to redline the development. Inability to get financing caused values there to drop $20,000 to $25,000 per unit! Of course, those same lenders would never dream of requiring a buyer of a regular house (no homeowners association) to have a $7,000 reserve for roof replacement and such.

A homeowners association property manager with 16 years experience told me that he wished he did not have any investor-owned units in the many developments he manages. He says the investor owners tend to vote against all increases in dues. That, in turn, causes the development to run down.

Also, he says investors tend to give their tenants the phone number of the homeowners association or its manager as the **only** number to call for maintenance. But the homeowners association **cannot** and will not make repairs to the **inside** of a unit. When the tenant calls the owner's number (typically the real estate office where they mail their rent), the bookkeeper refers the tenant back to the homeowners association. The investors try to remain anonymous as far as the tenants are concerned.

And, of course, the tenants cause problems for the homeowners association just as they do for landlords. But homeowners associations are less willing or able to deal with tenant problems because they have no power of eviction. And the owner-occupants resent having to pay for the extra time required to supervise tenants. Some investors think a condo association takes care of **all** their management duties. Wrong. Common area maintenance only. And even if you are a responsible condo investor, the other investors in your condo can foul you up. In a rental house with no association, you suffer only for your own failings, not the failings of the guy around the corner.

I suspect that a tenant in a homeowner association property is more likely to sue **both** the investor who owns his unit and the association than a tenant in a house with no homeowners association would be to sue the owner of the house. The big, impersonal corporation syndrome.

Opportunity

Slumping resale values in association property resulting from minor problems appear to be **overreactions** in many cases...like the $20,000 to $25,000 per unit drop in value due to a $7,000 per unit shortfall in reserves. Overreactions create **bargains**. In general, the problems that cause these value drops are eventually **corrected**...allowing the values to go back up to normal.

Theory versus reality

Association experts I spoke to said they could not cite any examples of lawsuits against associations. One said my theory would probably prove correct in the not-too-distant future.

Non-lawsuit problems (title, slides, etc.) have been occurring right along, though. And homeowners associations are frequently in court as plaintiffs suing the builder who built their development. The resulting publicity is not likely to enhance the resale value of your property.

Before you buy into a homeowners association, check pending litigation, percentage of rented units, existence of hazards (especially deep water), title problems, redlining, etc. JTR

70
Condo Investment Return Well Behind Houses

May 1988

Al Canella bought a condo in Chicago in 1979 for $59,000. He'd be lucky to get $40,000 for it now. But if he had bought a **regular house** in Chicago for $59,000 then, it would be worth about $90,000 today. (I changed the name to protect privacy.)

Lagging condo prices

In market after market all across the country you can find condo owners whose units have stagnated or dropped in value. Yet they can look out their condo windows and see **houses** which have gone up dramatically in value since they bought the condo.

- *BusinessWeek* (4/25/88) reports prices of some western ski condos falling 11% to 58%. Aspen Realtor® Richard Cohen says prices are going **up** there, but that houses generally "hold their value better than condos."

- Arlington, Virginia tax assessors say the average **house** assessment there will rise 16% over last year; average **condo** assessments, only 9%.

- According to *Banker and Tradesman*, the average condo price in Suffolk County, Massachusetts (Boston) **fell** from $160,592 in July to $150,418 in November.

- The DC Board of Realtors® reports that house prices went **up** 4% there in '87; condos went **down** 4%.

- House prices are going up smartly in my area of Northern California. But a Realtor® friend says prices of all but a few expensive condos in the area are stagnant. Units in one condo building which sold for about $135,000 in '82 are now barely saleable because of construction defect litigation.

- According to the San Fernando Valley, CA Board of Realtors®, **house** prices went up 18.4% there between March '87 and March '88 while **condo** prices only went up 2.8%.

Why is this? Several possible causes come to mind.

Condos have appreciated slower than homes...

Average Regional Rate

| Single-family homes |
| Condos |

Chart showing Average Regional Rate from 0% to 12% for years 1982–1986:
- 1982: Single-family homes ~3.8%, Condos ~7.2%
- 1983: Single-family homes ~3.6%, Condos ~1.5%
- 1984: Single-family homes ~5.2%, Condos ~2.2%
- 1985: Single-family homes ~8.7%, Condos ~5.7%
- 1986: Single-family homes ~11.3%, Condos ~6.6%

Source: National Assoc. Of Realtors®

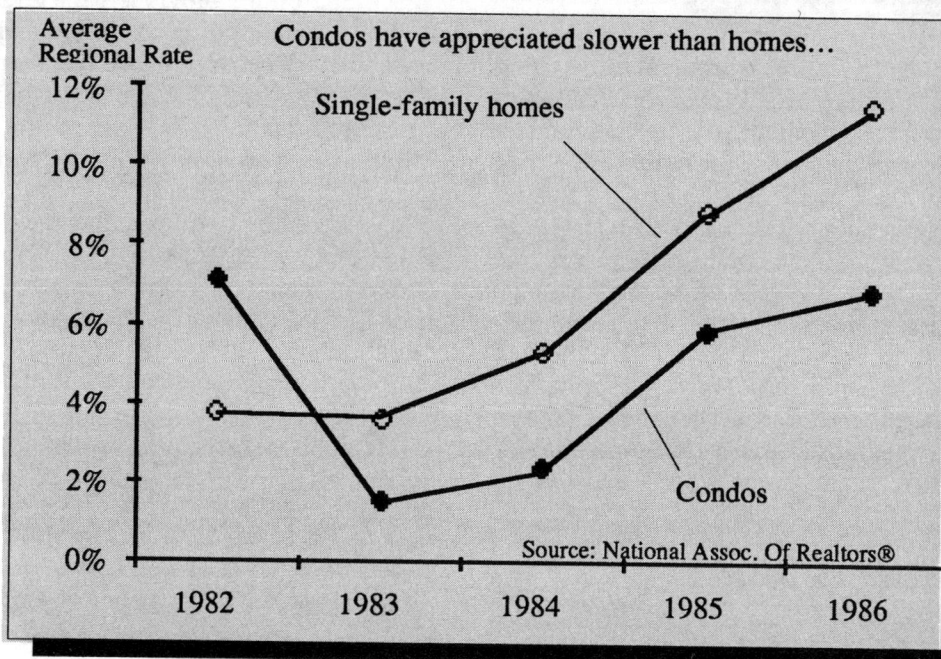

The IPO syndrome

Initial public offerings (IPOs) of stock in public companies are notorious for dropping in value after they are first offered. According to *Venture Economics*, the average IPO that was issued during 1986 (a bull market) sold for 1.5% less than its issue price by year-end. Money manager and author, Ken Fisher says the letters IPO stand for "It's probably overpriced." The same can frequently be said of new condos and condo conversions...especially high rises.

A *New York Times* reader complained that he agreed to buy a New York condo conversion at $107,000. The seller later dropped his asking price to other buyers by about $30,000. The $107,000 buyer presumably had to buy the unit at the higher price.

And I've read many a story about failed condos which managed to sell a few units to a handful of suckers who paid far more than the subsequent offering prices.

Litigation

Condos have participated disproportionately in the recent litigation trend. As I reported in the November issue, a study by the California Department of Real Estate found that a third of condo developments reported construction defects. About 25% had either filed suits or contemplated suing.

Condo association litigation is so widespread that attorneys find it cost-effective to solicit the business by **advertising** in community association newsletters. Banks and stock brokers man booths at condo community association trade fairs in part to become managers of the lump sum proceeds of condo litigation settlements and judgments.

Demographics

Glen Crellin of the National Association of Realtors® Economics Departments says the gap between house and condo appreciation rates may be explained by the fact that condos are disproportionately **starter** homes. Baby boomers are now rising into the move-up housing market. As they do, you have a large number of baby **boomers** selling their first homes to a smaller number of baby **busters**.

Data to support that theory is sparse and inconclusive. To wit, Crellin could only note that 2-bedroom homes appreciated at rates of 8.5% in '86 and 3.6% in '87.

Rates, not prices

I had a recurring problem researching this article. Virtually everyone I talked to would tell me houses appreciated faster because they were more desirable than condos. But prices are **not** what this article is about. There's no mystery as to why the median condo price in, say, the Northeast, was 96% of the median home price in '82.

The mystery is why the median Northeastern **condo** price **fell** from 96% of the home price in 1982 to just **75%** of the median Northeastern **home** price by 1987.

Easier to build

Leigh Robinson, author of the book, *Landlording*, thought the explanation might be that condos are more overbuilt than houses because the condo builder pays less per unit than the home builder to put them up. Thus making it easier to overshoot the market in condos. I'll add that condo **converters** spend less yet.

Buy houses, not condos

Buy houses, not condos, if you want to invest in the single-family market.

I'm a bit tentative because the figures are somewhat crude. For example, a National Association of Realtors® news release on February 26th said that *"...price appreciation for condos and co-ops, which was 7.4% from 1986 to 1987, outstripped the 5.1% price appreciation rate for homes for the same period."* That's because homes are more or less **equally** distributed nationwide... but 52.3% of condo and co-op sales were in the hot **Northeastern** market. In fact, houses appreciated **much more** than condos in every region but the Midwest.

Regional appreciation rates				
1987	NE	MW	S	W
houses	27%	4%	4%	12%
condos	17%	5%	1%	5%

My graph on the previous page does **not** show condos going up faster than houses in 1987 because I used the average **regional** appreciation rate rather than the **national** rate.

Similarly, condos went up faster than homes in 1982 because of a **Western** region phenomenon. As you may recall, interest rates were 16% in 1982. That retarded appreciation. In the West, which was by far the highest priced region then, the high interest rates made condos the only thing many people could afford.

Regional appreciation rates				
1982	NE	MW	S	W
homes	14%	3%	3%	-5%
condos	1%	1%	4%	23%

That seems to be a pattern. Condos can appreciate faster than homes briefly when there is a lurch upward in home prices or interest rates. I suspect that's because the people who had their heart set on becoming home owners switch to condos. But later, would-be buyers just sit out the market.

Houses, condos, & timeshares

We all know people who have made money in **houses**. Newspaper columnist, Bob Bruss, says he and others have occasionally made money in **condos**. But he knows of no one who ever **systematically** made money investing in condos. Furthermore, he asked his 500-newspaper reading audience to let him know if any of **them** knew of such a person. He got **one** letter...from a banker who had lots of foreclosed condos to **sell**.

To go one notch farther out on the condo spectrum, as far as I know, no one on earth has ever made money investing in **timeshare** condos as a buyer. The profit spectrum, then, looks like this:

Profit spectrum		
houses	condos	timeshares
frequent	occasional	never

Invest in condos only when you find a special "situation." JTR

71
Timeshares Stink

May 1989

In the May '88 issue (See Chapter 70), I said that, "as far as I know, no one on earth has ever made money investing in timeshares as a buyer. A survey by the Resort Property Owners Association pretty much supports that. It found that 38.7% of timeshare owners have listed their units for sale but only 2% have actually been resold and the overwhelming majority of those sold for the seller's cost or less.

The survey also seems to roughly confirm P.T. Barnum's observation that, "A sucker is born every minute." 1,300,000 suckers own timeshares. There are 525,960 minutes in a year which means it took 1,300,000 ÷ 525,960 = 2.47 years to produce the current crop of timeshare owners. The timeshare concept has been around a bit longer than that...but then some of the folks of whom Barnum spoke were needed to buy get-rich-quick home study courses. JTR

72
Rooming Houses

Most people only think of rooming houses as places with blinking neon lights outside the window…places police search after they arrest an assassin and find out where he lived. Why should you think of them more often than that? Because they produce as much as **300%** more rent per square foot than apartments according to one investor.

Definition

A rooming house is a residential building with one-room rental units and common bathrooms… sometimes limited common kitchen facilities.

You probably lived in a rooming house when you were in college or the military. Only they were called dormitories or barracks. The point is that using a common bathroom doesn't prove you're John Hinckley, Jr.

Who lives in them?

Generally, rooming houses cater to one sex, usually male. Many tenants are, indeed, lonely, economically marginal men who have received less of the grace of God than you.

Some rooming houses, like the late great Barbizon in New York, even manage to attract an **upscale** clientele. Another in Haddonfield, New Jersey has been on that proudly colonial community's annual Open House Tour and includes such upscale quaintness as brass beds and hand-made quilts.

New Jersey investor, Vincent Ortiz (201-369-7387) says rooming house tenants are typically divorced or separated men, married men who go home on weekends, foreigners, young people who don't get along well enough with their parents to live at home, and young people who like the camaraderie of living with others of similar ages and marital status. It's easier to find three guys for a pick-up basketball game in a rooming house than in an apartment house. In college areas, rooming houses frequently cater to **students**

Terms

Ortiz leases rooms on the same terms as typical apartment owners except for the following:

- All units are **furnished.**
- Rent is due **weekly** and personal checks are not accepted ("Too much rubber" says Ortiz).
- Leases are for **90 days.**
- Two-weeks **notice** required.
- **Security deposit** equals two weeks' rent.
- No separate **meters.**
- **Parking** at night only.
- Clean **sheets** are traded for dirty ones each week (tenant must make the bed).
- Tenants generally do **not** get **mail** delivered to them at the rooming house.

Management

Rooming house management is the same as apartment management except for:

- More **government** involvement, e.g. fire drills, licenses, increased reporting requirements
- Manager must **clean** bathrooms
- Common baths mean **hallways** which also must be cleaned
- **Parking** can be a problem because of the number of tenants per 1,000 square feet
- More **rowdiness** problems
- Check employment but **not** landlord references.

The numbers

A typical room would be 10 x 12 = 120 square feet and rents for $65 to $100 a week in Ortiz's North Jersey market. That's about $85 ÷ 120 square feet = 71¢/ square foot per week x 52 weeks per year = $36.83 per square foot per year. Ortiz gets $575 to $625 (tenant pays all utilities) for one-bedroom units of about 700 square feet in his normal apartment buildings in the same area. The apartment generates $600 ÷ 700 square feet = 86¢ per square foot per month x 12 months = $10.29 per square foot per year.

An outside laundry service charges $25 per week for 20 rooms worth of sheets. (Ortiz owns the sheets. It's cheaper that way.) Ortiz's manager vacuums the

hall, shovels the sidewalk, cleans four bathrooms three times a week, light maintenance, and enforces the lease. He does not handle leasing or rent collection. He gets a free room as his only pay.

Other expenses are about the same as a furnished, master-metered apartment building. Ortiz guesses his operating expense ratio on the apartment building is 45%; on the rooming house, 19%.

At $85 a week, a 20-unit rooming house would have gross annual income of $85 x 52 x 20 = $88,400. An operating expense ratio of 19% would mean total operating expenses of 19% x $88,400 = $16,796 leaving net operating income of $88,400 - $16,796 = $71,604. Ortiz paid about $470,000 for the rooming house portion of the building (it also has 3,500 square feet of office space). So his cap rate is $71,604 ÷ $470,000 = 15.23%.

Oakland, CA investor, Frederick Morse added five bedrooms to a three-bedroom fixer he bought for $175,000. He expects gross monthly income of $2,200 to $2,500 from eight students. As a single-family house, it would rent for about $1,200.

Legal status

Homeowners do not like rooming houses. And they use zoning to try to keep them out or restrict their size. I suspect that many rooming houses are illegal or contain more units than the law allows. I can't be more specific because there obviously are no government statistics on buildings whose owners are hiding them from the government.

Legality of anti-rooming house laws

However, governments are limited in their ability to restrict occupancy. In *Moore v. East Cleveland* (431 US 494), the U.S. Supreme Court said cities could not prohibit the members of an extended natural family from sharing the same "dwelling unit."

In *Santa Barbara v. Adamson* (610 P 2d 436), the California Supreme Court outlawed an ordinance which limited the number of unrelated people allowed to live in one house. But in *Belle`Terre v. Boraas* (94 SCt 1536), which predated *Moore*, the U.S. Supreme Court said it was OK to prohibit six unrelated college students from living in the same house.

Oakland, CA residents have lately been complaining about real estate investors who convert single-family houses into "collective households" for eight or more students who attend the University of California at Berkeley.

You **must** find out whether all the units in the property you are considering are legal. One of my friends owned a large house which had been converted to a rooming house. He had lots of cash flow until a neighbor complained to the city. They made him **reduce** the number of roomers he could rent to and dramatically reduced his cash flow and resale value. I recommend that you have a lawyer who specializes in such things tell you, in writing, how many of the units are legal, before you agree to buy.

Income tax aspects

Rooming houses are the same as apartment buildings or single-family rental houses for tax purposes. The only exception would be if your typical tenant's **stay**, not lease term, were **less than thirty days** [reg. §1.48-1(h)(1)(i) and (2)(ii)] and you provide "**substantial services**" [Senate Finance Committee Report 99-313, Title XIV, A, page 720]. In that case, your building would be treated as a **hotel** for income tax purposes. (See "Hotels, Motels, and the Passive Loss Limits" Feb. '88.)

That means all personal property in the building would be eligible for first-year expensing [IRC §179] up to the annual limit of $10,000. It also means income could be **non-passive** in nature and losses might not be subject to the **passive loss limits**. But keep in mind that rooming houses have extraordinarily high rents per square foot...without having extraordinarily high expenses...so there are no tax losses...even when depreciation is added.

Rooming houses are the long-sought PIG

When the Tax Reform Act of 1986 came out, there was a frantic scramble for property which would generate passive income which could absorb the passive losses generated by properties purchased in the pre-Tax Reform era. Parking lots, S Corporations, and free-and-clear buildings were suggested as solutions. I explained why they were **not** in the September, October, and December '86 and January '87 issues.

Rooming houses **are** the long-sought passive income generator (PIG). They make sense for **any** investor. But they **especially** make sense for an investor who has significant suspended losses.

Renting rooms in your house

Renting rooms in your home is a variation on the rooming house theme. But it only makes sense for bachelor "real estate bums" or cash short families.

A subscriber who used to rent out rooms in his residence says make sure you have very clear rules of the house (in writing). Spell out such things as who takes out the trash, permissable noise levels, cleaning requirements, the need to repair any damage promptly. The biggest problem that subscriber had was non-payment of last month's rent. He got tenants by word-of-mouth or classified ads. "Houses to share" seems logical but the "apartment for rent" heading drew better.

There is no financial advantage to renting a rental house to three or four roomers instead of to a family. Because the rent would be about the same either way.

To find rooming houses

Some states or towns require rooming houses to be registered. If yours does, use the registration lists as your mailing list to find properties for sale. Or you could just answer classified ads which offer rooms for rent. Ask for the address. Then look up the owner's name in the tax records. It's extremely hard to spot a rooming house even from street right out front. Even the mailman probably doesn't know because roomers use post office boxes.

Financing

I thought getting a mortgage on a rooming house would be tough because it's an odd ball property type. But Ortiz said he had no trouble. He called seven banks and three said yes. The loan he took was a $560,000 ARM which started at 10%. Interest rate increases were limited to 2% per three-year period with a cap of 14.75%. The seller took back another $60,000.

The reason the **banks** liked the rooming house was the same reason I like them: **cash flow**. Banks finance all sorts of odd ball **businesses**. So they're used to looking past the unusual to the underlying cash flow. In rooming houses, the underlying cash flow is great.

Rooming houses pencil out. They also generate passive income which can absorb otherwise wasted suspended losses.
JTR

73
Followup:
Rooming Houses

December 1988

Rooming Houses: Oakland, CA investor Frederick Morse, who was mentioned in my October article (See Chapter 72) as converting a three-bedroom house to an eight-room rooming house is the target of complaints by neighbors who claim he's violating planning rules. Supporters of the conversions labelled the complaining neighbors "single-family fascists" (they talk like that in Oakland and Berkeley). Oakland City Council ordered an investigation.JTR

PART EIGHT

LEASE-OPTIONS

74

Lease-Options:
What You Need to Know—
Part I

December 1987

Creative finance gurus say the lease-option is one solution to the problem of negative cash flow in rental houses. By leasing the property combined with an option, the story goes, tenants behave like **owners**. That manifests itself in two beneficial ways:

- The tenant takes care of the property like an **owner** would
- The tenant pays **more** per month, thereby eliminating negative cash flow.

The excess over straight rental value which the tenant pays is either consideration for the option or consideration for the purchase of the property or both.

Option itself has value

Let's say you sign a come-heck-or-high-water agreement to **buy** my property for $1,000,000 two years from now. If the property is worth $1,200,000 then, I lose out on $200,000 of gain I could have had if I had **not** sold the property. On the other hand, if the property is only worth $800,000 in two years, I am

$200,000 better off because you **have** to buy the property from me for $1,000,000...come heck or high water, remember. That's not an option. That's a **purchase agreement**. Purchase agreements are, in theory at least, **two-way** streets.

Options, on the other hand, are **one-way** streets. Let's say that instead of agreeing to a purchase agreement, I give you an **option** to buy the property for $1,000,000 two years from now. An option is the **right**, but not the obligation to buy the property during a limited period of time. If the property is worth $1,200,000 at the end of the two years, I again lose out on the $200,000.

But if the property is worth anything **less** than $1,000,000, the option will **not** be exercised and I'll lose out on the $200,000 I would have been ahead if I had **sold** you the property rather than just an option to buy the property.

With a purchase agreement, I can lose out or I can win. But with an option, I can only lose out.

If I give up the right to all of the profit above $1,000,000, I ought to get something for it. In the case of the **purchase agreement**, what I get is a sort of guarantee from you that my property value will not decline **below** $1,000,000. In the case of the option, I get no such guarantee. So I'd better get something else…like cash. That's why straight options (without leases) cost money.

When people get tangled up with lease-options, they often lose sight of the fact that compensation is due for the possible greater profits the seller gives up.

Credit toward purchase

Lessor/optionors generally give the lessee/optionee credit toward the option price for all or part of the rent. Don't give **too much** credit.

If you lease a property, you are entitled to **fair market rent**. The fact that there is an option involved is irrelevant.

Let's say that in your case, the fair market rental value of the house is $800 a month. Should you charge $1,100 for the lease-option payment and credit it **all** toward the purchase price? Absolutely not. If you did…and the option purchase price were fair market value of the property as of the expiration of the option…you'd have let the tenant live in the building **rent-free**! In this example, the credit cannot exceed $1,100 - $800 = $300.

Furthermore, even $300 is too much if you have not received adequate payment for the **option** …as opposed to the **property**… elsewhere in the deal.

The property price

The house is now worth $100,000. You and the lessee/optionee agree to an option price of $117,000 expiring in two years.

If you collect $1,100 a month for 24

months, you've gotten $800 x 24 = $19,200 in rent. That leaves $1,100 x 24 = $26,400 - $19,200 = $7,200 to cover part of the $117,000 purchase price and the value of the option itself. If you give **full** credit for the $300 a month excess rent toward the purchase price, you will get a lump payment of $117,000 - $7,200 = $109,800 in two years if the option were exercised.

Pricing the option

Reed: "What do you think the probability is that the property will be worth $125,000 instead of $117,000 in two years?"
Seller: "About 20%."
Reed: "How about $130,000?"
Seller: "Maybe 10%."
Reed: "$135,000?"
Seller: "5%."
Reed: "$140,000?"
Seller: "In two years? Zero probability."

That dialogue can be quantified using a decision tree. For more information on decision trees, see Chapter 3 of my book, *Aggressive Tax Avoidance for Real Estate Investors* (800-635-5425). For now I'll just say that the value of giving up the right to those higher gains is the weighted average of their probabilities. The table below shows how.

The seller should get:

• $3,800 just for granting a $117,000, 2-year option, plus
• $800/month fair market rent, plus
• $300 a month or $300 x 24 months = $7,200 credit toward the purchase price, plus

Property value	option price	Lost gain x	Probability =	Weighted amount
How to price an option…				
$117,000 or less	$117,000	$0 x	65% =	$0
$125,000	$117,000	$8,000 x	20% =	$1,600
$130,000	$117,000	$13,000 x	10% =	$1,300
$135,000	$117,000	$18,000 x	5% =	$900
		Total	100%	**$3,800**

- $117,000 minus $7,200 = $109,800 at exercise of the option, plus
- The amount of any money to be received in the **second** year needs to be increased a bit so that after it's discounted to its present value it gives you the above numbers.

This calculation is only as good as the probabilities you put in. But it makes the point that the option itself has value. Do **not** leave that $3,800 on the table.

When are option payments taxable?

The optionor doesn't have to pay tax on the option money he receives until the deal's over, right? Not so fast.

It **used** to be that option money received by the seller was not taxed until the option was either exercised or expired (*Dill Co.*, 33 TC 196). But that **only** applied **if**

- the option money was to be **applied** to the purchase price **and**
- the gain in question **could** be long-term.

But if the seller can **only** have ordinary income regardless of whether the option is exercised or expires, the payment for the option is taxed **in the year received** (*Commissioner v. Pickard*, 401 F 2d 615).

They eliminated the long-term capital gains exclusion in the Tax Reform Act of 1986. So the *Pickard* rule now applies to **all** option payments.

Actually, there is **still** a sort of long-term capital gains exclusion in 1987 only...a 28% limit on the rate at which long-term gains are taxed even if you are in the 38.5% bracket. But starting **next** year, the seller can only have ordinary income from an option no matter what happens to the option. Therefore the Pickard rule says all option payments are taxable in the year **received** starting January 1st, 1988. That's a startling change...and one that I have not seen a single word written about thus far. Continued next month.JTR

75

Lease-Options:
What You Need to Know
Part II

January 1988

A lease-option looks a lot like a mortgage. If it looks **too** much like a mortgage, it may **be** a mortgage...an **equitable** mortgage. This comes from the legal doctrines of:

- Substance over form, and
- Equity.

Substance over form says that the courts can ignore what you **call** a transaction and decide a case based on what it really is instead (*Golden States Lanes v. Fox*, 42 Cal Rptr 568 usury case).

Equity is the legal word for fairness. Sellers prefer lease-options to mortgages because if the lessee gets behind in his rent they can quickly **evict** him. Foreclosing on a mortgage they've taken back is much more cumbersome.

The borrower typically has some equity in the property. The courts hate to see someone lose a significant amount of his net worth just because of a couple late payments. It's as if there were an enormous penalty for lateness.

Stops your eviction

So a lessee/optionee may be able to stop you from evicting him for some breach of the lease if he can convince the court that he really has an equitable mortgage... and I **don't** mean trust deed. Then, you'd have to **foreclose**, not evict him. And all the (judicial) rules of foreclosure would apply. Most notably, you could not keep any excess equity above what the court said was the amount of your equitable mortgage...typically the equity you had the day you began the lease-option. I kid you not.

The vast majority of lessees probably know nothing about equitable mortgages. But their **attorneys** know. And the more equity they have to protect if and when you try to evict them, the more likely they'll ask an attorney if there is "some way" to stop you.

How IRS can use the equitable mortgage doctrine against you

This equitable mortgage doctrine could be used against you not only in state court to stop eviction. It could also be used against you by the **IRS**. The IRS's line would be that the lease-option was really an **installment sale**. That would make most of the payments you receive **interest**.

Furthermore, if you are deemed to have **sold** the property when you lease-optioned it, you no longer have the right to claim **depreciation** deductions... currently or carried forward.

Interest is **portfolio** income, **not** passive income. So you can't deduct rental property expenses from it. Furthermore, capital gains tax would typically be due on the lease-option which IRS is recharacterizing as an installment sale. (*W.D. Swigart,* 40 TCM 1215 and CCH SFTR ¶1382.548)

Are lessor/optionors active participants?

If your adjusted gross income (not counting real estate) is less than $150,000, you want to be considered an **"active participant"** under the Tax Reform Act of '86. So that you can deduct up to $25,000 in rental property losses from your non-rental property income. According to Senate Finance Committee Report 99-313, to be "active participant" you must,

"participate, e.g. in the making of management decisions or arranging for others to provide services (such as repairs), in a significant and bona fide sense. Management decisions that are relevant in this context include approving new tenants, deciding on rental terms, approving capital or repair expenditures, and other similar decisions."

But wait a minute. Isn't one of the great virtues of the lease-option that it makes the tenant think he's an **owner**? He takes care of the place and doesn't bother you, right?

Will the **real** active participant please stand up. If you want to do lease-options as the seller...and preserve your tax deductions...you'd better write a real buttinski of a lease. That is, require the lessee to come to you for practically everything. There goes the lessor/optionor's reputed Life of Riley. No management, no deductions.

But as experienced lessor/optionor, Dan Kinter (916-965-6716) points out, with the lease-option, you get so much cash flow you don't **have** rental property losses any more. Kinter is a dealer so he claims no depreciation.

Case study

Kinter says he gets houses below market value by buying them from rental house investors who lost interest in them when the Tax Reform Act of '86 took away their tax deductions. In a typical deal, Kinter says he buys a house worth $67,000 for $61,000. He then lease-options it for $850 a month. That's $300 a month over the straight rental value.

He gives the lessee $100 a month credit toward the purchase price of $77,000. The option can only be exercised at the three-year point...not before. This system enables Kinter to buy far more houses than he could if he did it the regular way and had negative cash flow on each.

What's in it for the lessee/optionee?

We know why the lessor/optionor wants the lease-option. He thinks it will minimize his management hassles and turn negative cash flow into positive cash flow.

But what about the lessee/optionee? Why should he want to take care of some landlord's building and pay $300 extra a month plus pay $3,800 for an option...all so he can he buy a house for $117,000...at a time when it will probably be worth $117,000? (These figures are from an example in Part I of this article in last month's issue.) Logically, no tenant would enter into this lease-option if he agreed with the lessor's probability analysis and could finance the deal through a bank.

But as I've often acknowledged, logic does not always reign in real estate. The lessee/optionee generally does **not** have the money for the down payment. For him, the lease-option represents the nothing-down deal he needs to become a home owner but cannot get from institutional lenders. And/or maybe he cannot save money and needs you to **force** him to save $300 a month (rent credit) toward a down payment via the lease-option.

Finally, even if he has the down payment or self-discipline to save it, he may disagree with your probability analysis. He may feel the probability of the property being worth $130,000 in two years is 35%, not the 10% that you estimated. If he's right, the $3,800 you want for the option is too cheap and he should take it.

Lessee/optionee's taxes

Taxwise, the lease-option stinks from the buyer's perspective. Lease payments on your residence are **not** deductible. Property taxes and interest on a home mortgage **are** deductible if the taxpayer itemizes...as most homeowners with large mortgages do. Option payments which are credited toward the price simply become part of the optionee's basis in the property.

Lease-options are dangerous **titlewise** from the buyer's perspective. For example, what if the property appreciates rapidly to a point well above the option price before the expiration date...and the seller refinances it so that the new loan eats up part of the lessee/optionee's equity? Or the seller refuses to deed the property upon payment of the final option payment?

There ought to be clauses to prohibit that. But people don't always abide by clauses. And if the seller allowed any kind of lien to be placed against the lessee's equity, the lessee would have a problem ...the kind of problem he would **not** have had if he had done a straight purchase with title insurance instead of a lease-option.

Real estate newspaper columnist, Bob Bruss says the buyer should at least record a memorandum of option. "Beware of any seller who would not allow such a recording," he says. Kinter says he allows it...but only one ever asked...and then he didn't even record it after all.

According to the Jan.-Feb., 1985 *Lawyers Title News*, you cannot record an option in many states. Therefore, you cannot get title insurance on lease-options in those states.

Not usually a way around due-on-sale clauses

One of the myths of the real estate business is that you can use lease-options to get around due-on-sale clauses. In fact, the phrase "due-on-sale" is a misnomer. The most common due-on-sale clause is the Federal National Mortgage Association clause. It says the mortgage must be paid off in full not only if you **sell** the property...but also if you **lease** the property for three years or more...or if you lease-**option** it for **any** term.

The only time you can use a lease-option to get around a due-on-sale clause is when the due-on-sale clause is poorly drawn. And even then, the doctrine of substance over form might be used to say that the lease-option is really a sale and therefore the due-on-sale clause has been triggered.

As a practical matter, the lease-option might succeed in getting around a due-on-sale clause as a result of the lender not learning of the transfer the way they would be in a purchase. But the loan would be in default...and if the lender found out...look out.

More talked about than done

Bruss says there's a lot more **talk** about lease-options than there are lease-options. Bob himself, who is one of the leading advocates of lease-options, says he only did **one** in 1987. According to the National Association of Realtors®, 8% of the house sales in January '82 were lease-options. That's probably as high as it gets. In '82, fixed conventional mortgage interest rates on existing single-family homes averaged 15.82%, thereby inspiring sellers to try all sorts of "creative finance."

Extreme high leverage

Bruss likes to use the lease-option as a **buyer**. He notes that it enables you to control a property for little or no money.

Whereupon you can renovate, hold, resell, etc. His best lease-option cost him a year's rent in advance and he got a 15-year, fixed-price option for one dollar. The option price was $125,000 which was also the market value of the property at the time. The property's now worth about $200,000 four years later. Bruss understandably is in no hurry to exercise the option.

Of course, the key to that deal was that the seller foolishly failed to build expected future appreciation into the option price. To the extent that there are other such fools about, you can make similar profits. But for ethics' sake, you should only part **sophisticated** sellers from their money.

For more information: See my book, *How to Use Leverage to Maximize Your Real Estate Investment Return* and Bob Bruss' *Real Estate Newsletter* #87154, "How to Make Real Estate Profits With Leases and Options." (800-322-3068, 305-422-8181 in FL) JTR

76
Lease-Option Defaults, Walk Aways, etc.

May 1989

The incremental 'cash flow' lease-option guys brag about is nothing but an advance sale of the property in monthly pieces. It's borrowing from the future to make the present look better." :John T. Reed

"Theoretically, you're right. But, in fact, 95% of the tenants don't exercise the option even when they have significant equity (difference between option price and market value)." :A student at one of my seminars

Most do walk away

That statement intrigued me so I called several guys I know who are lease-option users. I found that the incidence of lease-option tenants walking away from equity is not 95%...but it's generally quite high. And it varies according to the terms of the deal and the amount of equity. In any event, tenant defaults and walk aways are probably the **main** yield enhancer produced by lease option of rental houses...but a benefit which I've never seen discussed.

Richard Gardiner (916-797-0444), who has done about 250 lease options over nine years, says that in his experience about 15% exercise their option to purchase when market interest rates are high and about 50% when interest rates are low.

Gardiner's percentages may be different because of the structure of his lease-options. His lessee-optionees can buy the property within three years for its **appraised** value at the time of exercise less 25% of the amount of appreciation since the lease option began. (They also get rent credit toward purchase price in the $100 to $150 per month range.) My student with the 95% no-exercise rate may have structured his lease options so that the tenant had less equity at the end of the option period.

Given the lower rate of walk aways that Gardiner has I wonder if he might not be better off with an 80%/20% split (lessee gets 20% of the appreciation). Gardiner rejects the 80/20 split as being over the "hog line." I presume there is some optimum sharing percentage which maximizes both

- The attractiveness of the deal to the tenant and
- Probability that the tenant will walk away from an option that has equity.

Lease options are, indeed, attractive to would-be home owners. One Chicago reader told me he advertised a condo for sale and got no calls. Then he advertised that same condo for lease option and got fifty calls.

John Schaub, who has been doing lease options for about five years, says about 70% of his lease-option tenants have failed to exercise their options. (You can get his booklet, "Lease Options: How to Buy and Sell Real Estate for Maximum Profits" 26 pages $15, 1938 Ringling Blvd., Sarasota, FL 33577, 800-237-9222).

Atlanta investor Bill Manley says 90 to 95% of his lease-option tenants walk away. He says the more equity they have, the greater the probability they'll exercise. And he says they are more likely to walk away of three-year options than one-year...because there's more time for unexpected stuff like divorces to happen. Also, the three-year optionees are more likely to exhibit the Ever-Receding-Bonanza syndrome: "We can't qualify for the mortgage now but surely our fortunes will have improved three years from now." Manley says he uses lease options for the better quality tenant it gets him; not additional income.

Why they walk away

Gardiner says tenants don't exercise valuable options because of inability to qualify for the mortgage which, in turn, is caused by:

• Job loss
• Bad credit
• Inadequate income
• Divorce or separation
• Job transfer.

A typical Gardiner lease option has the tenant renting a house with a fair market rental value of $695 per month on this schedule:

year 1: $795 with $100 per month credit toward purchase
year 2: $895 with $125 credit
year 3: $995 with $150 credit.

The worst case is no appreciation or negative appreciation in which case Gardiner is ahead as long as the tenant stays because the tenant is paying **more than market** rent. However, the tenant is likely to bail out as soon as he or she concludes that there will be no appreciation.

Sharing appreciation

If the property appreciates, and the tenant exercises the option, Gardiner has given up 25% of the appreciation plus the sum of the monthly credit amounts. That leaves him slightly worse off than if he had just leased the house for market rent to a regular tenant who had no option to purchase. Because he has to give back all or most (depending on how soon the option is exercised) of the extra "rent" he collected and he has to give up 25% of the appreciation.

Gardiner will give the tenant a one-year wraparound or straight second when they exercise if they have generally paid on time. Most of his tenants who paid on time prefer a new institutional mortgage to Gardiner's one-year loan.

Walk away

The best case...and usual case thus far...is that the property appreciates...but the tenant does **not** exercise the option. Then Gardiner gets to keep the extra "rent" as well as all the appreciation.

How much equity do the tenants walk away from? Gardiner cites a recent example where a woman walked away from $15,000 to $20,000. He notes that the tenants who can't or won't exercise the option themselves could profit by selling their option to someone who **can** exercise it. Gardiner has brokered the sale of about ten of them for his tenants.

Bob Bruss, the nationally syndicated real estate columnist, has done about 12 lease options. All but one of his tenants exercised their option. That person was transferred out of Bruss's area. The transferred tenant tried to **sell** the option...even listing the property with a real estate company. But he overpriced it and didn't find a buyer by the expiration date.

Bruss's low incidence of walk aways may be due to his more generous terms. In a typical deal, he gets $5,000 up front on a one-year, fixed-price lease-option to buy a $315,000 (that's a top of the market price) house. $1,500 of the $5,000 is the first month's rent and $3,500 is option consideration which is applied to the purchase price if the option is exercised. Bruss advertises, "$5,000 moves you in" under both the "houses for rent" and "houses for sale" newspaper classified categories.

The market rent on the house would be $1,200. Bruss gets $1,500 a month on the lease option but he gives $500 per month credit toward the purchase.

Offering long-term seller financing

Sacramento investor, Dan Kinter (916-965-6716) gives his tenants long-term wraparound seller financing when they exercise so he has had **no** walk aways. But he **has** had about a third of his tenants **default** on the monthly payments... usually in the first year of the lease option. Since his properties have always appreciated, he has welcomed the defaults because they enabled him to re-lease-option the property at a higher rent and sale price.

Seeking them out

Because of the desirability of default and/or failure to exercise the option, investors might well seek out lease-option tenants who are likely to default or not exercise. If there's no front-end option consideration, you would **not** want an immediate default. The transaction costs of finding the tenant and readying the house would exceed the profit if the tenant defaulted within a month or two. But in a case like Bob Bruss's, where you get $3,500 option consideration up front, an immediate default would even be welcome.

Ethics

I believe it's wrong to use a sophisticated financial instrument to bamboozle unsophisticated people. The lessor-optionors I spoke to in writing this article seemed to have no such intention. But that may be the effect, however unintentional.

I have this same beef when it comes to those who advocate high leverage seller financing.

Persuading a seller to take back a mortgage is the equivalent of persuading them to mortgage their property and invest the proceeds in a junk bond. Actually, it's **worse** because the vast majority of high-leverage seller mortgages are **inferior** to junk bonds when it comes to liquidity and risk.

By the same token, persuading a young couple eager to own their own home to agree to a lease option is the equivalent of asking them to invest their meager savings in an over-the-counter Wall Street option. (About 85% of all lawsuits filed against securities firms involve options and 75% of those involve "suitability.") Actually... as with seller mortgages and junk bonds...it's much **worse**. Same reasons: lack of liquidity and greater risk. The greater risk stems from the difficulty of arranging financing to buy the real estate.

Reputable Wall Street firms have "suitability" criteria which say roughly, don't sell junk bonds or options to widows or orphans. Reputable real estate investors ought to follow a similar rule.

Lease options **seem** totally understandable to an unsophisticated young couple. But as the experience of my interviewees indicates, young couples usually **understimate** the risk that they will be unable to exercise the option before expiration and thereby forfeit the extra money they paid.

In addition to the ethical issue of "suitability," there is also the legal docrtine of equitable mortgage. In short, that says that a lease option is really a **sale** to the lessee/optionee and that you must **foreclose**, not evict them. For more on "suitability" and equitable mortgage doctrine, see "Lease-Options: What You Need to Know, Part II" in the January 1988 issue (See Chapter 75) and my book, *How to Use Leverage...*

Mortgage default

Most mortgages say a lease-option triggers the **due-on-sale** clause. So if your property has such a mortgage, it is in default as soon as you lease option it.

Lease-option investors invariably poo poo the possibility of foreclosure on the grounds that the lenders never check. But your state law on fraud and such probably requires you to **disclose** the default to the lessee/optionee and to specify the rights and responsibilities of each party in the event the lender forecloses.

The lease option has "magical powers" to transform rental house negative cash flow into positive cash flow. But as with any exotic financial arrangement, it comes with complexites which far exceed the usual seminar description of such "creative" techniques. JTR

PART NINE

MATHEMATICAL ANALYSIS OF REAL ESTATE

77
Cost Accounting in Real Estate

January 1990

Manufacturing companies often hire cost accountants. In the typical case, the company is profitable, but it doesn't know how much profit each of its products produces. The cost accounting study usually shows that some of the products are actually **losers**, some average, and some producing far more of the company's profit than previously realized.

Real estate investors would benefit from a similar analysis.

Separate service lines

Real estate investors see themselves as having only one "product," the service of providing rental space. In fact, real estate investors have five service lines. They are:

- Acquisition
- Property management
- Owner operations
- Income tax return filing
- Disposition.

Cost accountants think of each service line as if it were a **separate** business.

So that's what we'll do here. Let's say a $500,000 rental property is being acquired, managed, and disposed of.

- Mr. Brown negotiates a five-year option to acquire the property for $500,000.
- Mr. Black net leases the entire property on a master lease for the amount of the mortgage payment then hires a property management firm to manage the property and sublease it to individual tenants.
- Mr. White owns the property management firm that agrees to manage the property for 5% of the gross income.
- Mr. Green acquires title to the property and leases it to Mr. Black on the master lease. His ownership entitles Mr. Green to claim the rent from Mr. Black as income and to deduct the mortgage interest and depreciation as expenses.
- Near the end of the five year period, Mr. Brown lists the property (actually his option) for sale with Mr. Blue, a real estate broker, and agrees to pay a 4% commission.

After five years

Let's say the property appreciates to a value of $650,000. (Holding a property for five years is generally a speculation on market-wide appreciation rates which I do not recommend. But it's also the most common approach to real estate investing. That's why I'm using this example.) The mortgage amount is $400,000 and the monthly payment is $3,659 (10.5% fixed, 30 years, self-amortizing). The gross income starts at $55,000 a year, the expenses at $30,000, and each increases 5% per year. The improvement ratio is 85% and it's residential property. (I'll ignore personal property and land improvements to keep it simple.) Mr. Green's non-real estate adjusted gross income is $90,000. The acquisition month is January.

Here's how each party does:

Brown makes a $150,000 gross profit less the 4% x $650,000 = $26,000 commission for a net profit of $150,000 - $26,000 = $124,000.

White gets 5% of the gross income which is:

year	1	2	3	4	5	Total
gross	$55,000	$57,750	$60,638	$63,669	$66,853	$319,200
mgmt. fee	$2,750	$2,888	$3,032	$3,183	$3,343	**$15,960**

Black gets the operating owner's net loss which is:

year	1	2	3	4	5	
N.O.I.	$25,000	$26,250	$27,563	$28,941	$30,388	
mgmt. fee	$2,750	$2,888	$3,032	$3,183	$3,343	
rent	$43,908	$43,908	$43,908	$43,908	$43,908	
loss	(21,658)	(20,546)	(19,377)	(18,150)	(16,863)	(96,594)

Green gets the amortization and the tax savings (assume 33% bracket) from the depreciation deductions:

year	1	2	3	4	5	
deprec.	$15,470	$15,470	$15,470	$15,470	$15,470	
savings	$5,105	$5,105	$5,105	$5,105	$5,105	
amort.	$2,002	$2,222	$2,468	$2,739	$3,042	
total	$7,105	$7,227	$7,573	$7,844	$8,147	$37,896

Blue gets the 4% commission of $26,000.

In sum, here is each guy's profit:

Brown, the optionee:	$124,000
White, the manager:	$15,960
Black, the sandwich lessee:	($96,594)
Green, the owner:	$37,896
Blue, the sales agent:	$26,000

Overall it was a good investment

If one person did all this stuff himself including selling without a real estate agent, his net profit would be:

Option:	$124,000
Management fee:	$15,960
Sandwich lease:	($96,594)
Amortization and tax savings:	$37,896
Resale commission:	$26,000
Net profit:	$107,262

I'm mixing apples and oranges to an extent here by not taking into account the tax savings from the negative cash flow and the tax payable on the gain. But you get the idea. Would this person be pleased? You bet.

Shoveling fries

Should he be pleased? Well, his appreciation speculation (the option) turned out very nicely ($124,000 profit).

He got $15,960 for managing the property...but he earned it. He probably would have made as much money, without the lawsuit risk, shoveling french fries at McDonalds for the same number of hours.

His sandwich lease was a **disaster** losing $96,594 over five years.

He got $12,473 of amortization. That's nice but if he had personal liability on the mortgage, it wasn't worth the risk.

He got $25,423 worth of tax savings from depreciation. That's also nice but he'll have to give it back if he sells the property rather than exchanging.

For sale by owner

Finally, he got $26,000 in commission savings by selling the property himself. As with the property management, he probably **earned** it. Although agents are paid much more per hour than property managers for the work involved in selling the property *per se*. That's aside from the number of hours they spend trying to get listings and the hours they spend holding sellers' hands. Our for-sale-by-owner obviously does not have to do either of those time wasters. On the other hand, agents, with their offices and contacts may have been able to sell the property for a higher price.

In all, the option speculation produced a spectacular profit, the sandwich lease a spectacular loss, and the rest was average, white-collar compensation for hours worked.

"Cash machines"

One of the real estate seminar phenomena which amuses me is audiences which are enthralled with the "cash machine" sort of technique. In those techniques, you either do sandwich leases, or lease-options, or buy properties, then sell them and take back wraparound mortgages with payments slightly larger than the payments you have to make on the underlying first mortgages.

In the typical scenario, you get a hundred bucks a month from each property and you are supposed to "get rich" by buying lots of properties. If the people who take those seminars think about it, cash machines require working a great many hours to arrange and oversee deals, investing capital, taking considerable risk, and probably only making about $5 an hour when all is said and done.

My point in this article is that many investors who are smart enough to see the low pay per hour inherent in the "cash machine" techniques overlook the same problem when it's presented to them as a **package deal** in the form of a traditional buy-manage-and-sell-or-exchange investment.

What to do

Given the example in this article, the ideal thing would be to just go around buying five-year fixed price options. Unfortunately, most sellers are unwilling to do that. (Although, as with any other real estate investment technique, I suspect there are ways to do it. For example, I've heard that property owners often do let their guard down and give very favorable options as part of a lease or to persons who buy one of two or more adjacent properties from them. But that's for a future article.)

Hire someone?

Most people would react to this cost accounting by saying, "Fine, we'll hire out the grunt work and just spend our time on the important, high-paying stuff."

Would that it were so easy.

A good property manager is extremely hard to find. Virtually impossible for most people. I recommend that you **never** hire a fee-paid independent property manager, especially real estate agents who normally sell houses. If you have to manage, either do it yourself or hire an employee to do it.

Less holding, more dealing

Simply shortening the holding period to zero or a few months and specializing in bargain purchases or fair-market-value purchases of properties with unrealized potential are two ways to get rid of or minimize the time you spend on unprofitable or inadequately profitable service lines.

You would sell the bargain purchases immediately and the upgraded properties as soon as they were ready. (See "The Wisdom of Making Less Money Per Deal" in the 1/89 issue, Chapter 32, and "Ranger Real Estate Investing" in the 2/89 issue, Chapter 33.)

Fundamentally, the point is most real estate investors spend too much time on losing or nickle-and-dime activities. That, in turn, prevents them from acquiring more bargain-purchase and/or upgrading skills...and from profiting from the use of those skills is more deals. Bargain purchases and upgrading are where the **deliberate** profits are in this business. Even the speculators (most investors) who seek **accidental** profits from market-wide appreciation would be better off buying options rather than fee simple ownership with all its management duties and ever increasing liability and political risks. JTR

78
Why You Should Use Cap Rates to Analyze Small Properties

October 1987

Income property investors generally use capitalization or cap rates (net operating income divided by sale price) to analyze properties they buy. But rare is the house or duplex buyer who uses cap rates. And since the people you'll be **selling** the small property to do not use cap rates don't use cap rates, why should you?

To get a **higher cash flow** return and thereby raise your overall return on the investment.

Forget appreciation

For the rest of this item, I'll assume that appreciation rates are the same on all the similar properties in your market... which is probably correct.

Property taxes

When I was a real estate salesman in Southern New Jersey, I noticed that some communities had **higher tax rates** per dollar of property value than others. Dramatically higher in some cases. Unless the **rents** in the high tax communties were proportionately higher than the low

tax comunities, the **cap rates** on the low tax properties were higher. In fact, there was **no** correlation between the rents and the property taxes. (Taxes are roughly uniform in California because of Prop 13).

Heat

My first duplex had oil hot **water** heat. Three years later, I bought my second property, a triplex with oil hot **air** heat. The landlord paid for fuel in both cases because of central systems.

The hot water-heated duplex used an average of $400 worth of oil a year. So when the seller of the hot **air**-heated triplex told me the annual heat bill was $220, I puffed up my then 26-year old chest and informed him that I was an **experienced** apartment owner and knew that it cost $400 a year, not $200, to heat a **duplex**. And a **triplex** would certainly cost at least that much.

The owner assured me that $220 was the correct figure. I called the oil supply company and they confirmed it. Then I bought the triplex. And darned if it didn't use $220 a year worth of oil.

Why leave $800 a year on the table?

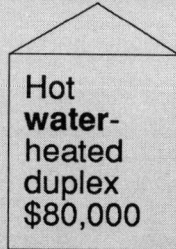

Hot water-heated duplex $80,000

Hot **air-**heated duplex $80,000

Tax Benefits: Same

Appreciation: Same

Amortization: Same

Rent	$9,600
Heat	$1,600
Other Exp.	$2,400
Net Op. Inc.	$5,600

Rent	$9,600
Heat	$800
Other Exp.	$2,400
Net Op. Inc.	$6,400

If 20% down, debt service is 80% x $80,000 = $64,000 @ 10% for 30 years = $6,740 annual debt service

Cap Rate = $5,600 ÷ $80,000 = 7%

Cap Rate = $6,400 ÷ $80,000 = 8%

Before-tax cash Flow:

Hot water: $5,600 - $6,740 = -$1,140

Hot air: $6,400 - $6,740 = -$340

It turns out, hot air heat is much less expensive fuelwise than hot water. And a heck of a lot cheaper on **repairs**, too. Having a hot water or steam heating system is like having a **second** plumbing system. So your plumbing bills about double, too.

In **today's** prices, the hot air building uses about $800 less fuel a year than the hot water building. If you put $16,000 down on an $80,000 duplex, that $800 represents $800 ÷ $16,000 = 5% additional return on your investment.

Other items

Buildings with fireproof **roofs** have lower insurance premiums. **Utilities** rates are higher in some communities. And some properties need much more water than others because of pools or large landscaped areas. Although tenants usually pay their own gas and electric in one- and two-family buildings, in some cases the landlord pays. In those buildings, abnormally high **usage** by the building or abnormally high local **rates** reduce the property's cap rate.

Overlooked advantages

Many small properties have significant investment advantages which are overlooked by both the sellers and the other buyers. But don't **you** overlook them. JTR

79
Eleven Percent Cap Rates Really are Obtainable

July 1988

You can't shake the feeling that you are overpaying for property. What are other investors paying? What cap rates (net operating income divided by purchase price) are they getting?

Thus far, I can't answer the question **nationwide**. But there is one area where we can get a reasonably accurate answer: Seattle.

Seattle

The reason is that Cain And Scott, Inc. (206-285-7100) does an exhaustive annual survey of the Seattle market and publishes the results. Cap rates in the survey are based on interviews with either the buyer or the seller or on data collected by Cain and Scott, Inc. itself if they represented either party. They claim to have interviewed at least one principal in 95% of the apartment sales done in the Seattle...including the deals in which Cain and Scott played no part.

In "Real Estate Investing..." in the May issue (See Chapter 25), I said you had to look at between 50 and 200 properties to find a deal that made economic sense. It occurred to me call Mike Scott of Cain and Scott and ask if he could tell me the cap rates on the last 200 apartment building deals done there. I hoped it would show that the vast majority of those 200 deals had mediocre or low cap rates...but that a handful were up in the 11% to 12% range.

Mike surprised me at first by saying he could do that but that, "To get you two hundred deals I'll have to give you the last **two years**. Only about a hundred apartment buildings of 20 or more units change hands in the Seattle each year." That's **total** deals done in the **market**...with or without a real estate agent...and not just Cain and Scott deals.

That fuels my belief that you should be willing to invest absentee. If you are selective enough to only buy the best deal you see in two hundred you look at...like a couple investors I quoted in May...restricting yourself to one metropolitan area means it'll be a **long time** between deals. A Seattle investor who refused to invest absentee might have to do three or four years of hot and heavy looking in his market to find one double-digit cap rate deal in his price range. (The twenty units or more range covers about five layers of investors. For example, one layer would consist of those who have a hundred unit minimum. Few, if any, investors consider properties across all five layers.)

Bell-shaped curve

On page 67 of the October '87 issue, I used a bell-shaped curve or normal distribution as it's known in statistics to illustrate the point that the vast majority of deals are unacceptable to a competent

9.1 cap rate

Investors who bought an average deal got about a 9.1 cap rate. That means if the building had net operating income (NOI) of $100,000 a year, the sale price was $100,000 ÷ 9.1% = $1,098,901. But a few investors...11 guys out of 190...were able to buy on terms that gave them cap rates around **11%**.

At 11%, you buy that building with its $100,000 NOI for $100,000 ÷ 11% = $909,091. I'll round the two prices to $1,100,000 and $910,000. With a 75%-

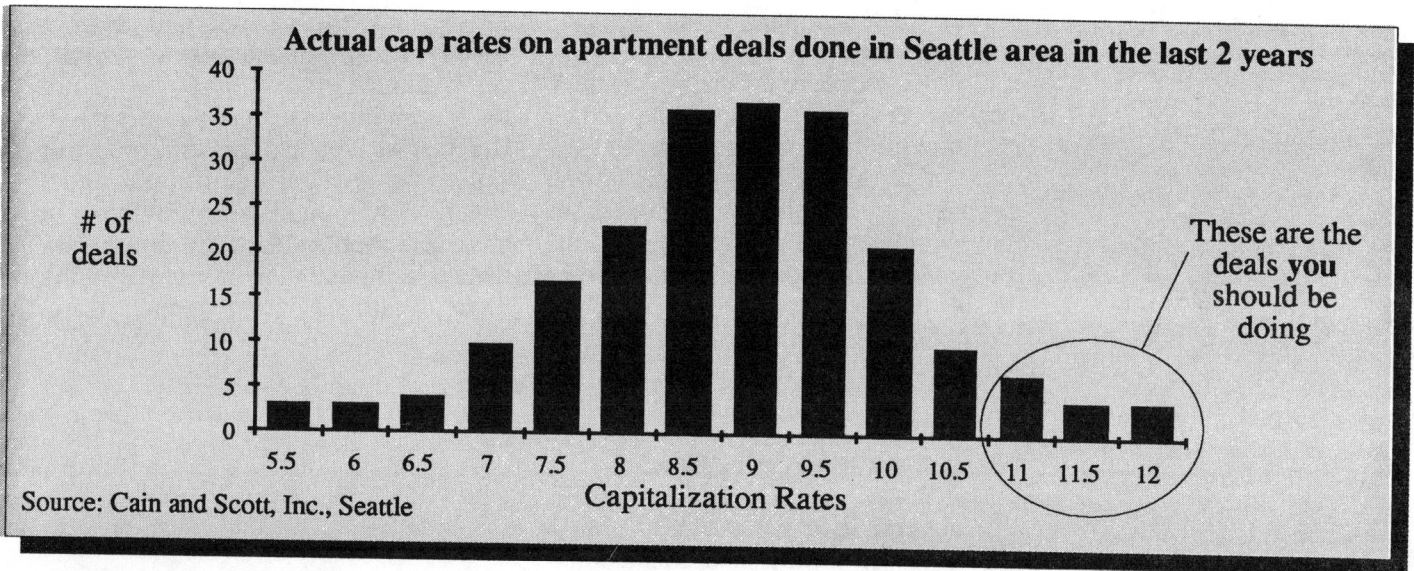

Actual cap rates on apartment deals done in Seattle area in the last 2 years

# of deals (vertical axis). Capitalization Rates (horizontal axis). These are the deals **you** should be doing

Source: Cain and Scott, Inc., Seattle

real estate investor. He needs to do deals in the top .5% to 2% or so to achieve the double-digit cap rates that make sense. There are a lot of average deals, a few decent deals or lousy deals, and a **very** few few good deals or terrible deals. Those very few **good** deals...the few, the proud, the double-digit cap rate deals ...the only ones you should be doing...are way out at one end of the bell-shaped curve.

That's **theory**. Scott's statistics are **reality**...as best we can ascertain it. Does reality confirm this particular theory?

Yes.

Above is a graph of the last two years of Seattle apartment deals. The horizontal axis shows the cap rate range of the apartment deals done in the Seattle area. The vertical axis shows the number of deals in each particular cap rate group.

of-value, 11% interest, 30-year mortgage in each case, your monthly payments would be $7,856.67 and $6,499.61 respectively. **Annual** debt service (d/s) would be 12 x $7,856.67 = $94,280.04 and 12 x $6,499.61 = $77,995.29 respectively. Here's your before-tax cash flow (btcf) and cash return on investment (ROI) in each situation:

	9.1% cap	11.0% cap
NOI	$100,000	$100,000
d/s	$94,280	$77,995
btcf	$5,720	$22,005
down	$275,000	$227,500
ROI	2%	10%

Over a, say, five-year holding period, the guy with the 11% cap rate collects about $17,000 a year extra or 5 x $17,000

= $85,000 more return. Plus, he made another $190,000 ($1,100,000 - $910,000) more than the 9.1% cap rate guy the day he bought the property.

No free lunch

Of course there's no free lunch. The eleven guys who got the 11% cap rate deals probably **hustled** far more than the guys who got the 9.1%. They looked at far more properties, contacted far more prospective sellers **before** the properties were for sale, moved much **faster** when they heard of a property being available, and so forth.

It is reasonable to assume that the 11% cap rate properties were on the market the **shortest periods of time.** Indeed, most, if not all, of those top deals were probably never offered to anyone but the guy who bought them. And he was the man on the spot because he made it his business to be everywhere ...like a star linebacker who seems to be in on every tackle.

Other property types

Cain and Scott's figures are for normal deals on normal apartment buildings. If you looked at the kinds of **abnormal** "leper" properties I've been pushing lately...like those with bad foundations, title problems, one-bedroom houses, etc...you'd find the curve shifted to the right. That is, the median cap rate would be more like 11% than 9.1%. And the top 5% deals would have cap rates in the 15% to 20% range. There's more **risk** dealing with leper properties. But you can make them **calculated risks** by acquiring appropriate expertise.

Other cities

If we could get a cap rate curve for **other** cities, we would no doubt find it was shifted to the right or, more likely, to the left from Seattle's. In California and Northeastern major metropolitan areas, for example, I suspect the **median** cap rate on apartment building deals (20 or more units not under rent control) would be about 8%. And 11% cap rates would be proportionately harder to come by.

Tough, but doable

The **bad** news is that it's tough out there. The **good** news is that you **can** find deals that make investment sense...if you have the necessary specialized expertise and you are willing to make the necessary effort. That expertise is tougher to come by than the average would-be investor thinks. But it **can** be acquired.

And the effort necessary to get your hands on some of the few worthwhile deals is much greater than most would-be or even intermediate investors think. But just as you got into the habit of expending great effort in high school athletics or military basic training or graduate school studies, you **can** get into the habit of making the effort necessary to do investment deals that make sense. JTR

80
Do You Really Need Positive Cash Flow?

August 1987

Since the Tax Reform Act of 1986, I've been saying income property buyers needed positive cash flow. They generally are not finding it. So I thought I'd better reexamine the advice. After all, a real estate investor is a guy who **buys** buildings. Not a guy who **rejects** them all...for whatever reason. I write for the real world.

Breakeven OK when tax savings

Real estate investing needs to return about 150% of what second mortgages return...because it's more risky and involves management. Today, seconds go for about 14%. 150% of 14% is 21%. That's the minimum return you should get from real estate.

Let's assume you can take full advantage of the tax deductions. That is, your adjusted gross income (AGI) is $100,000 or less not counting rental property income or loss. And you have not used up your $25,000 rental property loss limit (You need about $850,000 of newly purchased residential property or about $950,000 of non-residential to use up the $25,000.)

Assume you buy a $100,000 rental house with $20,000 down. The personal property that comes with the house is worth $1,500 leaving real property of $98,500. Assume an 85% improvement ratio and you get 85% x $98,500 = $83,725 of depreciable improvements ($98,500 - $83,725 = $14,775 of undepreciable land). With a 27.5-year recovery period, your annual straight-line depreciation deduction is $83,725 ÷ 27.5 = $3,044.55.

If your AGI is $85,000 not counting rental property...and the rental house breaks even on a before-tax cash flow basis...the $3,044.55 rental property loss will save you 28% (from tax rate tables) x $3,044.55 = $852.47 a year in income taxes. That's a $852.47 ÷ $20,000 = 4% return on your down payment. You need an overall return of 21%. So 21% - 4% = 17% must come from appreciation and amortization.

Amortization during the first year of a 10%, 30-year, $80,000 mortgage is $444.39 or a $444.39 ÷ $20,000 = 2% return. That leaves 17% - 2% = 15% to come from appreciation.

Leverage multiplies appreciation return

Since you are leveraged 80% to 20%, the appreciation rate on the property is multiplied five times when translating it into return on investment. So 15% ÷ 5 = 3% is the appreciation rate you need to get an overall 21% return on a rental house when you get full benefit of the possible tax savings.

Is 3% realistic? I think so.

Do investors who get full benefit of the tax savings need positive cash flow when their property is appreciating 3% per year? No. (Actually, transaction costs are such that the appreciation rate would have to be a bit higher.)

Suppose you don't get any tax benefits?

Now suppose the investor makes $160,000 AGI not counting rental property. And he's buying a $1,000,000 apartment building for $200,000 down. Can he afford to accept breakeven in a 3% appreciation market?

No. He'd fall 4% short of his 21% to 17% if he did. Real estate involves too much hassle and risk to settle for 17%.

However, if the investor assumed the appreciation rate would be 4% per year, breakeven cash flow would be OK. Because 4% x $1,000,000 = $40,000 and $40,000 is a $40,000 ÷ $200,000 = 20% return on the $200,000 investment. Amortization, if any, would add about 2% more.

Is 150% enough?

Some might wonder if getting 150% of the second mortgage return is enough. After all, real estate has gotten much riskier in recent years. What with massive overbuilding, toxic chemicals, increased litigation, and a Congress willing to pass retroactive tax laws.

If you require **200%** of second mortgage rates, you are at 200% x 14% = 28% overall return. That requires a (28% - 2% amortization) ÷ 5 = 5.2% appreciation rate on the breakeven apartment building. And a (28% - 2% amortization - 4% tax savings) ÷ 5 leverage ratio = 4.4% appreciation rate on the breakeven house for the tax savings user.

To accept breakeven is to assume an appreciation rate

When I urge you to insist on positive cash flow in income property, I am implicitly assuming that appreciation rates will be less than 4%. If you think it'll be 4% or higher, buying on terms that get you breakeven cash flow will not keep you from getting an adequate return.

Rather than adopt a positive cash flow standard, run the numbers above using your situation and assumptions about appreciation rates. The main point is to recognize that tax benefits are gone for many investors. So the breakeven and negative cash flow deals that could make sense before the Tax Reform Act of 1986 need to be improved upon.

Negative cash flow

I do not care for negative cash flow. But on a strictly numerical basis, there's nothing wrong with it as long as you have the appreciation rate you need to make up for it. In this example, for every percentage point your cash flow falls, you need 1% ÷ 5 leverage ratio = .2% more of appreciation to compensate for it. For example, a 5% negative cash flow (5% x $20,000 = $1,000 in the rental house case) requires the appreciation rate to be 1% higher to compensate for it.

High income persons must pay less for rental property

During the first half of the '80s, I often said that real estate had become a high bracket investment like municipal bonds. The Tax Reform Act of '86 reversed that. Now, rental properties are most valuable to people with AGIs **below** $100,000 and who have not already used up their $25,000 loss limit.

Upgraders have higher appreciation rates

If you upgrade...that is, raise the value of your property by rent raises, renovation, upzoning, etc., your appreciation rate will be the general appreciation rate **plus** the percentage attributable to your upgrading. Consequently, competent upgraders can afford to buy on terms that yield breakeven or negative cash flow prior to the upgrade.

On the other hand, upgrading is riskier, more time-consuming, and requires a higher skill level. So it may be appropriate for upgraders to demand a higher premium over second mortgage returns to compensate them. Maybe 250% of mortgage rates or 35%.

The competent upgrader suffers opportunity cost if he snubs his nose at a profitably upgradable building because the seller will not sell on terms that yield positive cash flow. JTR

PART TEN

RISK
AND REAL ESTATE INVESTING

81
Calculated Risks:
Part I

February 1990

Gamblers take risks for the thrill of it. Investors take **calculated** risks because their calculations show they will be better off financially if they do.

Coin flip

For example, a gambler would take an even money bet on a coin flip. An investor would **not**. The investor would **only** invest in the outcome of a coin flip if he would receive **more** than his bet if he called it right...like he gets $11 if he wins on a $10 investment.

Furthermore, the calculated-risk taker requires that the number of **iterations** be adequate to insure that the outcome will approximate the probability. For example, the calculated-risk taker with a $1,000,000 net worth will **not** make the 11-to-10 coin flip investment if the minimum investment is $1,000,000. Because although there is a 50% probability that he will come out $100,000 ahead, there is also a 50% probability that he will lose his entire life savings.

Many little bets

If you cut the minimum investment down to $10,000, he'll invest because he knows that over a 100 coin flips, the heads and tails will probably be evenly split and he **will** come out ahead.

Must have valid data

In order to take a calculated risk, you must accurately measure **all** the possible **outcomes** and the **probability** of each. Do the vast majority of people who call themselves real estate investors do that?

No way.

Could they do it if they made the effort?

Nope. Accurate outcome amount and probability data do not exist and cannot be obtained.

So the vast majority of real estate investors are really gamblers?

Right.

What should they do?

Knock it off. And confine their risks to insurable ones.

Uninsurable risk

Ever since I learned it, I have been intrigued by the concept of uninsurable risk. And I've written about it on occasion (See "If You Have an ARM, You're an Insurance Company" in the 9/88 issue). Another concept that I came across in graduate school is the notion that all investors are insurance companies in a sense.

Insurance companies are supposed to be calculated-risk takers. Life insurance is a good example. Compare it to the coin toss above. Do we know the probabilities of various people dying? Yes. Can we get lots of iterations? Yes. Do we know the financial outcome of a death to the insurance company? Yes, it's specified in the policy. Can everybody die at once thereby bankrupting the insuror? Not unless there is a war and wars are excluded in the policy.

Life insurance is an excellent example of an insurable risk...a calculated risk.

Insurable risk

The minimum requirements of an insurable risk are:

- **Lots of chances** to win or lose
- **Probabilities** of winning or losing are known to a reasonable degree of accuracy
- **Value** of winning or losing is known
- Probability of **massive simultaneous loss** is very low.

Investing is insuring

Banks are really insurance companies which insure the availability of capital. For example, a line of credit says if you need money for certain purposes, the bank will guarantee that you will be able to get it. That's very much like a fire insurance company saying that if you need money to rebuild your property after a fire they will guarantee that you get it. True, you don't have to pay back the insurance company. But it is only the **availability** of credit which the bank insures, not the thing for which you needed the money.

The principle goes beyond banks. You and I are insurors (even if we don't have the ARMs of my 9/88 article).

Tenants/policyholders

Let's say Sam needs space for his business. He's worried about toxic liability for prior users' behavior if he **buys** a building to house his business. His insurance agent says no insurance can be bought to protect him from that risk. So he decides to **rent** the space from you, instead.

He's eliminated the risk, hasn't he? Or more precisely, he's **transferred** it to you. Just as buying an insurance policy would have transferred it to the insurance company.

He may also be worried about the value of the building going down if he buys it. Again, he cannot buy insurance against that risk but he can transfer that risk to you by renting.

So if you own rental real estate, you are an insurance company. Who are your "policyholders?" Anyone who has an interest in the property which is less than equity ownership. Tenants have a leasehold interest. Mortgage lenders have a security interest. You provide them with a sort of "all risks" policy which places upon you the burden of such problems as overbuilding, toxic liability, higher mortgage interest rates, federal tax reform which adversely affects property values, etc.

Gloom and doom

Real estate investors would respond that they are **optimists**. Bankers and insurance company executives, they would say, are gloomy, doomy, suspenders-and-belt conservatives. Why should we financial he-men follow the lead of the financial 90-pound weaklings when it comes to analysis of risks?

To discuss the issue in terms of optimism versus conservatism is to descend to mere name-calling. The question is not who is optimistic or who is conservative. The question is who is right? Either you have the data to calculate your risks or you don't. Inadequate data combined with optimism is still inadequate data. Indeed, that combination is **more** dangerous than inadequate data alone.

You could get killed crossing the street

Often, when I discuss real estate risk and the proper response to it, listeners dismiss my concerns with the line, "Heck, you could get killed crossing the street, too."

"Getting killed crossing the street" is an insurable risk. Good data is available on the subject.

For example, in 1986 (the most recent year in my *Statistical Abstract of the United States*), according to the National Safety Council, 6,800 people who were struck by vehicles died. The population of the United States that year was 241,078,000. So the average person's chances of being killed as a pedestrian by a vehicle were $6,800 \div 241,078,000 = .00003$.

Furthermore, more detailed analysis would probably reveal that avoidable factors like alcohol in the pedestrian's blood, dark clothing, bad neighborhoods, late weekend nights, no sidewalk, etc. increase the probability of being killed crossing the street. By avoiding those increased risk factors, you could reduce your risk of getting killed crossing the street to **much lower** than the average .00003.

So clearly it is absurd to lump the risk of, say, higher mortgage interest rates, with the risk of "getting killed crossing the street." Indeed, crossing the street is an excellent example of a true calculated risk. On the other hand, putting yourself in a position where you could be financially "killed" by a jump in interest rates is an excellent example of a pure gamble that should only appeal to a thrill seeker.

Past trends

To figure the risk of getting killed crossing the street, I used past data. Roughly speaking, real estate investors do the same when they express confidence that real estate values will go up in the future. But I claim the use of past data is **invalid** for predicting appreciation rates. Why is it valid for one but not the other?

Pedestrians generally get killed by vehicles because of lack of visibility or impaired judgment on the part of either the pedestrian or the vehicle operator. The incidence of poor visibility and/or impairment (alcohol, drugs, senility) is relatively constant from year to year.

For example, the number of pedestrian/vehicle fatalities ranged from a low of 6,800 to a high of 9,200 (1972) during the ten years reported in my *Statistical Abstract*. The population of the United States in 1972 was 209,284,000 so the probability that year was $9,200 \div 209,284,000 = .00004$. That is, for most purposes, the same as the .00003 at the other extreme of the 10-year period.

Wild swings

Mortgage interest rates, on the other hand, swung wildly from 9.00% in 1977 to 16.55% in 1981.

The things that affect real estate values...interest rates, tax reform, toxic liability, rent control, overbuilding, recession, etc....swing wildly in short periods. In terms of predictable patterns, they are **light years** away from the factors that contribute to pedestrian/vehicle fatalities.

Indeed, past appreciation rates are virtually **irrelevant** to predicting future appreciation rates. Appreciation rates have repeatedly shown that they can rapidly stop and reverse direction on a regional or national basis (Houston, New England, the Depression)...even after a prolonged run up in property values. And on a property-by-property basis, where such individual risks as rent control, toxics, radiation, and earthquakes come into play, your appreciation rate can be a big **negative** at the same time properties around you are going **up** in value.

You gotta go on something

Another line I hear when I urge investors to avoid real estate's uninsurable risks is, "Well you gotta go on something.

If you you don't go on past trends, which is the best data available, what **do** you go on?"

The short answer is that you don't "go" at all. Let's say I offered to bet you even money on whether it would rain in New York City **three** days hence. You get to pick whether you bet on rain or non-rain. That's a bet you ought to take. Because the weather forecasters are right more than 50% of the time on such a short range forecast.

But if I changed it to **thirty** days hence, you should pass. Even if I give you 200 years worth of the weather history for that date. Because weather forecasters can't make accurate forecasts more than five days hence. 200 years of history don't change that.

"But," I protest, "you gotta go on something. Past history is the best information available." If you understand weather forecasting and probability, you'll say something like, "Past history may be the **best** data available regarding whether it'll rain thirty days hence, but it is **not adequate**. I cannot calculate the risk of rain thirty days hence so I refuse to take the bet."

Just so. Now if I can just get you to see the parallels in real estate.

Next month: Part II: Implications for your strategy. JTR

82
Calculated Risks: Part II

March 1990

You cannot accurately forecast appreciation rates. Not even within a range. The fact that you **appear** to have done so in the past is **coincidence**. If you had applied your real estate appreciation forecasting skills to Houston in 1980 or New England in 1987, you would almost certainly have been wrong.

Risk taker's credo

The calculated risk taker's credo is,

"If you can't forecast it or control it, don't mess with it."

But the vast majority of real estate investors **are** messing with appreciation rates (betting they'll continue to be positive and greater than two or three percent) even though they can't forecast or control them...and those investors **believe** that they are calculated risk takers.

Most successful real estate investors take great pride in their accomplishment. I'm dismissing that accomplishment as mere luck...the product of a strategy based on an incorrect assumption (that one can predict appreciation rates within

a reasonable range) combined with a time and place where the appreciation rates happened to be favorable.

Arguing with success

Successful real estate investors would say, "I believed that real estate would be a good investment during the seventies and eighties. I bought real estate on that assumption. In fact, real estate went up in value. I made a fortune. Therefore I was right."

You can't argue with success, right? Actually, you **can** argue with success. And you **should** far more often than people do.

Success is defined as achieving one's goal. If a kid fresh out of high school adopts becoming a millionaire as his goal and achieves it, he is a success. Should those others of us who wish to be millionaires emulate his methods?

Lottery tickets

We can't answer that until we know **what** his methods were. For example, suppose his strategy was to buy state lottery tickets at the local 7/11. And his 17th ticket purchase was a million-dollar winner. Does that prove that buying lottery tickets is a good way to become a millionaire? Of course not. The lottery millionaire has **success** at making money...but no **skill**.

I congratulate success no matter what ethical way it was achieved. But I try not to write a newsletter based on invalid logic or mysticism (the near religious belief that real estate is a "good" or "sound" investment). Rather I try to learn and impart to you **skills** you can use to make money **on purpose** in the real estate market.

The lottery millionaire's conclusion that his success **proves** the validity of his strategy is a classic example of the *post hoc ergo propter hoc* logic fallacy. *Post hoc ergo propter hoc* is latin for "after which therefore because of which." The vast majority of successful real estate investors who believe their success proves the validity of their position-yourself-to-benefit-from-market-wide-appreciation strategy are drawing the same illogical conclusion.

Everybody wins

When I've used that lottery ticket analogy with real estate investors in the past, they have protested that it is invalid. "Only a tiny few lottery ticket buyers win," they say. "But in real estate in the past, virtually **everyone** who owned it won."

Actually, the notion that virtually every real estate owner has won in the past is **incorrect**. In this century, there have been times (e.g., The Depression, mid-seventies) and places (e.g., Oil Patch, Northeast) and property types (e.g., pre-shopping center downtown retail stores, office buildings in the '80s) where virtually every real estate owner lost.

Furthermore, projecting the past into the future is only valid when the relevant variables change very little over time. As I pointed out in Part I of this article last month, you **can** predict how many people will die crossing the street in the future because the relevant variables (e.g., the incidence of impaired visibility or judgment) are relatively **constant** over the years. But you **cannot** similarly predict

real estate appreciation rates because the relevant variables (e.g., interest rates, tax reform, toxic liability) are **not** at all **constant** over the years.

Change

What happens when businessmen **wrongly** believe they are taking a calculated risk? They often get their financial clock cleaned.

Pre-Paid Legal Services, Inc., which specialized in truck drivers, figured the risk of truck drivers being sued was a predictable and therefore insurable risk. They figured wrong.

Federal legislation setting new, higher safety standards caused truck drivers to get sued far more often than before, starting in early 1989. As a result, the company lost $600,000 in the second quarter of that year. Assumption is the mother of all screw ups. The incorrect assumption that Pre-Paid Legal Services, Inc. made was, "The lawsuit incidence among truck drivers in the future will continue to be similar to what it was in the past."

The red hot, very savvy, leverage buyout firm of Kohlberg Kravis Roberts & Co. took Jim Walter Corp. private in 1987. They split off a subsidiary (Celotex Corp.) which had 58,000 asbestos suits (seeking $3 billion) against it on legal advice that the remaining company (Hillsborough Holdings) would **not** have any liability for the asbestos claims. That assumption proved to be **possibly** incorrect and Hillsborough Holdings filed Chapter 11 bankruptcy last month as a result. KKR has also now been sued by the asbestos plaintiffs and the courts have refused to dismiss the suits.

Pre-Paid Legal Services, Inc. got hit by a new **law** which caused massive simultaneous losses to their policyholders; KKR by the courts' **expansive attitude** toward liability law.

We real estate investors have also been hit by new laws (e.g. Tax Reform Act of 1986) and expansive liability decisions (being held liable for acts of criminal third parties against tenants). Not to mention overbuilding, interest-rate increases, changes in federal lending and prepayment policies, recessions, and so forth.

These are all unpredictable and therefore uninsurable and "uninvestible."

The right way

The insurance industry is the correct model of calculated risk taking. As I said last month, insurable risks are characterized by:

1. Lots of chances to win or lose.
2. Probabilities of winning or losing are known to a reasonable degree of accuracy.
3. Value of winning or losing is known.
4. Probability of massive simultaneous loss is very low.

Now what are the implications for real estate investment strategy? You'd want to invest **small amounts** in a **large number** of different investments. You'd want **actuarial tables** covering all the possible outcomes. The **amount** you could win or lose would be clear. And there would be virtually no chance of **all** your investments going sour at once.

What kind of deals?

The typical pattern of acquiring from a half dozen to a couple dozen properties is somewhat diversified...but not enough when compared to the thousands of policy holders of a typical insurance company.

"But," you may protest, "small real estate investors with limited funds can't make more than a couple dozen investments."

Well, let's think about that. Let's say you have $100,000 to invest. To invest in 100 different properties, you'd have to average just $1,000 per investment. Is that possible?

Not if you invest in the **traditional** manner, i.e., buying single-family rental houses or larger properties.

How about **partnerships** where you buy $1,000 worth of each? You could probably find 100 diferent partnerships which you could buy into for $1,000 each on average. But I don't like putting your fate in the hands of others. Somebody's got to pick the property to buy, manage it, etc. I want that person to be **you** in general. The notion that you can pay others to do those things seems fundamentally and fatally flawed to me.

Are there properties you can buy for $1,000 a piece? Yes. Abandoned vacation lots and timeshare condos. Useless properties, slivers, and postage stamp-size lots. Should you buy such properties? Probably not when it comes to abandoned remote vacation home sites and time share condos. But useless urban area lots **can** be profitable. (See "Buyers Who Overpay" in the 11/89 issue.)

Now let's expand your thinking a bit. Instead of asking are there properties I can buy for $1,000 ask are there **interests** in properties I can buy for $1,000?

You bet. For example, in the 7/89 issue (See Chapter 12), I told you how Lloyd Walters buys judgments which he can use to create liens on real estate. The face value of his typical judgment is $1,100. But he only pays 8¢ on the dollar or $88 each for them. At $88 each, a guy with $100,000 to invest could buy $100,000 ÷ $88 = 1,136 different investments.

In the 2/89 and 3/89 issues, I told you of the spectacular profits made by investors who bought partial (tenant in common) interests. The actual case histories in those articles included a $500 investment and a $475 investment.

Another article I wrote where cash outlays were in the $1,000 range involved rights of redemption (11/89 and 12/89 issues). And there are options and nonrecourse, high-leverage deals available for an investment of $1,000 or less.

So there **are** ways to make multiple small ($1,000 or less) investments in real estate.

Actuarial tables

Life and other insurors can get reliable actuarial tables covering death rates, etc. Can we real estate investors get reliable actuarial tables on the incidence of Tax Reform Acts, the probability that fiberglass insulation will be declared a health hazard, the likelihood that mortgage interest rates will exceed 15% in 1995, the chances that an endangered butterfly will be found on our land, etc.?

Nope.

So how do we not mess with properties which will be adversely affected by tax reform and such?

One way is **short holding periods** ...like days or weeks or months. Or even **zero** holding periods using assignment of options or purchase agreements.

Another way is to do only **wired** deals. In a wired deal, you don't commit to do it until you are sure or nearly sure that you will make a profit. Like stock market arbitrage where the arbitrager buys and sells the stock at the same time knowing that he profits.

Value of win/lose

Generally, you do not know how much you can win in real estate. It used to be true that the most you could lose in real estate was the purchase price. Then they invented toxic liability where it's possible for the clean up cost to far exceed the purchase price.

However, you **can** contractually or legislatively limit winnings and losings. For example, with an option, the most you can lose is the option money. In a rent-controlled community, the most rent you can collect is determined by the rent control law. Obviously, there's no benefit to a limit on your **winnings**. But a limit to your **losses** goes a long way toward enabling you to make calculated risks.

The boundless negative value of toxic liability is a horrific possibility which must be eliminated. One way is to completely stay out of the chain of title as with assignment of purchase agreements and options.

A thorough environmental audit is the minimum for an investor who takes title. But the law is nebulous and toxics are elusive. The list of toxics grows yearly thereby adding substances to which you paid no attention to when you bought the property.

Simultaneous wipeout

The vast majority of successful real estate investors have become wealthy as a result of simultaneous appreciation of all properties in their market. Unfortunately, many investors believe that's a one-way (up) street. It's not. As many Oil Patch and other investors can now attest, it works in both directions.

Diversification by owning several properties reduces your exposure to **some** risks. But not all.

For example, the Tax Reform Act of 1986 cut the value of all income property. The only way to diversify against such adverse federal laws is to invest in **foreign** real estate.

Interest rate increases hurt **all** capital assets including real estate. And they are now global. There is nowhere to hide from higher interest rates. Although you **can** protect yourself **contractually** with fixed-rate mortgages or by hedging in the interest rate futures market (See the 11/87, 12/87, and 7/89 issues). I've said it many times...but it bears repeating ...adjustable-rate mortgages are financial Russian Roulette.

Buying in more than one town can reduce your exposure to such risks as municipal rent control or extraordinarily high property taxes (outside of California). But it will not protect you against a downturn in the **regional** economy. Buying in more than one region can reduce your exposure to regional downturns but not to national or worldwide downturns like recessions and depressions.

The best protection against the risks that you cannot diversify against is **time sequence diversification**. That is, you do, say, a deal a week. You only use a small part of your cash on each deal. If you happen to hit the future equivalent of 1929, it's only one deal and only a small part of your overall net worth.

After 14 years of writing for real estate investors, I have no illusions about how quickly my readers will change their strategies as suggested by this article. Heck, it took me years to get a lot of you guys to exchange.

If I can get **some** of you to allocate a **small portion** of your portfolio and time to this approach on an **experimental** basis, I'll be satisfied. JTR

83
Protection Against Uninsurable Catastrophes

June 1989

Case histories

- In August of 1985, an Odessa, TX tenant was raped at knifepoint in her apartment. The rapist entered through a patio door which the tenant alleged was not fixed in spite of her asking for repairs nine times. On April 10, 1989, an Odessa, Texas jury awarded the tenant $956,000 in damages from her apartment management company. $825,000 of that was for **punitive** damages. (AP)

- On March 21, 1989, a group of Baltimore residents filed suit against eight landlords who own 10 vacant houses. The suits complain that the houses have become nuisances and seek $600,000 per house in compensatory and **punitive** damages. (UPI)

- The Fair Housing Amendments allow federal courts or administrative law judges to assess unlimited damages including **punitive** damages.

- On June 17, 1988, a jury awarded 23 tenants of a San Francisco low-income hotel $3,000,000 in **punitive** damages for "malicious harassment" by their landlord. (UPI)

- In February of 1988, San Diego became the eighth California city to pass a law allowing actual or suspected AIDS carriers who are discriminated against in housing or business because of AIDS to sue for "potentially large **punitive** damages." (*LA Times*)

- On August 11, 1987, a San Francisco jury awarded Eileen Becker $60,000 in actual damages and $200,000 in **punitive** damages. She said her landlords promised to let her move back into her studio apartment after renovation. They say she agreed to vacate permanently in return for $1,000. (UPI)

No insurance

You cannot buy insurance against punitive damages. State legislatures have outlawed liability insurance which covers punitive damages as violating "public policy." Punitive damages are supposed to hurt.

Toxic substances are another uninsurable risk. Most liability insurance policies have a pollution exclusion clause which excludes contamination caused by the insured or prior owners. (They **will** insure against pollution occurring as the result of an **accident during** the policy period.)

You have far more liability risk now

Peter Huber, attorney and author of the 1988 book, *Liability* (Basic Books $19.95), says that nothing less than a "revolution in liability law" has occurred "in the last thirty years." Paul Pesek, a Dallas real estate lawyer (214-922-9393), says environmental pre-purchase inspections and contract language (representations, warranties, clauses which let the buyer out of the purchase, and indemnifications) have lately become crucial elements of virtually all commercial real estate deals.

From 1977 to 1981, the number of civil lawsuits filed in the U.S. grew four times faster than the population. The first million-dollar verdict came in 1962. According to Jury Verdict Research, Inc., there were 407 verdicts of a million dollars or more by 1984. The probability that a plaintiff would win a civil suit in the '60s was 20% to 30%. In the '80s, the probability had risen to over 50%. The average judgment rose from about $50,000 in the '60s to about $250,000 in the '80s. And those figures are adjusted for inflation.

From the time a lawsuit is threatened until it is settled or tried, it hangs over your head. You are required to tell prospective lenders about pending suits when you apply for a mortgage. And it's one of the things you worry about when you wake up at two in the morning.

If not from insurance, where **can** you get protection? Incorporating and other non-traditional forms of ownership come to mind. Those forms of ownership are more complex and costly than we real estate investors are used to. But today, a non-traditional ownership form may be an "insurance policy" worth buying.

Incorporate rental properties?

When someone starts a small business, they almost invariably assume they should incorporate. Incorporation probably occurred to most landlords when they bought their first rental property.

But the landlords typically decided to go the sole proprietor or partnership route after consultation with their accountant, attorney, and other investors. Ruth Furey, Executive Director of the Contra Costa County (CA) Rental Housing Association says only about ten of their 750 members are incorporated.

Bottled-up tax benefits?

My book, *Aggressive Tax Avoidance for Real Estate Investors*, recommends **against** owning real estate in corporations ...in-cluding S corporations. The main reason for avoiding C (regular) corporations was that they bottled up the tax benefits.

Remember tax benefits?

With tax benefits dramatically restricted by the Tax Reform Act of 1986 (TRA '86)...and liability for punitive damages, toxics, Fair Housing violations, etc. explod-ing...corporations and other estate preservation techniques deserve another look.

"Piercing the corporate veil"

Most laymen believe that incorporating absolutely protects an owner of a business from all liability. Legal people call making a corporate officer **personally liable** for a corporate action "piercing the corporate veil." Indeed, it **is** very difficult to "pierce the corporate veil." Courts are reluctant to permit it in the absence of fraud or other misbehavior in the use of the corporate form.

But plaintiffs in **toxic** cases can frequently make you personally liable without piercing the corporate veil...if you are **personally involved** in the running of the corporation. One case (*N. Y. v. Shore Realty Corp. and Donald LeoGrande*, 759 F 2d 1032) even said the corporate officer was personally liable because he was an "**active participant.**" Of course in tax law, "active participant" is exactly what you must prove you **are** in order to deduct up to $25,000 in rental property losses from non-passive income.

In toxic substance cases, the corporate veil means little if you are the guy in charge. The Comprehensive Environmental Response, Compensation, and Liability Act of 1980 (CERCLA) lays the liability on the "owner **or operator**" [emphasis added] of the property in question. Another anti-toxics law, The Rivers and Harbors Appropriations Act of 1899 (33 USC 411) says, "every **person** and every corporation that shall violate, or that shall knowingly aid, abet, authorize, or instigate a violation..." [emphasis added] is liable.

In toxic matters, the protection of the corporate veil applies mainly to stockholders who are **not** involved in day-to-day operations. For example, a Manville shareholder would not be personally liable by mere ownership for Manville's asbestos personal injury liability. But Joe Smith who is president, manager, and major shareholder of JS Elm Street Corp. (which owns his apartment building at 123 Elm Street) **can** be held personally liable for toxic contamination based on his **management** rather than his ownership of the property.

Alter ego

A corporation **can** possibly help when it comes to **punitive damages**, however. As I understand it, the plaintiff would have to pierce the corporate veil in those cases where pertinent statutes did not create individual liability.

In order to pierce a rental property owner's corporate veil, the plaintiff would generally have to prove that the corporation was a mere *alter ego*. To invoke the *alter ego* doctrine, the plaintiff must show that the stockholders:

- Disregarded the entity of the corporation
- Made the corporation a mere conduit for the transaction of their own private business
- The separate individualities of the corporation and the stockholders ceased to exist.

(*Sefton v. San Diego Trust & Savings Bank*, 106 P 2d 974)

In layman's terms, the *alter ego* doctrine means if you want the protection of the corporate veil, you can't just incorporate then forget about it. You have to keep separate books, bank accounts, minutes of corporate meetings, and generally genuflect to the corporate altar at every opportunity. That's a pain but it's doable and probably worth the protection it creates.

Trusts, etc.

Attorney Jay W. Mitton (801-595-1200) is a guru who does seminars and sells books (*Creating Your Financial Fortress*) and tapes on the subject of protecting your assets from various uninsurable liabilities. (His seminar/book/tape number is 800-654-6606) Among the protective forms of ownership he advocates are:

- Limited partnerships (you and spouse not a syndication)
- C corporations
- S corporations
- Family trusts
- Business trusts
- Children's trusts
- Insurance trusts.

No definitive answer

Whenever possible, I like to tell my readers to do this or don't do that. The question of which form of ownership to use is too complicated and situation-dependent for me to do that. Also, it's outside my area of expertise.

You need to discuss it with a local attorney who knows your state laws regarding the personal liability of corporate officers, trustees, etc. And you need to discuss the tax and transferrability aspects with an accountant or estate-planning attorney. Mitton's firm, although based in Salt Lake City, takes clients nationwide.

Your accountant and attorney can explain the amount of "punitive-damage-insurance coverage" you'll be getting under your current state law if you switch to a non-traditional form of real estate ownership...as well as the "premium" (legal and accounting fees, extra taxes, transferability restrictions, bookkeeping, etc.) you'll have to pay to get that "coverage." Then you decide whether it's worth it or not to you.

My main purpose in writing this article is to impress upon you to the fact that there have been revolutionary changes in tax and liability laws...changes which may have pushed your sole-proprietor-or-not decision past the tipping point. Our old habit of rejecting incorporation, trusts, etc. out of hand no longer makes sense.

This is a defensive article. Offense is more fun than defense as a general rule. But to win in sports, as well as real estate, you have to be able to play **both** offense and defense. JTR

84
Where Punitive Damages are Insurable

August 1989

In the June issue, I said punitive damages were not insurable. Last month, I reported that insurance consultant Greg Crouch (512-467-7299) told me that they **are** insurable in **some** states. Greg has now brought to my attention an article on the subject ("The Insurability of Punitive Damages," *The Risk Report*, January 1989). The article tells where each state stands on the question of whether punitive damages are insurable.

Directly assessed punitive damages are those assessed against you because of something **you** did. **Vicariously** assessed punitive damages are those you have to pay because of what a **third party** (like your employee) did.

According to the law firm of Peterson, Ross, Schloerb & Seidel, **direct** punitive damages cannot be insured in:

CA	KS	NY
CO	ME	OH
CT	MN	OK
FL	MO	PA
IL	ND	RI
IN	NJ	

The question is **undecided** in:

HI	NV	VA
MA	SD	WA
NE	UT	

Vicarious punitive damages cannot be insured in:

KS	OH	PA

and that question is **undecided** in:

CA	ND	RI
CO	NE	SD
HI	NH	VA
MA	NY	WA
ME	NV	

The list changes from year to year.

If you operate rental property in a state where punitive damages **cannot** be insured against...or in a state where the question is **undecided**...you should consider the non-insurance protections suggested in my June article.

The U. S. Supreme Court is currently considering a case which argues that punitive damages violate the prohibition against "excessive fines" in the Eighth Amendment to the Constitution. JTR

85
Drug Seizures
Of Property

In the 9/88 issue, I wrote about the Republic National Bank of Miami losing their $800,000 mortgage on a house because the borrower was a drug dealer and the feds said the bank knew or should have known that.

The 10/89 issue of *Real Estate Today* has a brief summary of laws governing seizure of property because of drug activity. They include:

The **Comprehensive Crime Control Act of 1984** (21 USCA 881) allows the feds to confiscate property, including real estate, when they believe that drug-related activity is being conducted on the premises and that the owner either knows about or consents to that activity.

Portland, OR has a law under which a citizen complaint about drug activity triggers a letter to the owner. If the owner does not evict the tenants within ten days the city can go to court seeking to have the property **boarded up** for as long as a year and to fine the owner up to **$500 for each day** the drug activity occurred in the property.

There are other such laws and more proposed. Typically, they call for ultimate sale of the property with the sale proceeds going to pay off any liens. Proceeds in excess of the liens (i.e. your equity) go to the government for drug enforcement programs (i.e., the salaries of the guys who confiscated your property). In some cases, the government takes over your building for government use.

What's going on here is terminal frustration over how badly the war on drugs is going. In fact, it's not a war on drugs at all. It's a **civil** war between drug users and their suppliers on one hand and non-users on the other. The users and pushers are winning because it's impossible to stop people from smuggling, selling, or using easily-hidden drugs in a 3.5-million-square-mile country occupied by 245,000,000 people…tens of millions of whom **want** the drugs.

I am a lifelong teetotaler. I've never used tobacco. And I'm one of the few of my baby-boom generation who has not even tried marijuana or any of the other stuff that was cool in the '60s and '70s. But I recognize the second coming of the **Prohibition** mistake when I see it.

The only solution to the drug problem is to legalize the stuff. Like alcohol and tobacco, drugs are bad for you. But as with those substances, so many idiots insist on using the stuff that prohibition accomplishes nothing but criminalizing the business by giving the bad guys a monopoly.

Prohibition made the Mafia and corrupted society. Anti-drug laws are strengthening the Mafia, enriching street gangs, and corrupting society. Not to mention turning law-abiding citizen against law-abiding citizen as in these property seizure laws.

Laws which permit **landlord** property to be confiscated because of **suspected** drug activity by a **tenant** are blatantly unconstitutional. But I fear the courts will play for the anti-drug grandstand and look the other way.

What should you do about this? Tell your legislators that you don't appreciate being punished for the acts of others who are beyond your control. If you suspect drug activity in your property, take all legal action vigorously. But remember the Massachusetts lawyer who broke down the door of one of his apartments and put the tenants' stuff in the street. (See "Miscellaneous" in the 6/89 issue.) He was arrested and charged with breaking and entering and assault and battery. The lawyer said they were drug dealers (250 visitors in one night) and that Massachusetts law required him to get rid of them. Basically, landlords of America, you are damned if you do and damned if you don't when it comes to drug dealer tenants. JTR

86
Kaplan:
"Too Much Risk"

May 1989

I have quoted Jay Kaplan on a number of occasions. He used to be the main acquisitions guy for Consolidated Capital, one of the largest syndicators in the country.

In his May 14th column in the *San Francisco Examiner,* he said,

"Personally, it's depressing for me to consider how badly skewed the risk/reward ratio has become [in today's real estate market]. Except possibly in the single-family development market, I feel there's just too much risk for the forseeable rewards."

He adds that he's still looking in the hope of finding "that one special deal."

I mention this because it dovetails nicely with my 1959 article on page 217 of this issue. But real estate offers so many alternative ways of structuring deals that the solution to the problem Kaplan talks about can be found **within** real estate.

Solutions I plan to explore in future issues include incorporation, shorter holding periods, more bargain purchase techniques, upgrading (which is a relative of single-family development), and geographic areas where positive cash flow is common. In short, I think Kaplan's remarks describe today's **mainstream, traditional** investment market in **most** geographic areas...but **not all** of real estate. JTR

87
Long–Term Investment Is a Contradiction In Terms

November 1988

Real estate is a long-term investment, right? You've heard that and read it numerous times. I've said it myself.

There is **no such thing** as a long-term investment. When you go long-term, your ability to either predict or control the relevant variables drops rapidly to near zero. Long-term "investments" are really speculations. Most assumptions you make about two years hence or later are "garbage in."

Weather forecasting

Long-term weather forecast is another contradiction in terms. The accuracy of weather forecasts is inversely proportional to the length of the forecast. The same is true of real estate...although some variables...most notably completion of buildings under **construction**... **can** be forecast accurately for a year or two into the future.

The ability of weather forecasters to predict long-range varies around the world. For example, in San Francisco, we can probably predict the summer weather with a high degree of accuracy for the next hundred years: low coastal cloudiness morning and evenings. Because it rarely varies.

By the same token, real estate investors can probably predict the apartment vacancy rate in New York City accurately for the next ten years: extremely low...because of that city's addiction to rent control.

But predicting vacancy rates in the Oil Patch is like predicting the weather in the Eastern part of the U.S. If you don't like today's, stick around for a while and it'll change.

Dr. Gilman, a meteorologist at the National Weather Service says his colleagues have **"no skill"** when it comes to predicting, say, precipitation beyond five days. "No skill" is a good way to put it. Millions of real estate investors credit themselves with investment skill when they made money on properties they held longer than anyone could possibly have forecast pertinent variables at the time they bought. The old In-A-Bull-Market-Everyone-Thinks-He's-A-Genius syndrome.

The variables

Real estate net operating incomes and property values are determined by:

1. Interest rates.
2. Supply of similar properties and labor and materials used to operate them.
3. Demand for such properties and labor and materials used to operate them.
4. Government confiscation of valuable property rights as happens in tax reform, rent control, and down zoning.

Interest rates

Interest rates are totally unpredictable. If you think you can predict interest rates movements, get out of real estate and make a billion dollars in the interest rate futures market. *The Wall Street Journal* (July 2, 1984) asked 20 of the top economists in the country to forecast what 30-year treasury bond rates would be six months later. Their forecasts ranged from 9.5% to 12.5%. The actual rate six months later was 13.64%.

An increase in interest rates reduces the value of all capital assets...including real estate. For example, a 10% increase in mortgage interest rates...from, say, 10% to 11%...would reduce property values by about 10%.

You can eliminate interest rate risk by **hedging**. You do that by getting a fixed-rate assumable mortgage...which is easier said than done these days.

Or, if you have a higher tolerance for complexity, you can hedge in the interest rates futures market or with interest rate swaps. (See "The Best of Both Worlds: A Hedged ARM" in the 11/87 and 12/87 issues.) A **non**-assumable, fixed-rate mortgage hedges the interest rate risk to your **cash flow** if not to your resale value.

Supply

Supply is **the most predictable** variable in real estate. Or at least, **additions** to supply. To create new supply, a developer has to acquire or get control of land, obtain government approvals, and construct the building. That takes at least six months and as long as two years ...absent extraordinary delays. So if you find out what approvals are being sought in your market, you can get a very accurate idea as to how much space will be added to supply in the next six months to two years. But I suspect few investors could say accurately how many competitive buildings are under construction in their market...or how many they would regard as enough to make them get out of the market.

Demolitions...which are more numerous than most realize...also affect supply. But they can take place almost overnight.

Demand

Demand, too, can change overnight. In my 19 years as an investor I've seen many an absorption rate (annual increase in demand for rental space) forecast rendered hopelessly inaccurate by unanticipated changes in demand. A California developer whose fall was chronicled in *Urban Land* magazine said demand for space in their properties didn't tail off. It all but stopped **overnight**.

Anyone who has been in the apartment business for any length of time knows that you can go for months with virtually no traffic then rent five apartments in one day.

Recessions are generally caused by fear. People fear losing their jobs or a down turn in their business. As a result, they **postpone** major purchases. The collective postponing by millions of people becomes a self-fulfilling prophecy as car and home sales drop. That fear can be triggered overnight by events like the stock market crash of '87 or the 1979 increase in the Federal Reserve discount rate.

Or it can be triggered by an **accumulation** of bad news that "breaks the camel's back." No one can predict recessions. I failed in the August '87 issue where I said a recession was overdue and that '88 seemed like "the prime suspect."

Tax laws

If you think you can predict tax law changes, you haven't read *Showdown at Gucci Gulch*, the inside story of the Tax Reform Act of 1986 (book review in this issue). On April 28, 1986, no less an expert legislation-forecaster than Senate Majority Leader Bob Dole said tax reform was "hanging by a thread." Less than a month later, the Senate Finance Committee passed it **unanimously** and it rolled down hill from there, knocking 15 to 25% off the value of income properties.

Other political risk

I've seen rent control go from a standing start to being law in three weeks in San Francisco. Down zoning can happen literally in the night...at a council meeting you're unable to attend.

What to do

The obvious answer to the conclusion that the long-term is a speculation is to only hold **short**-term. That's possible. There are many real estate strategies ...like the building-moving related in "How to Buy for Half Price and Nothing Down" in the August issue...which enable you to get in and out in a matter of weeks or months.

Or you could make your decision to continue holding on an incremental basis. That is, you structure the deal so that you can make an adequate profit within the first eighteen months then get out if necessary. But if the next eighteen months look good when the first eighteen months ends, you can decide to continue to hold.

Transaction costs are higher in real estate than in other investments. That militates **against** short holding periods. But there ways of minimizing transaction costs...like avoiding real estate commissions, institutional lenders, and states with high transfer taxes.

Hedge; fatter margins

Hedging risks by investing in perenially tight markets, getting fixed-rate mortages, long-term leases, statutory prohibitions against rent control, etc. can minimize some of the risks.

Finally, you can and should reduce your exposure to risk by seeking deals with **higher profit margins** than the run-of-the-mill deal. Today, the typical national median real estate investment shows a breakeven cash flow and relies on future appreciation for an adequate return. That's a crap shoot... notwithstanding the fact that appreciation has occurred fairly steadily since the sixties.

I constantly hear real estate investors say, in effect, my market has steadily appreciated for many years therefore I conclude that steady appreciation is an inalterable characteristic of my market. Invariably, they overlook times when their market wasn't so hot. More importantly, they overlook the tenuous nature of the specific **causes** of whatever appreciation they've enjoyed. Appreciation is not caused by some mysterious chemical in the local water.

The list of recent markets which have learned that past appreciation does not guarantee future appreciation includes:

- The Oil Patch which flew so high in the seventies
- Boston which flew so high in the mid eighties
- Silicon Valley (Envy of the world in '83)
- Resort condos
- Office building markets almost everywhere

In the October '86 issue (Chapter 67), I wrote an article with the title, "Are You Aware of Your Investment Assumptions?" **This** article tells you to ask yourself the **additional** question, "To the extent that those assumptions pertain to future years, is there really any basis at all for relying on those assumptions?"

The honest answer must be that hardly any of the variables which determine real estate investment performance can be forecast with any accuracy beyond the next month or two. And even the most forecastable variable...new construction ...cannot be forecast beyond a year or two.

Crap shoot

A real estate "investment" which relies on third year or later returns is really a crap shoot. And even "investments" which **don't** need third year or later returns contain a larger crap shoot component than most real estate investors are willing to admit.

But the crap shoot aspect of real estate investing...while not totally eliminatable ...can be reduced to an acceptable level by the kinds of short-duration, high margin techniques I've been writing about of late...combined with the various hedges I've described in this and other articles.

Refusal to speculate is not wimpy...it's just smart. Willingness to speculate is not macho...it's just dumb. The money you're risking represents your children's education, your retirement, and your ability to obtain future health care. Gambling with it is irresponsible.

Some risk is unavoidable. My message is not, "Take no risk." Rather it is, "Calculate your risks." And plunge in **only** when the odds favor your success.

JTR

88
Big Profits...and Big Losses...from Toxics Panic

September 1988

The Comprehensive Environmental Response, Compensation and Liability Act of 1980 (CERCLA) says landlords are strictly liable without limit for abatement of toxic substance hazards unless you can prove that you did not know or have reason to know of the hazard when you bought the property even though you conducted an investigation which was consistent with good commercial or customary practices [42 USC §9601(35)(A)(B)].

A couple court decisions say you are liable **regardless of fault** [*US v Nepacco*, 579 F Supp 839; *US v Argent*, 21 ERC, 354 BNA, Dist. NM].

Landlord's duties

According to Gary Andrews of Maxim Engineers, Inc. of Dallas, (800-526-2946) lawyers agree you have a common law duty to:

• **Inspect** for toxics,
• **Monitor** them continuously,

• **Warn** your tenants if indeed you have hazardous toxics,
• **Train** your employees to safeguard both the public's and their own health regarding proximity to or contact with toxics and
• **Remove** or encapsulate any substances which are in a hazardous condition to the public using **state of the art**, not just legal minimum, methods.

Andrews says 99 out of 100 buildings which have asbestos do **not** need any more action than awareness, warning (ask your attorney), and monitoring.

Toxics are forever

You **never** escape responsibility for the removed toxics. Wherever it's taken, it's still yours. If the dump itself is later determined to be a hazard, you will be required to pay for removing your toxics from there and taking them to yet another dump.

Feds can bill you

If you fail to discharge your hazardous substance duties, the government has the authority to do it for you...and bill you.

Furthermore, there is the **personal injury lawsuit** liability from future tenant or employee or visitor suits. Even if you or the government remove the toxic substance immediately and by state-of-the-art removal technology, you may **still** be held liable for someone's illness by a jury if, for example, they feel you should have acted sooner.

Common sense tells us that these substances are more likely to cause harm if they are disturbed than if they are simply left alone. But when trial lawyers are part of the equation, common sense is an uncommon commodity.

Insurance and trash

You're generally **not** covered by your insurance policies for toxics. In recent years, insurance companies have added endorsements which **exclude** toxic substance coverage.

Trash colletion companies are now slipping sweeping toxic clauses into the faint gray print on the back of container service agreements. One clause...which I crossed out on the contract pertaining to one of my properties...says,

"Non-hazardous waste only. Customer shall use the container only for the disposal of its non-hazardous solid waste, and agrees that if it places waste which is liquid, radioactive, reactive, toxic, ignitable, corrosive, pathological, acidic, or waste which is otherwise listed as a hazardous or toxic substance (as defined by local, state, provincial or federal laws or regulations) in the Equipment: (a) it shall indemnify company for any and all damages, losses or claims which may be incurred by Company; and that title to any such waste shall not pass to Company but shall remain with Customer. Customer shall not place any waste which requires special handling in the equipment, including but not limited to items such as tires, brush, demolition or construction waste, white goods, and foam products."

Real Estate Investment Strategy

That clause prohibits most of the stuff you put in the trash. Furthermore, it makes you the trash company's insuror. If the trash company was faced with a suit or regulatory action which threatened to bankrupt its owners, they would likely sue all their customers who had signed these indemnification agreements.

The cost of all this

Maryland Bank & Trust Co. foreclosed on a $335,000 mortgage a couple years ago. So far, they've had to spend $500,000 cleaning up toxic waste they found on the property.

Four banks decided not to foreclose on a $57,000,000 mortgage they had made to a Colorado refinery. They feared toxic cleanup costs. Note that amount again: $57,000,000! A California jury awarded one tenant $600,000 in a "sick building" case.

According to *Means Repair & Remodeling Cost Data 1988*, it costs $2.86 to $3.13 per square foot to remove **ceiling** asbestos, a common application. The *1988 National Construction Estimator* puts the cost of removing asbestos **pipe** insulation at $3.02 to $10.96 per linear foot. Subscriber Ernie Kaluzhny adds that asbestos-removal contractors generally have a $1,000 to $1,500 minimum.

An executive of Brand Companies, a Park Ridge, IL asbestos removal contractor, says it costs $10 to $30 per square foot to remove asbestos. The September '88 issue of *Sunset* magazine has a diagram showing the common locations of asbestos in a house. That article puts the cost of a home inspection at $150 to $500 and the cost of removal from a ceiling at $3 to $30 per square foot. Restoring the ceiling to normal appearance is extra.

Underground worse

As bad as asbestos is, it's a picnic compared to underground toxics. And they can occur not only in industrial property but also in other property types because of a previous use or someone who dumped stuff on the premises.

Underground **tanks** can cause a buried toxics problem, too. In the Northeast, many houses and other buildings have buried tanks to hold heating oil. The Environmental Protection Agency says as many as 35% of motor fuel tanks leak. The percentage for heating oil tanks is probably higher.

Steps to take

You must take several precautions as a result of the new risk to real estate investors which toxics represent:

- Have the property **inspected** for toxics before you buy.
- Investigate the **history** of the property regarding toxic-substances as best you can.
- Seek **indemnification** agreements from sellers and tenants.
- Take common sense **precautions** to prevent injury.
- Make full **disclosure** when you lease or sell.
- **Fight** unreasonable cleanup demands and litigation.

Inspection requires experts. For example, ascertaining whether asbestos is present often requires that samples be examined under an electron microscope (The fee for such microscopy is $330 to $580 according to *Means*).

You investigate the history of a property by talking to neighbors, the local fire department (which pays particular attention to properties where flammables are used), checking with the reference librarian for local history books, title chain search, and checking with concerned government agencies like the Evironmental Protection Agency, state equivalents, local board of health, etc.

Indemnification

Seek indemnification by putting a clause in your purchase agreement which says the seller agrees to cover the cost of any toxic substance which was put on the property during or prior to his ownership. Make sure the clause survives closing. I suspect sellers will **refuse** such clauses except where virtually all buyers are demanding them. The more professional the average buyer for the property in question, the more likely all buyers will be damanding such clauses. That is, sellers of institutional-size properties will probably find they have to agree to such clauses. But sellers of homes, duplexes, etc. will probably find that they do **not**.

Prohibit your tenants from polluting your property...and make them promise to pay for it if they do. As with any prohibition clauses, remember that an ounce of **prevention** is worth a ton of litigation. So inspect periodically. Remember also that an indemnification clause is no better than the credit of the indemnifier.

Use an attorney to draw up indemnification clauses. That helps in two ways: attorneys are more likely to draw an effective clause and they and thereby, their errors and omissions insurance carriers, can be sued if they don't. The July '88 issue of *Leasing Professional* (602-860-0659) contains suggested hazardous waste lease clauses.

Consult with estate planning and bankruptcy attorneys on ways to rearrange your affairs so as to limit the amount of your net worth which can be taken if you are held liable for a cleanup.

Politics not health

Toxics are a **political** risk. Obviously, tobacco and alcohol kill far more people than leaking heating oil tanks or asbestos-containing ceiling coatings. But tobacco and alcohol companies reap billions in profits...in spite of the injuries they cause...while landlords may be ordered to give up their life savings...to fund cleanup of the remotest hazards...by methods which arguably do more harm than good. Clearly, these cleanup laws are the result of a dash of genuine health concern combined with a ton of dislike of landlords and big business.

Since cleanup laws are leftist- rather than health-inspired, you can expect that the laws will appear in a pattern similar to that of **rent control**. That is, leftist states and communities will pass such laws. And politically powerful groups like homeowners will be allowed to ignore the "hazard."

The profit opportunity

So where's the profit in all this? Many are **overreacting**. Maxim's Gary Andrews cites one example where a major insurance company owned a vacant 240,000 square foot office building in Dallas. It had asbestos. Consultants hired by the insurance company said it would cost $22 per square foot to remove. The insurance company decided to let the **new** owner remove it and offered the building for sale for $22 per square foot **less** than the asbestos-free market value.

Andrews' clients bought it because Andrews' firm said the correct removal cost was **$7** per square foot, not $22. Subsequent estimates from certified removal contractors confirmed that. Furthermore, Andrews said the asbestos-containing material was in good condition so a mere "operations and maintenance program," not removal, would suffice.

Andrews' clients bought the building for $22 - $7 = $15 x 240,000 = $3,600,000 less than market value if the asbestos has to be removed. And if they just go the operations and maintenance route, their bargain purchase price was $22 x 240,000 = $5,280,000 below market value even with the asbestos. Some people work all year to make that kind of money.

Andrews has seen many other similar cases. And I read of a Los Angeles office building which sold for a $90,000,000 discount when the asbestos removal cost was only $50,000,000.

Who is most likely to panic? Litigation-phobics and people and entities who usually respond to pressure for other leftist causes: governments, non-profit institutions, mass market companies, people who invest in "socially conscious" mutual funds.

Opportunity won't last

I suspect that the window of opportunity for profiting from asbestos panic will be brief. The profits are too spectacular to last. Also, remember that the leftist communities will probably mandate not just monitoring but **removal** by owners of four units or more or non-residential buildings. Finally, remember that there's a big difference between toxics like asbestos...which can be accurately surveyed...and **underground** toxics which have spread God only knows how wide and deep. JTR

89

Reader Feedback on Toxics

In September, I put a post card poll in this newsletter asking readers to tell me if they had run into the toxics issue in their real estate dealings. Here are some of the reports I got back.

Next to gas station

Subscriber offered $83,900 to buy a property next to a former gas station. Her lawyer said soil might be contaminated. She rejected an environmental audit because it would have cost $2,500. She got a "mini-soil test" instead for $500. No contamination was revealed so she bought the property.

Developer's contract

Subscriber sold a former farm to a developer. The developer's purchase agreement required the seller to guarantee that there were no toxic materials on the site and to indemnify the developer if there were. The subscriber refused to sign and the developer settled for a state-ment by the seller that they had never allowed toxic materials to be used on the property during their ownership.

Refi requires soil test

Subscriber refinanced a commercial property in Massachusetts. The lender required "test borings" around the property at a cost of $3,500. The subscriber also says New Hampshire real estate agents are being warned that residential testing is to come there in the near future.

$300K asbestos bill

San Francisco subscriber says he encapsulates or removes asbestos because he has the kind of tenants "who would try to sue me." He "discounts for it at purchase to the extent possible." He spent $300,000 removing asbestos from a five-story, 105 unit apartment building in San Francisco...one 21-unit floor at a time ...which meant 21 vacancies at a time.

$250,000 sale lost

A subscriber who is a real estate agent sold a Continental Trailways bus station for $250,000. It had two 6,000-gallon underground petroleum tanks. The seller was willing to remove them and provide the buyer with "an EPA inspection giving clean bill of health."

But the buyer refused on the grounds that future legislation **might** create additional liabilities and that the seller **might** then be bankrupt leaving the buyer holding the bag.

Dead industrial deal

Subscriber was doing a delayed exchange with an eight-figure cash amount to spend. He considered buying a 250,000 square foot warehouse complex. But his environmental auditor found "enough oil & chemicals to put the Arabs out of business." He bought a 300-unit apartment complex instead.

Pesticide on farm land

Subscriber sold farm land. Buyer put a clause in the purchase agreement allowing him to get out if toxics were found. His environmental auditor found them: pesticide residue. But the buyer decided to go ahead with the purchase anyway. No change in terms.

Asbestos on heat pipes

Subscriber owned a $300,000 rental house which had asbestos pipe insulation. A $40 test revealed that. He called a certified asbestos removal contractor listed in the *Yellow Pages* and had 228 linear feet and some suspect dirt removed at a cost of $2,000.

There was no particular reason for removal. The subscriber and his attorney simply felt it would be a good idea. He hopes to find a cheaper, but legal method next time he encounters the problem.

Asbestos and tank

Subscriber owns a former car dealership property. When he tried to sell, the buyer required an environmental audit. It revealed asbestos insulation on an abandoned steam boiler and a petroleum storage tank under the building slab.

The subscriber says the asbestos and tank have to be removed although he does not say whether that is a government, lender, or buyer requirement. Local and federal laws must be complied with regarding removal. He adds that most lenders in the New York City area now require environmental audits.

Hassles

In selling a property, a subscriber "was hassled by potential buyers' lawyers over all manner of potential problems including asbestos, radon, buried oil tanks, was there ever chromium plating done on site? This, plus the potential liabilities under the so-called Fair Housing Act Amendments of 1988 take some of the joy out of rental property ownership."

Lender required audit

Subscriber wanted to finance a strip center which used to be a gas station. Lender required Phase I audit which cost $3,000.

$500 asbestos credit

An audit by a general contractor found possible asbestos in a vent line. Test for asbestos was positive. The seller credited the buyer $500 to cover the cost of removal.

Phase I needed for refi

Long time investor encountered a Phase I environmental audit requirement for the first time when he applied to refinance an industrial building. The investor competitively bid the environmental audit. He sought six bids and got four: $2,800, $3,000, $4,500, and $6,400. The $2,800-guy had excellent references so he got the job. My subscriber noted that there was a direct correlation between amount of paperwork the bidder sent and the amount of the bid.

The environmental audit has been held up because the government building which contains some necessary records regarding nearby properties is condemned for earthquake damage.

That same subsciber also just removed 11 underground storage tanks (they held solvents) from another property. It had previously been occupied by a **paint manufacturer**. The subscriber had negotiated long and hard over the toxics clause in the purchase agreement. He, as buyer agreed to pay to remove the tanks; the creditworthy seller agreed to pay the cost of cleanup, if any.

Before closing, the buyer removed the tanks and had extensive soil testing done under the supervision of the government and an environmental engineer. The property turned out to be **clean.** A monitoring well (about $2,000) is the only clean-up type requirement required by law. The tank removal was required by the lender.

Seller silent on fumes

Subscriber is negotiating to buy a 26,000 square foot warehouse building. The 40-year old property has buried gas, diesel, and heating oil tanks. The gas and diesel tanks have not been used in years …except that a heating oil deliveryman mistakenly pumped 4,000 gallons into one.

Leaks are so bad the building has to be evacuated from time to time because of the fumes. The seller did not mention any of this to the buyer. Rather they learned it from a guy who works in the building.

The news accounts I cited in my September and October articles may have seemed remote and improbable to you. I hope these subscriber stories convince you this problem is here now. JTR

90
Environmental Liability

There is an excellent, comprehensive article on the new environmental risks in real estate investing in the March/April 1990 issue of *Units*, the magazine of the National Apartment Association. Unfortunately, the article is also depressing because it points out, without saying it in these words, that it is impossible to be confident that you have taken adequate steps to avoid liability or loss of property value due to contamination.

For example, the article provides the first list I've seen which claims to be a "complete" list of the elements of an environmental audit. That's the **good** news. The **bad** news is there are **35** such elements and I guess it would cost about $100,000 per property to do them all. And that's on a property you are only **considering** buying.

Ain't gonna happen, folks. All the king's Congressmen and all the king's trial lawyers aren't gonna make real estate investors spend $100,000 checking out a prospective purchase.

The article also points out your duty to:

- Inspect **nearby** properties (a one-mile radius is favored by the Federal National Mortgage Association)
- Clean up contamination you find **after** purchase
- **Report yourself** to the EPA if your property has any contamination
- Pay for clean up of contamination caused by **tenants**.

I note that in the aftermath of the recent oil spills...and the resulting astronomical liabilities...Shell Oil has announced that it will no longer transport oil. Think about that. One of the world's largest oil-transporting companies suddenly wants nothing to do with transporting oil.

Similar outright abandonments have occurred in other areas of business. All American makers of intrauterine birth control devices (IUDs) stopped making them to avoid product liability...in spite of the fact that only the Dalkon Shield brand has been found harmful. Many lifelong baby-delivering doctors have stopped delivering babies to avoid malpractice liability.

The obstetricians, oil companies, IUD makers and others have all concluded that liability in those businesses has reached **intolerable** proportions. Me thinks a similar point either has been reached or is about to be reached in some parts of real estate.

We are now told we must inspect the uninspectable (nearby properties), bear unbearable audit and cleanup expenses, and expose to loss an unthinkable percentage of our life savings (100%—There is no insurance or corporate-veil protection). All this we must do for the privilege of maybe getting a real estate return not any better than, and often not as good as, the return we got **before** these astronomical liabilities were conjured up by environmentalists.

So far, the response of the real estate industry has been to manfully soldier on as we have in the face of the countless new, anti-real-estate-owner laws enacted in the **past**. But these environmental laws are not just more annoying laws. They are potentially **ruinous**.

I again urge you to consider the **deedless real estate investing** I've written about in recent years and to consider increasing the **single-family-rental-house** percentage of your portfolio. In general, home owners are not subjected to such liabilities for obvious political reasons. JTR

91
Earthquakes and Real Estate Investors

The common belief that you can neither predict earthquake damage nor prevent it is incorrect. You can avoid high risk properties and, in many cases, greatly reduce the risk in others.

Soil and structure

The U.S. Geological Survey publishes maps showing predicted maximum earthquake intensity. My current house is in an E (weak intensity) zone. Our only loss on October 17th was three glasses. In contrast, the very expensive Marina District of San Francisco is rated B (violent). The Marina District suffered severe property damage in the recent quake. The Cypress section of Interstate 880, which collapsed, is also partly on B-rated soil.

The **structure** is also key. Unreinforced masonry is bad. Wood and steel frame buildings are much better. The '88 Armenian earthquake was not as strong as the October 17th quake. But tens of thousands died because of unreinforced masonry buildings.

In addition to soil and structure, you need to be concerned about **distance to a fault**, geology and structures **uphill** from your property, upstream **dams**, and **adjacent** buildings. On October 17th, a woman was killed in Ford's Department Store in Santa Cruz...by masonry falling off the building next door.

The worst quake in U.S. history hit New Madrid, MO December 16, 1811. Seismologists estimate it was a Richter **10**. Charleston was hit in 1886, Boston in the 1700s. An *NBC News* earthquake map of the U.S. showed fault lines in about two thirds of the states. Quakes occur less often in the Midwest and East. But, because of different geology, a quake that would have a 50-mile damage radius in the West would have perhaps a 500-mile damage radius in the East. Plus non-western states lack quake-resistant buildings.

Earthquake insurance

Buy earthquake insurance. If the building is **not** eligible for quake insurance, do **not** buy it. One company, for example, will not earthquake insure buildings with numerous garage doors. The $300K earthquake policy on my six-year old home cost $414/year and has a $30,000 deductible. You generally cannot buy quake insurance within 100 miles of an epicenter for about 30 to 60 days after one occurs.

Use only insurance companies which are highly rated as to **financial strength**. Avoid companies which **specialize** in earthquake insurance. That's because earthquakes trigger many simultaneous claims. After the 1906 quake, 12 companies were overwhelmed by the claims...including Firemen's Fund. Firemen's Fund, which had $7 million in assets and $11.5 million in claims, paid the claims at 56.5¢ on the dollar and gave stock in a new, debt-free Firemen's Fund for the rest. California Ins. Co. paid every cent of $2.55 million in claims in spite of the fact that it had only $450,000 in assets...by assessing its stockholders the difference.

But 43 American and 16 foreign companies resisted paying 1906 quake claims. German and Austrian insurance companies, which had many immigrant clients in the U.S., either refused to pay claims or chopped off an arbitrary 20 to 25%. You can find out the financial strength and specialization, if any, of an insurance company from the *A.M. Best Guide* which is available in most libraries.

standpoint. Do **not** directly solicit owners of such properties. Do not make low-ball offers. Only make offers with normal offer-to-asking ratios on low offering prices advertised in the classified section or multiple-listing services.

After an earthquake, expect buyers and lenders to increase scrutiny of the earthquake resistance of properties in so-called earthquake country. Also expect the government to ratchet up earthquake-resistance standards for new buildings. In some cases, they may even impose **retrofit** requirements, like sprinklers being required after a major fire.

The most important thing in acquisitions is to avoid properties that are ineligible for earthquake insurance (unless they can be made eligible by economically viable changes to the structure). You must even avoid high-risk, properties which **are** eligible for insurance because of the high deductibles and because the insurance only covers **replacement** cost of the structure, not the **market** value of the property which may also be diminished by the quake.

If you already have a building which is susceptible to earthquake damage, you can frequently have it strengthened cheaply. There are a number of books available on the subject including *Peace of Mind in Earthquake Country* by Peter Yanev. ▥

Effect on property values

Severe earthquake damage causes a temporary reduction in the market value of properties there. I expect that will happen in the Marina District in San Francisco...and other severely damaged areas. The town of Montara, CA suffered a similar downturn in 1982 when severe slides cut off Route 1, its only road to San Francisco, forcing residents to commute by a long circuitous route. The effect was **temporary** in Montara in 1982 (and in San Francisco in 1906 for that matter) simply because the memory fades in about six to 18 months.

In theory, you could profit by buying property in disaster areas cheap after the disaster then holding it until people forget about what happened. But you could get **shot** if you did not handle such investing properly from a public relations

92
War

In my recent articles on the many risks that real estate investors seem to ignore, I included such wide-ranging problems as earthquakes and depressions. But I left off wars. In retrospect, I don't know why.

Wars are less common than recessions...but more common than depressions. We've had four big wars in this century.

Do wars affect real estate? You betcha. But in different ways in different places. There is no such thing as bad economic news. Because economics is the study of transactions and it takes two to transact. All economic news is good for one end of the transaction and bad for the other.

Iraq's annexation of Kuwait and the ensuing worldwide trade embargo will probably **raise** property values in the Oil Patch. But it will **hurt** values near military bases where troops have deployed. I was a member of the 82nd Airborne Division in 1969. That division is now partly in Saudi Arabia. When I lived in Fayetteville, NC (next to Fort Bragg, home of the 82nd), people were still talking about the economic hard times when the division was sent to Santo Domingo in the mid '60s.

To the extent that the Kuwait tension causes higher interest rates and/or recession, it hurts **all** real estate. And higher oil prices and the threat of gas lines hurt remote properties like those in **resort** areas. Master-metered buildings are probably also less desirable now than before Iraq invaded Kuwait, although that is an illogical response. Owners of master-metered buildings should be able to raise rents to match any utility expense increases because master-metered buildings become more attractive to tenants when their electric bills shoot up.

In short, people who confidently predict that their properties will increase in value are implicitly claiming to be able to predict the behavior not only of earthquake faults and macroeconomic forces but also the behavior of the Saddam Husseins of the world.

The fact is, real estate values are determined by countless forces which no one could possibly predict. There certainly is no basis for belief that real estate always appreciates.𝕁𝕋ℝ

PART ELEVEN

REGIONS
AND REAL ESTATE RETURNS

93
Huge Regional Differences in Returns

February 1988

You knew that rents and home prices in the New York area were higher than in the Detroit area. But did you know that the New York prices were more **double** the Detroit prices...while the rents were only **8%** higher. That has investment implications.

Detroit

Let's say you bought a suburban Detroit house for $88,100 and rented it out for $621. With 20% down, your mortgage would be 80% x $88,100 = $70,480. At 10% interest for 30 years, the payment would be $618.51. That takes up **all** the rent. The property taxes, insurance, repairs, vacancy loss, etc. would all be **negative cash flow**.

That's an unacceptable return unless you assume appreciation rates of about 10%. But if the **median** figures for the Detroit area get that close to break-even, you can probably find positive cash flow in some of Detroit's submarkets.

New York

With 20% down, your $181,100 house will have a mortgage of 80% x $181,100 = $144,880 and payments (10%, 30 years) of $1,271.43. It's going to be hard to make that payment with a $671 rent check. Not to mention the taxes, insurance, etc.

Imprecise Figures

Before I go any farther, I hasten to add that these figures are very imprecise. I suspect the New York rent figure includes **rent-controlled** apartments. If you avoid them...as you should...your rent would be higher...but probably not high enough.

Also, the rent numbers were compiled by **government** officials. If they compile rent figures the way they run the government, I wouldn't bet my life savings on them.

Finally, these figures are regional **medians**. Real estate investors who know what they are doing would reject **most** of the property in any region as overpriced for investment purposes.

Huge Difference In Gross Rent Multipliers

Area	Home price	3br rent	GRM
Detroit	$88,100	$621	142
Cleveland	$78,500	$535	147
Miami	$102,500	$662	155
St. Louis	$86,400	$546	158
Chicago	$114,400	$701	163
Philadelphia	$108,600	$615	177
Kansas City	$93,900	$520	181
San Francisco	$184,400	$1,018	181
Portland	$104,300	$570	183
Boston	$176,200	$948	186
Baltimore	$118,600	$624	190
Atlanta	$120,300	$631	191
San Diego	$152,100	$783	194
Houston	$100,600	$500	201
Seattle	$124,600	$615	203
Los Angeles	$170,300	$840	203
DC	$155,900	$741	210
Minneapolis	$139,200	$645	216
Denver	$141,000	$624	226
Dallas-Fort Worth	$127,000	$535	237
New York	$181,100	$671	270

Sources: Prices, *U.S. Housing Markets*; Rents, HUD Fair Market Rents for Section 8, 52 *Federal Register* 48205

My purpose in showing you these figures is not to declare Detroit the nation's best rental house area. Rather I am suggesting that just because the area where you live is so high priced that you can't make the numbers work does not mean the whole country is the same. And for those of you who oppose absentee investing with religious fervor, the point to be made is that you will probably find similar huge variations in yield in the various **submarkets** of the market where you live.

It's A Numbers Game

Investing is a numbers game. Your goal is the highest return on investment. There is no prize for investing close to your residence. Nor is there any investment prize for investing in the most "desirable" neighborhood near your home. Indeed, there is an investment booby prize for that. Some of the cities that score **best** (lowest gross rent multiplier is best) on the accompanying chart are considered less desirable. The same is probable true of your market. Typically, the best investment submarkets are the lower priced, but non-slum, neighborhoods. That's where you get the **highest cap rates** (net operating income divided by price). And the **appreciation** over the long run is generally the same on both high and low priced neighborhoods.

I used to kid a Realtor® friend of mine who sold real estate in depressed Camden, NJ...until he pointed out that low-priced properties there had been appreciating at **10%** per year...at a time when the affluent suburbs of Cherry Hill and Haddonfield were **also** appreciating at 10% per year.

When the appreciation rates are the same, you invest where you get the best cap rate. ЛTR

94

Should You Invest in One-Industry Areas?

August 1986

In recent years, a number of one-industry areas have made news as lousy places to invest in real estate. Farm land. Detroit a few years back. Oil-producing areas recently. Silicon Valley industrial property. The Mexican border.

Don't do it

Should you invest in one-industry areas? I think **not**. Especially if it's outside of a major metropolitan area. I used to think there were two exceptions to that rule: Houston and DC. Houston was a one-industry town. But what an industry! Who could ever imagine a glut of oil after the gas lines of '73 and '79?

That leaves DC. Could something happen to make **its** "industry," government, go into decline? I don't know what. But after seeing what happened to Houston, I doubt even DC is invulnerable. (*Indeed, DC was overbuilt in the late 80s.*)

Big metropolitan areas like Houston and Detroit will ultimately pull out of their slumps even if their major industries do not. Too much human and infrastructure capital are in those areas to not attract other industries eventually.

But I have no such confidence in **smaller** areas. I fear that their economies can turn down and stay down much longer than the average real estate investment holding period of five to ten years.

Investing in real estate or oil?

Investing in real estate in the oil area of West Texas is probably a lot like buying oil futures...only **worse**. Because in **boom** times, small, isolated towns have so much buildable land on which competitors can put up property. But in **bad** times, there are such great distances to other employment opportunities. So you can **lose** big, but it's hard to **win** big in such places.

Oil towns will be back economically when oil comes back. And if oil does **not** come back, oil towns probably won't either. Same goes for other small one-industry areas.

Don't invest in one-industry areas. That includes agricultural areas, mining areas, military bases, college towns, factory towns, and government towns. But if you **must**, make sure they are **big** one-industry areas. JTR

95

Texas Marketing in The Northeast Market?

I once wrote an article titled "Positive Cash Flow Makes You Lazy." Northeastern real estate investors who have owned their properties for more than a couple years have positive cash flow. In addition, their rental market is amazingly tight. They can rent apartments by putting a business card in the window... on the second floor. So the contrast between Texas, where I own apartments, and the Northeast, is extreme. Here's a comparison:

There's still a point to be made, though. Especially to those Northeastern owners who are just order takers. You guys are leaving money on the table. Lots of it. In both your cash flow and your property value.

Raise rents until your vacancy rate is 5%

Raise your rents. Raise your vacancies higher than you ever have before... by a

Marketing	Texas	Northeast
"Now Leasing" banners	Always	Never
Office hours	8 to 6	By appointment
Classified ad	Display	No need
Paint, clean, etc.	Always	WYSIWYG
Features signs	Usually	Never
Rent decreases?	You bet	Are you kidding?

I'm overstating it, of course. Some Northeastern apartments market. Especially the larger ones. And as I've stated on a number of occasions, many Texas apartment owners are flailing... wasting money on marketing gimmicks which are not cost-effective.

larger jump than ever before. If you don't **have** any vacancies, issue larger, and larger **renewal** raises until you **get** some vacancies. If you **get** the higher asking rent, raise the next vacancy to even **higher** levels.

At the same time, make **renewals** pay the same as the most recent move-in. Not a penny less. I know what many landlords will say. That'd mean $100 rent increase notices. Send them. I don't have room here to explain why it's the right thing. See Chapters 1, 2, and 3 ("Setting Rents," "Signs of Low Rents," and "Excuses for Not Raising Rents") in my book, *How to Manage Residential Property for Maximum Cash Flow and Resale Value* ($21.95 800-635-5425).

Eventually, after you've dramatically increased your cash flow and property value, your vacancy rate will rise to 5%. That's when I want you to go Texan...or at least moderately so.

Texas marketing

Clean up the vacancies. New drapes and carpet when needed. Clean ovens and refrigerators. Fresh paint. Put up a "Now Leasing" banner or two ($22 for 3 x 10 banner from World Division, USA, 800-433-9843). Establish office hours if you have 50 units or more. Stick a few Burma Shave-type signs along the street saying "Dishwashers" or whatever. Put a big enough ad in the paper to tell about your main selling points. Have a well-groomed, pleasant, sales-oriented, leasing agent.

If you've never lowered rents, you're too low

I asked the audience at a recent Long Island, NY Real Estate Investors Association speech to raise their hands if they had ever **lowered** rent. Not one hand went up. The only way to never need to lower rents is to always be well **below** market value.

Texas apartment owners have lowered rents. Negative cash flow makes you energetic...open to new approaches ...more objective.

With the exception of climate and regional fashion, there is no reason why non-rent controlled apartments in Long Island should be marketed any different from apartments in Dallas. But visit each and you'll see that they sure **are** being marketed differently.

The optimum approach is a moderate version of what Texas apartment owners do. Don't adopt such extreme measures as give aways or dressing your managers in clown suits to hand out brochures at Safeway. (You think I'm kidding?)

But **do** mimic the less costly marketing techniques. And, of course, don't forget that **raising rents** is the whole reason for doing this. Until you get rid of your 100% occupancy by raising rents, marketing is a total waste of money.

The most valuable advice I've ever given

Of all the advice I've given over the years, the most valuable has been the admonition to raise rents on both new and existing tenants until your vacancy rate hits 5%. Every year, people call or write or approach me in person at speeches and say they tried it and were **amazed** at how much they were able to raise rents.

One example I mentioned in my apartment management book resulted in the owner of $20 million worth of apartments (in the late '70s) getting an average $70 per unit monthly increase ...thereby raising the value of his apartments by $6 million.

And this took place in the span of **ninety days** after the lunch during which I told him to raise the rents. JTR

96
"Places Rated"
For Investment

Would you believe Lawton, Oklahoma tops a statistical study of rental property investment yields?

Places Rated Almanac

Rand McNally's *Places Rated Almanac 2nd edition* contains detailed information for 329 metropolitan areas about:

• Rents
• Energy utility costs
• Property taxes and
• Home prices

I wrote that investment returns vary greatly around the nation in "Huge Regional Differences in Returns" in the February issue (See Chapter 93). But I used **gross** rent multipliers in that article. In the October '87 issue (See Chapter 78), I wrote "Why You Should Use Cap Rates to Analyze Small Properties" in which I urged you to also take **expenses** like taxes and utilities into account when selecting even small properties. *Places Rated Almanac* gave me the data to look

at the **net** income yields around the country.

Partial yield

I calculated the yield a rental house would have after taxes, energy utilities, and mortgage payment but before other expenses. Because *Places Rated* does not give other expense figures. But since those left-out expenses are either small or similar nationwide, the results shouldn't be too far off.

Also, *Places Rated* was published in 1985 and relies heavily on the 1980 Census. That's hard to avoid because this kind of detailed data is not gathered annually.

Here's the formula I used:

[(monthly rent x 12) - (annual property taxes + annual energy bill + annual mortgage payment)] ÷ home sale price = "yield"

Here are the 25 best and worst. If you want the all-329 areas printout, send me a self-addressed, stamped, business-size envelope.

Best Investment Yields		Worst Yields	
1. Lawton, OK	-4.64%	329. Pittsburgh, PA	-10.07%
2. Richland, WA	-4.79%	328. Fall River, MA	-9.59%
3. Odessa, TX	-4.89%	327. New York, NY	-9.43%
4. Yakima, WA	-5.05%	326. New Orleans, LA	-9.43%
5. Pascagoula, MS	-5.06%	325. Newark, NJ	-9.31%
6. Casper, WY	-5.07%	324. New Bedford,MA	-9.06%
7. Spokane, WA	-5.13%	323. Salem, MA	-9.01%
8. Enid, OK	-5.15%	322. Stamford, CT	-8.94%
9. Clarksville, TN	-4.19%	321. Bergen, NJ	-8.84%
10. Jacksonville, FL	-5.20%	320. Norwalk, CT	-8.65%
11. Tacoma, WA	-5.20%	319. Lawrence, MA	-8.65%
12. Huntsville, AL	-5.21%	318. New Britain, CT	-8.56%
13. Phoenix, AZ	-5.23%	317. Atlantic City, NJ	-8.54%
14. Lake Charles, LA	-5.23%	316. Bridgeport, CT	-8.50%
15. Beaumont, TX	-5.25%	315. Jersey City, NJ	-8.48%
16. Alexandria, LA	-5.27%	314. Portsmouth, NH	-8.45%
17. Olympia, WA	-5.30%	313. Worcester, MA	-8.44%
18. Vancouver, WA	-5.31%	312. Boston, MA	-8.43%
19. Jacksonville, NC	-5.31%	311. Providence, RI	-8.43%
20. Boise, ID	-5.33%	310. Fitchburg, MA	-8.43%
21. Anchorage, AK	-5.33%	309. Manchester, NH	-8.40%
22. Oklahoma City, OK	-5.34%	308. Orange Cnty,CA	-8.38%
23. Chattanooga, TN	-5.35%	307. Pawtucket, RI	-8.37%
24. Florence, AL	-5.37%	306. Binghamton, NY	-8.33%
25. Fayetteville, NC	-5.38%	305. Waterbury, CT	-8.25%

Sources: *Significant Features of Fiscal Federalism* by the Advisory Committee on Intergovernmental Relations, Department of Energy *Typical Electric Bills*, Energy Information Administration, *1980 Census of Population and Housing*

All negative cash flow

Note that every single area...even champion Lawton...runs negative cash flow...and that's **before** taking into account six other expense categories. One reason is the rent figures are for both apartments and houses. The **good news** is these figures are the **average** for the area. *Real Estate Investor's Monthly* readers don't do average deals.

In "Sellers Who are Likely to Sell Cheap" in the October '87 issue, I said "about 98% of the properties are **off limits** to you." Because they are overpriced in relation to their net income. Roughly speaking, that's true in places like Lawton, too. Although a higher percentage of Lawton properties make investment sense than Pittsburgh properties.

In other words, there are indeed huge differences in returns from community to community. But there are still **no** places in America where an **average** deal makes investment sense. Shifting your acquisition search to a better area will make it easier for you to find a deal that makes sense. But **no** amount of shifting will make it **easy**.

If real estate investing were easy, everybody'd be doing it.

.5% to 2%

Nationally, you need to buy a property on terms that rank the deal in the top .5% to 2% of all deals to get a proper cash return. If you invest in an area at the bottom of the net income chart...like Pittsburgh...you have to get a deal in the top .5% or maybe even top .1% or .2% of the market. Whereas in communities at the **top** of the net income chart, you can probably find the same return by buying in the top 2% or maybe even top 4% or 5% of the market.

That translates into time. If you only buy .2% of the properties you look at, you have to look at 1 ÷ .2% = 500 properties for every deal you do. It may take years in the Pittsburgh area for 500 properties which fit your size requirements to become available to buy. Meanwhile, deals with the numbers you are waiting for are popping up ten times as often in other areas of the country.

Travel, wait, speculate

So if you refuse to invest absentee ...and you live in an area with relatively bad yield numbers... you are sentencing yourself either to a life of years of property inspection for every purchase...or to **speculation**. A speculator is one who buys losers (negative cash flow) and hopes market-wide appreciation in value will cover his negative cash flow and then some. In contrast, an **investor** buys properties with **positive** cash flow and/or unrealized potential. His return on investment is wired from the start. If market-wide appreciation occurs, he benefits from that just like the speculators. The **difference** is that the speculators are **completely** dependent on market-wide appreciation.

Gold mining

Mining terms turn up in real estate discussions. Real estate investors and agents "prospect" for properties. Val Cabot wrote a book called "*Gold Mining in Foreclosure Properties.*" The analogy is apt.

So apt, I went to the library and got a book on real gold mining to see if it would give me any insights into investing. Apparently, it's not hard to find gold. The trick is finding it in sufficient **quantity** and with sufficient **speed** that you earn more than the minimum wage. You do that by looking in places where the **probability** of finding gold is **higher**. The book had both maps of the U.S. showing gold find areas and diagrams of streams and rock formations showing where gold is most likely to be found.

This article is analogous to the gold mining book's map of the U.S. Other articles I've written like "Profit Opportunities in Bad Foundations" (last month), "Case Study: Title Problem = Profit" (October '86), and "Sellers Who are Likely to Sell Cheap" (October '87, See Chapter 15) are analogous to the book's diagrams of streams and rock formations.

Can you imagine someone deciding to become a gold miner but refusing to leave the metropolitan area where he had been living for the last several years.

"Yep, I'm a gonna stop shaving and start prospecting right now."
"Where ya heading? To California or Nevada?"
"Nope. I believe in working the area you know best. I'm staying right here in the Chicago area."

It would be not quite as dumb...but still dumb...to go to a prime gold area in Nevada and select your digging site by throwing a dart at a map of the county.

To find real estate "nuggets" in sufficient quantities and with sufficient speed to make it worth the investment of time and money and risk...you've got to go where the "high-grade ore" is. That means selecting the high-yield geographical area and the high-yield properties within that geographical area. You're not likely to be looking in a high-yield geographical area if your only "selection" criterion is where your last job required you to live.

Limits of the analogy

Like any analogy, this one has its limits. Gold is a fungible commodity the price of which is set by world markets.

Real estate, on the other hand, is **unique** and its price is set in **local** markets. The fundamental skill of real estate investing is out-appraising the other players in the market. And appraising requires some local knowledge.

So, yes, there's more to real estate investing than just finding which community's properties have the highest net yield. But finding the high-yield areas is an important **part** of it.

Invest In Fort Sill?

I would not invest in many of the top 25 areas in this study. They are too small...their economies too narrowly based. According to the *Almanac of American Politics* 1988, Lawton's major industries are "Goodyear and the Army's Fort Sill." When you buy real estate in a place like Lawton, you are really investing in Goodyear and Fort Sill for the most part.

Phoenix is the only large, diversified economy in the top 25 in this study. Some of the Washington State cities are in or near the Seattle metropolitan area. Seattle is more diversified than it was in 1970 when Boeing's work force was cut from 101,000 to 38,000. But the *Almanac of American Politics* still describes Washington as a state whose "economy is vulnerable to slumps in a few industries...lumber...[and] Boeing." (The *Almanac* allows that "Washington may be on the way to overcoming these problems.")

Pittsburgh

Ironically, the city that fares **worst** when you rearrange *Places Rated* data by **investment yield**, Pittsburgh, PA...is the city that *Places Rated* said was "the **best place to live** in America." Investing only where you would live is a classic real estate mistake.

The best **overall** real estate investment yields (tax savings + cash flow + appreciation) are generally found at the low end of the price spectrum. JTR

97
Oklahoma City
Bargains

June 1989

According to real estate agent Mike Goodwin (405-691-6879), you can buy homes in Oklahoma City for $10,000 to $20,000 and resell them for $20,000 to $30,000 after spending about $5,000 fixing them up. After fix-up, the houses rent for $400 to $450 per month ...often with Section 8 assistance. The sellers are the Department of Housing and Urban Development, the VA, or the Federal National Mortgage Association.

Terms are good, too. Goodwin says VA will sell on a **no-money down** basis at 10% interest. For a limited time, they ran a special in which you could get a 7.5% interest rate if you put 5% down. Those of you in higher-priced areas may need me to call to your attention the fact that 5% of $10,000 is a mere $500. Non-owner-occupied HUD houses can be had for 15% down.

Goodwin says some junkers can be bought for **$2,000 to $3,000** and will sell for $25,000 or so after about $10,000 in fix-up.

Two actual case histories:

• Two duplexes bought for $25K each. **$1,475 positive cash flow**/month from the four units.

• Two duplexes bought for $22K and $23K. Leased to Section 8 tenants for $350 per month per unit. **Positive cash flow is $1,425** per month.

Goodwin says the investors buying these buildings also frequently qualify for **low-income tax credits**. One word of caution: As in Anchorage which I wrote about in the 1/89 and 2/89 issues, there are thousands of vacant housing units overhanging the market. JTR

98
More on Oklahoma City

September 1989

In response to my article on Oklahoma City (6/89 issue), real estate educator Ron Starr visited that city and looked at property. He more or less confirmed that deals were available on the positive-cash flow terms I reported in the article. He also talked to Oklahoma City apartment house broker Jim Alexander (405-685-3494) who said **luxury** apartment buildings there were selling at prices which gave their buyers 10% cap rates; **middle income** apartment buildings, **12%**. JTR

99
Double-Digit Cap Rates In Memphis

September 1989

According to Steven Levy of Olswanger & Michel, Inc. (901-454-6079), it's not unusual for attractive income properties in the Memphis area to sell at prices which give the buyer an 11% to 12% cap rate (net operating income divided by price).

One of his current deals is the sale of an 11-unit apartment building for under $200,000. Gross annual income is $36,000 which is a gross rent multiplier of $200,000 ÷ $36,000 = 5.56. If you put $50,000 down and got a 30-year, $150,000 mortgage at 10%, your annual mortgage payment would be $15,796.29. If the operating expense ratio was 47.5% (the 1987 Memphis median according to the Institute of Real Estate Management), your net operating income would be 100% - 47.5% = 52.5% x $36,000 = $18,900 leaving cash flow of $18,900 - $15,796 = $3,104.

Levy, who used to live in San Francisco, says one of the main differences between the California and Memphis markets is the absence of a history of high appreciaton rates and therefore an inability to use the greater fool theory to justify high prices in Memphis. I say that no one can predict the future appreciation rates in either California or Memphis and that the California market is far more speculative than the Memphis market. JTR

100
Median House $45,100
In Youngstown, OH

August 1990

The latest quarterly home price report from the National Association of Realtors® says the cheapest homes in any metropolitan area are now in Youngstown, Ohio where the median is $45,100. With all the lawsuits and environmental liability flying around these days, I find myself musing about living in such places. Say the feds tell me I owe $3,000,000 to clean up a leaking underground tank I didn't know I owned. I file Chapter 11, take the $45,000 California law lets me keep, and pay all cash for a home in Youngstown. I've never been there, but they must have tv, supermarkets, schools, Little League, and a shopping mall. And, after all, what else is there to life?

In 1983, I wrote an article on the subject of how much money do you need? At that time, I figured about $100,000 a year was all you could use. Above that level, all you could do with the money was show off or adopt expensive hobbies (boats, horses, planes, etc.). I got more comment about that article over the years than any other I've written. (I can't sell you a copy because I wrote it for another newsletter.)

Now, having lived a good part of my life at the all-you-need level, I find myself somewhat envying the shallow pocketed. The people who seemingly do not worry about being sued for $1,750,000, who do not agonize over how to fill Form 8582 ("Passive Activity Loss Limitations"), who do not read daily of some new proposed law which could subject them to some horrific liability for activities recently thought legal.

On the other hand, I know a guy who was head of his firm's San Francisco office for many years. Then they transferred him to Cleveland (50 miles from Youngstown). After being there two days on a house hunting trip, he resigned and west back to San Francisco. I also remember that I spent most of my life aspiring to be more or less where I've been for a decade or so.

I'm glad there are still places where you can buy a house for $45,100. No doubt there are rural homes for even less. However, I'm not so convinced the Youngstown life is adequate that I'd leave sunny California voluntarily. But if the feds or some plaintiff's attorney show up at the door with a million-dollar clean-up bill or judgment some day...well, Go Browns! JTR

101
Niche, Niche, Who's Got a Niche?

April 1988

All of America, it seems, is either overbuilt or overpriced. So I'm looking for a niche. Me and two million other investors.

Surely somewhere in this vast land of a hundred million housing units there must be an opportunity to make a real estate profit other than by just hoping prices will go up.

Waiting lists

My biggest successes came from buying waiting list buildings and raising their rents to market. That would still work. If I could find a waiting list building...that's not rent-controlled.

You can tell an overbuilt market by ads which offer rent concessions, security deposits in the $100 or less range, and leasing office hours in the 9 to 5 or greater range.

Virginia's DC suburbs

DC has rent control. And the whole Washington area is overrun with the kind of pro-government folks who oppose growth. That could mean a tight market. Plus, Virginia has a state law prohibiting cities from passing any landlord/tenant laws...like rent control.

Check the paper

To check out these assumptions, I call a college roommate who lives in Alexandria and ask him to send me the *Washington Post's* big weekly real estate section. When it arrives, I scan down the page looking for those dreaded words, "One Month's Rent Free."

Damn! I find lots of rent concessions, low security deposits, unspecified "specials," and office hours that start at 9 am or earlier. But on the other hand, I met a Northern Virginia landlord/Realtor® at a seminar last week...and she assured me the rental market there was generally tight.

Alexandria resident, Ted Jonas, says my idea might work there. But he's had to invest in Maryland. He says most low rent stuff in the DC area is vacuumed up by rehabbers.

Where rent control is prohibited or discouraged by law		
State	Authority	(Updated 11-90)
AZ	Title 33, Chapter 3 Article 1 AZ Revised Statutes §33-132-1329, Title 43, Chapter 10, Article 4 ARS §43-1060	
CA	(non-residential) Title 5,Prt.4,Div.3,CCC Ch.2.6,§1954.25	
CO	§1, Article 12, Title 38 CO Revised Statutes 1973, part 3	
FL	Chapter 77-50 FS 1985 166.043	
GA	Article 1, Chapter 7, Title 44, Code Of GA, § 44-7-19	
ID	H.B. 555 (3-28-90)	
LA	Chapter 1, Code Title IX, Title 9 LA Revised Statutes 1950 part V RS9:3258	
MI	pending Senate Bill 583	
MN	Laws of MN Chapter 551 S.F. No. 1683 471.995-6	
MO	H.B. 602 (5-18-89)	
MS	Senate Bill 2006 (3-16-90)	
NC	§1, Chapter 42, General Statutes of NC §42-14.1 (1987)	
NH	Girard v. Town of Allenstown, 428 Atlantic Reporter, 2d Series 488 (Supreme Court of NH, 1981)	
OK	OK Statutes §14-101.1 of Title 11 (3/21/88)	
OR	OR Legislative Assembly House Bill 2505 (1985)	
SC	Code Of Laws of SC §27-39-60 (1976)	
SD	Senate Bill 260 (2-23-90)	
TX	Chapter 472, Act of the 51st Legislature 1949 (Article 12691-1, Vernon Texas Civil Statutes) §1b	
UT	§1, Utah Code of 1953, §57-19-1 (1987)	
VA	Codes of VA Chapter 13-2 §55-248.3 with §15.1 - 839, 491.8	
WA	Chapters 35.21, 36.01 RCW	

That's a tight market

In contrast, try to find a concession in the Berkeley, California classified. For that matter, try to find an apartment-for-rent ad. Berkeley is an unbelievably tight apartment market. It's also under draconian rent control and no place for a landlord to hang around longer than it takes to watch a Cal football game.

That's one way to spot a tight market. Not only few rent concessions in the classified section but disproportionately few ads at all given the number of rental units in the area.

Minneapolis?

During a call to the National Multi Housing Council (202-659-3381) to verify that Virginia has a law requiring all landlord/tenant laws be passed at the state level, I learn that there are seventeen states with laws that prohibit or discourage rent control. And Minnesota is one of them.

Hmmm. I wonder if the Minneapolis area is overbuilt? Off to the out-of-town newspaper store to buy a *Minneapolis Star*.

Same as Virginia. Lots of concessions, low security deposits, "specials," and extended hours. Kansas City paper showed the same conditions there.

It appears the only waiting list apartment markets in the country are in or near severely rent-controlled towns...which controls preclude increasing the value of the building by raising the rent to market.

One could try buying buildings in adjarent or nearby un-rent-controlled towns. But in the absence of legislative protection against rent control, you are taking a chance of paying an uncontrolled price for a building that may subsequently **become** rent controlled. Rent control typically causes apartment building values to decline.

How about non-residential?

Could there be such a niche in non-residential? Find a non-residential building, like a retail center, with waiting-list-like, below-market rents. Buy it for a price which reflects the low rents. Then raise the rents up to market. Which might be 15% to 25% higher...thereby raising the building value 15% to 25%.

Rent control is not much of a threat to non-residential. The only state that ever had retail rent control, California, now has a state law which prohibits non-residential rent control. However, **lease** terms are longer in non-residential. So you would not be able to raise rents until the lease permitted.

Plus, it's harder to tell when non-residential rents are too low...because the market is thinner and more volatile than residential. And vacancies tend to last longer. So you'd want to play the nonresidential game in such a way that if you guessed **wrong**, it would not wipe you out. That is, structure deals so you could make your payments even if you had a prolonged high vacancy rate...say 33% for a year.

Micro-niches

At the moment, there are few, if any, **markets** which offer opportunity in a market-wide sense. Too many builders found those markets and spoiled them a couple years ago. Austin is an extreme example. When Houston became overbuilt, statistics showed Austin had the state's lowest vacancy rate. Developers poured into Austin and gave it one of the most severe cases of overbuilding in the country.

So you're going to have to look for micro-niches...one-property "**situations**." "Situations" can be found in all markets at **all** times. Although they are **harder** to find in times like these than in better times.

I may try looking for a tight **building**, not market...at the bottom of the income property range (4 to 10 units)...in a market where rent control is statutorily discouraged. Such a building would be big enough that a buyer would pay a price based on the rents. But it's small enough that many of the owners would

be incompetent managers who are ignorant of the fact that their rents are below market.

If real estate investing were easy, everybody'd be doing it. JTR

102
Profits in
View Liberation

June 1987

A property with a view is worth more than one without. Often, much more. Sometimes, the view is **blocked**. In many cases, you can remove what's blocking the view for less than the increase in value that results. That's a profit opportunity.

Trees and shrubs

Trees and shrubs sneak up on you. They're cute, harmless little things when you or your neighbors plant them. And they rarely block a view when planted. But then they grow.

According to a May 26th *San Francisco Chronicle* story, Berkeley home owner Madi Bacon built a home with a "million dollar" view 40 years ago. Since then, down-hill neighbors planted trees which grew up to block her view.

Some property owners in that neighborhood claim such blockages can reduce property values by 25%. Bay Area appraiser, Frank App, M.A.I., says, "25% is well within the realm of possibility." Ray Brown, past president of the San Francisco Board of Realtors®, says his firm recently was asked to appraise the value of a **partial** view blockage in that city. $60,000 was the figure they came up with.

U.S. Housing Markets (313-963-9441) said homes in the Los Angeles/San Diego area generally have 60% improvement ratios (value of building divided by total value of building and land) but that **view** lots in Orange County (between LA and San Diego) have 25% improvement ratios. That roughly means that the view adds 60% - 25% = 35% to the value of the property.

How to get rid of the tree or shrub

Brown says the simplest, most common way to get rid of a view-blockage is for the blockee to offer to pay the cost of trimming the offending vegetation.

With few exceptions, you cannot compel trimming or removal of someone else's trees or shrubs by suing. Common law gives you no such right. Some municipalities have tree/view ordinances. As far as I know, none of those laws has been tested for constitutionality.

Some laws give you the right to **solar access.** You may be able to use a solar access law to get your view unblocked.

View easement

Trimming is a temporary solution. Although it may be long **enough** if you immediately sell the property after the view has been liberated.

Better you should try to persuade the owner of the offending property to grant you a view **easement**...which **does** give you the legal right to sue to have a tree or shrub trimmed. You have to **pay** something for the view easement in order to make it enforceable. If the owner of the offending property is greedy, you may have to pay a lot. If he's too greedy, he will demand so much that there is no profit left for you.

Deed restriction

Another solution which gives you or your successors the right to sue to force trimming is a deed restriction. You could persuade the owner of the offending property to put such a deed restriction is his deed when he sells. Or you might even buy the property yourself, then resell it **with** the deed restriction. If the owner of the offending property is hostile, buy his property through a **third party** who appears unconnected to you.

The purchase/resale option has a substantial **transaction costs** disadvantage. But if the view's good enough, it's still worth it.

Other obstructions

Trees and shrubs aren't the only things that block views. Cooling towers, pitched roofs, parapets, etc. can do it. If the view is blocked by such inanimate, unoccupied objects, a profit opportunity arises. Cooling tower owners do not need for the tower to have a view.

You could pay to **move** the tower...to **your** property if no other suitable location is available. You could pay to **replace** the tower with a lower profile version.

If you **do** pay to remove such an obstruction, be sure to insist on an easement preventing any future blocking of the view. Otherwise, the property owner may come back for more. Like a blackmailer who's never satisfied.

Read the laws and records carefully

Although you do not have a common law right to sue to get rid of a view obstruction...and you rarely have a statutory (specific law) right to file such a suit...there are **other** laws which you might be able to use to accomplish the same purpose.

In addition to solar access laws, there are also **building codes, prior deed restrictions, prior easements, planning requirements,** etc. If you cannot get the obstruction removed on a friendly basis, you may find it profitable to go over all pertinent laws and restrictions and easements of record with a magnifying glass.

It may be that the current or previous owner of the blocking property built an **illegal addition** to the top of his property. The Russian Consulate did that in San Francisco...and had to remove it. Or that there already is a deed restriction or easement which was ignored or forgotten about.

For example, maybe the lower lot was originally owned by a previous owner of the upper (blocked) lot. And he was concerned about his view back in 1922. So he put an appropriate deed restriction or easement on the lower lot. Subsequent owners of the blocking property, however, either did not know about the restriction or easement (they'd normally be told in title papers at closing) or decided to ignore it. Owners of the **blocked** property would not ordinarily **ever** hear about the restriction or easement.

If you find a helpful law or recorded restriction or easement, bring it to the offending owner's attention in a friendly way. If that doesn't move him, go to court.

To find deed restrictions or easements, visit the county hall of records. Or you can get a title company to do it for a fee. To find pertinent laws, ask a local real estate lawyer.

How to find view properties

To find view properties, go to where the viewers are looking...and look back. Take telephoto pictures or use binoculars to identify targets for view-liberation. Hiring an aerial photographer might make sense. Then track down the likely candidates and see what you can work out. In cases where you need to buy **both** the blocking property and the blocked, you may find it necessary to get **control** of one or both, then wait until they are for sale.

A **right of first refusal** would be adequate and probably easier and cheaper to get than an option. Record it. **Don't** tell sellers you are a view liberator.

You might profit if you only owned the blocking property. Get control of the blocked property. Then offer to sell the owner of the blocked property a view easement...for **half** what the liberated view would add to his property value.

As with all the other value-increasing techniques I advocate, you can use this two ways. You can make it your **specialty** if you live near a view market. Or you can put it into your **check lists** for normal non-view acquisitions or things to do to your current properties. JTR

103
Greenmail for Real Estate Investors?

March 1989

Settlement offers and agreements are usually confidential. But I heard a rumor that a city with rent control laws offered to settle an anti-rent control suit out of court for big bucks. Other cities rewrote their rent-control ordinances so that they no longer applied to the landlord who sued.

Fontana, CA and El Monte, CA went the exempt-the-plaintiff route. (Such exemptions seem to violate the equal protection clause of the Constitution. Fontana is now being sued by another landlord who alleges unconstitutional taking.)

California's Center for Property Rights (415-386-0100) says in its 11/88 news-letter that Berkeley has made:

"...offers of economically viable settlements in order to evade adverse judgments when judicial success by an owner appears imminent."

Rent control is a fundamental part of the political base of most politicians in rent controlled towns. And rent control is increasingly coming under more effective legal attack (outside of New York).

Scared politicians would rather pay a sort of **greenmail** to the few landlords who sue than risk losing their jobs if the rent control bandwagon were judicially junked. In **corporate** greenmail, executives fearful of losing their jobs pay **shareholder's** money to get the attackers to go away. In **rent-control** greenmail, it's **taxpayer's** money.

Rent-control greenmail delays the judicial day of reckoning for rent-control laws. That hurts landlords as a group. But you can't blame the individual landlord who takes the greenmail and runs. It's a sure thing compared to a "maybe" in court.

Rent-control greenmailing leads to 2 conclusions:

1. If you are a rent-control victim, you ought to consider suing to collect **your** greenmail.
2. The industry as a whole should fund suits so the landlord whose case is being used has no incentive to bail out before a decision. Class action suits seem appropriate as well.

The more people who follow advice number one above, the quicker the politicians will run out of taxpayers' money for greenmail purposes.

I've heard of one settlement offer in the million-dollar range. So greenmailing may be a viable business strategy all by itself...just as it is on Wall Street. (Note: I believe the **payment** of corporate or municipal greenmail is an outrage which is arguably an illegal breach of fiduciary duty. And if it isn't, it **ought** to be. But I find no fault with **recipients** of greenmail who honestly admit what they're doing.)
JTR

104
Why You Can't Find An 8-Unit Apartment Building

Most real estate investors have probably read William Nickerson's book, *How I Turned $1,000 Into $5,000,000 in Real Estate in My Spare Time*. In that book, he moves smoothly from a single-family rental house to a five-unit to 24-unit and so forth. What he does **not** tell you is that many areas of the country have few, if any, five- or 24-unit buildings.

The "rental dwellings" columns in the classified section

Nickerson said to look for income property in the "rental dwellings" columns in the classified section of your local newspaper. I tried. I lived in southern New Jersey then. There **was** no "rental dwellings" column in the three local daily papers. Nor was there such a column by any other name. Occasionally there'd be a listing of an apartment building for sale under the "business opportunities" or some other catchall heading. But most of the time, there were no apartment buildings advertised at all.

The two-family capital of the world

What we **did** have in South Jersey was two-family buildings. So instead of moving **up** after my first property, I moved **sideways**. I bought a two-family, then a three-family, then two more two-families.

Two-family buildings are excellent for your **first** property if you can't afford bigger. But they have poor capitalization rates (net operating income divided by property value) compared to income property (four or more units). So you want to move up out of two-family buildings as soon as you can.

Apparently, not every area of the country has two-family buildings. When I was on a Financial News Network call-in talk show, a caller said he couldn't find any in his upstate New York area.

Nickerson did his thing in Oakland

I interviewed Nickerson in the late '70s. He made his millions investing in Oakland, San Francisco, and Sacramento.

Real Estate Investment Strategy

Regions and Real Estate Returns 281

Those three cities are crawling with small and medium size apartment buildings and non-residential properties.

They also have the support groups Nickerson referred to: large, active apartment associations and real estate agents who specialize in income properties. In my southern New Jersey area, there was only one very small apartment association.

Income property brokerage specialists starved in South Jersey. One I knew was collecting unemployment while working full time as the only apartment house broker for the largest commercial real estate operation in the area.

Today's *San Francisco Chronicle* (June 30, 1986) has almost two full columns under the heading of "Residential Investment Property." And that's on a **Monday.** In contrast, today's *Philadelphia Inquirer* lists a "Commercial and Industrial" section in its classified **index.** But there were **no listings at all.**

Other areas

In Dallas/Fort Worth, there are numerous real estate brokerages which sell nothing but income properties. D/FW also has huge, very active apartment associations. And there are plenty of small and medium size apartment buildings.

Houston, on the other hand, has no zoning. As a result, when they build apartments, they build them **big.** Hundreds of units per complex. That's one of the reasons I chose **not** to invest in Houston. I needed 40, not 400. So aside from its other problems, Houston is not a good place to try to move up from a two-family to a five-family.

Seattle and Tacoma appear to be more like the D/FW or SF areas with lots of small and medium size apartment buildings, strong apartment associations and strong specialized brokers.

The Boston area has zillions of triple-deckers (three flats) and other small investment properties, a strong apartment association, and brokers who specialize in income properties.

Rent control and bad neighborhoods

Unfortunately, many of the areas with lots of small and medium size income properties now have rent control or have turned into bad neighborhoods or both. Rent-controlled San Francisco, San Jose, Los Angeles, Berkeley, NY, and Boston have lots of small and medium size apartment buildings. Oakland has much more crime and poverty than when Nickerson came out with the first edition of his book.

What to do

The small and medium size income property is **nonexistent** in many areas of the country. In other areas, what small and medium size income properties that exist are unacceptable because of rent control or crime or poverty or all of the above.

If you're having trouble finding properties even to look at, you may be in one of those areas. The solution is to **invest elsewhere.** Do **not** do as I did and move sideways into more and more two-families.

You can find areas with the property sizes you need by visiting your out-of-town newspaper dealer and checking the classified sections of papers from other areas. You can also get very thorough data on sizes of apartment buildings ("number of units in structure") in every area of the country from the Census of Housing.ᴶᵀᴿ

INDEX

Roulac, Steve 69
rural 3, 13, 191

S

S corporation 237, 238
Sachs, Dwain 49, 80
Sacramento, CA 25, 80, 281
sale-leaseback 69, 82
Salem, MA 266
Salt Lake City 160
San Diego 236, 261, 276
San Fernando Valley, CA 196
San Fran-
     cisco 18, 158, 171, 236, 244, 246
San Francisco,
     CA 252, 257, 261, 271, 272, 281
San Francisco
     Chronicle 3, 75, 158, 276, 282
San Francisco Examiner 75, 166, 243
San Francisco Examiner. 140
San Jose, CA 282
Santa Ana, CA 161
Santa Barbara v. Adamson 201
Santa Cruz, CA 257
Scarsdale, NY 51
Schaub, John 213
Scher, Les 191
Scott, Mike 97, 110, 222, 223
Seattle *97,* 158, 161, 181
Seattle, WA 222, 261, 268, 282
secrecy 41, 43
securitization 138
Sefton v. San Diego Trust & Savings
     Bank, 238
senior citizen 191
septic tank 191
Sequoia National Forest 43
Shell Oil 255
sheriff's sale 36
Showdown at Gucci Gulch 246
Sierra Club 43
Silicon Valley, CA 102, 146, 166, 246
slide hazard 133
sliver 44, 234
Smart Trust Deed Investing in Califor-
     nia 35
soil test 252
solar access 277
sole proprietor 91
Sonoma County, CA 45
specific performance 52, 53, 54
speculation 168, 169, 170, 267
speculative mania 155, 156, 162
Spokane, WA 266
St. Louis 49, 80, 261
Stamford, CT 266
Starker. *See* exchange

Starr, Ron 44, 45, 270
Statistical Abstract of the United
     States 230
Stephenson, Jim 99
Stephenson System, The 99
Stevens, Mark 43
stock market 179
Stockton, CA 22
store room 1, 3
subdivide 116
subdivision 43
subject to 15, 17, 32
Substance over form 208
substance over form 210
substitution of collateral 185
"suitability" criteria 214
Sunset 249
survey 45, 114
swimming pool. *See* pool
Syracuse, NY 60, 62

T

Tacoma, WA 266, 282
tank 250, 253, 254
Tappan, Bill 97, 104
tax assessor 20
tax attorney. *See* attorneys fees
tax auction 45
tax reform 7, 90, 100, 103, 107, 108
Tax Reform Act of 1984, 75
Tax Reform Act of
     1986 131, 160, 166, 176, 202, 207, 209. *See*
     also TRA
Tax Reform Act of
     1986, 101, 105, 109, 110, 111, 115
Tax Reform Act of
     1986. 225, 226, 233, 235, 237, 246
Tax Reform Acts 234
tax reform law 148, 229, 233, 245
tax sales 44
tenant, bad 101, 124, 125, 133
tenant, drug dealer 242
tenant in common inter-
     est 42, 50, 95, 96, 234
Texas 178, 191, 263
Texas Monthly 96
Thomas,
     Ted 30, 31, 32, 34, 35, 65, 98, 99
Thompson, Paul 22, 23, 24, 25
Tiburon, CA 6
Time 177
timeshare 82, 198, 199, 234
title insurance 53, 66, 84
title prob-
     lem 101, 133, 167, 169, 193, 194, 224, 267
Toffler, Alvin 91
toxic 28, 39, 90, 107, 194. *See also*

environmental audit
toxic chemical   132, 226
toxic liability   100, 126, 229, 233, 235
toxics   230, 237, 248, 252
TRA   117, 131. *See also* Tax Reform
    Act of 1986
Trammel Crow   85
transaction cost   277
Trump, Donald   77, 187
trust, business   238
trust, children's   238
trust, family   238
trust, insurance   238
trust, living   39
TRW   38

U

U.S. Geological Survey   257
U.S. Housing Markets   *127, 261, 276*
unconscionable act law   132
underground oil tank   90
underground petroleum tank   253
underground storage tank   254
underground tank   250, 272
underground toxics   249, 251
Underwood   65
uninsurable   234, 236
Units   *255*
upgrading   85, 95, 118, 119
Urban Land   *245*
US v Argent,   *248*
US v Nepacco   *248*
useless property   44, 45, 47, 234
utilities   133

V

VA   5, 9, 89, 164, 269
vacation lot   234
value in use   42
Vancouver, WA   266
variance   71, 72
Venture Economics   *197*
view   278
view liberation   101, 276
Virginia   274
vulture fund   147
vulture strategy   146, 149, 150

W

W.D. Swigart   *209*
waiting list   273
Wall Street Jour-
    nal   *55, 74, 75, 127, 245*
Walters, Lloyd   35, 38, 39, 40, 234
war   259
Washington, DC   196, 261, 262, 273

Washington Post'   *273*
Washington, state   191, 268
Waterbury, CT   266
Wechsler, Steve   60
wells   191
Weseman v Latham,   *64*
Western Land Bank   44, 45, 46
Western Mobilehome Association   192
Worcester, MA   266
World Division, USA   264

Y

Yakima, WA   266
Yanev, Peter   258
Yoshimura, Connie   130
Youngstown, OH   272

Z

Zaccaro, John   187
zon-
    ing   3, 12, 45, 71, 122, 139, 201, 282
zoning, down   117, 120, 139, 245, 246
zoning, up-   96, 101, 119, 227

John T. Reed's Order Form

	Unit Price	Total
Newsletter		
_____ one-year subscriptions to *John T. Reed's Real Estate Investor's Monthly* (12 monthly issues)	$ 96.00	$_____
_____ two-year subscriptions to *John T. Reed's Real Estate Investor's Monthly* (24 monthly issues)	$186.00	$_____
_____ binders for newsletters (holds 24 issues)	$ 7.00	$_____
_____ back issues (Please see catalog for list. <u>Minimum order is 3.</u>) 1 to 11 back issues	$ 7.00 ea.	$_____
12 or more back issues	$ 6.50 ea.	$_____
All back issues starting Feb. '86	$ 6.25 ea.	$_____

Seminars

Current seminars will be listed in our catalog which we will send you upon request.

Books

_____ copies of *Aggressive Tax Avoidance for Real Estate Investors*	$23.95	$_____
_____ copies of *How to Increase the Value of Real Estate*	$19.95	$_____
_____ copies of *How to Manage Residential Property for Maximum Cash Flow and Resale Value*	$21.95	$_____
_____ copies of *Office Building Acquisition Handbook* (loose leaf)	$39.95	$_____
_____ copies of *Real Estate Investor's Monthly on Real Estate Investment Strategy*	$39.95	$_____
_____ copies of *Residential Property Acquisition Handbook*	$19.95	$_____

Cassettes   (Two 60-minute cassettes in a binder)

_____ copies of *High Leverage Real Estate Financing*	$29.95	$_____
_____ copies of *How to Buy Real Estate for at Least 20% Below MarketValue*	$29.95	$_____
_____ copies of *How to Find Deals That Make Sense in Today's Market*	$29.95	$_____
_____ copies of *How to Manage Residential Property for Maximum Cash Flow and Resale Value*	$29.95	$_____
_____ copies of *How to Save Tens of Thousands of Tax Dollars by Exchanging*	$29.95	$_____

Software

_____ copies of *Landlording™ On Disk* software by Leigh Robinson		
IMPORTANT: <u>Circle one</u>: Macintosh OR IBM 5 1/4" OR IBM 3 1/2"	$39.95	$_____
	Subtotal	$_____

Discount 5% for orders over $100 $_____

California residents: add your area's **sales tax** (except on newsletter subscription) $_____

Shipping: $3 per item (If you need a **Rush Order**, add $5 to the total.) $_____

(Including shipping, a subscription is $99 for one year and $189 for two years

and there is one $3.00 charge for any number of back issues.)   **Total** $_____

════════ **Satisfaction guaranteed** ════════
or your money back

Method of Payment: _____ Check enclosed payable to John T. Reed   _____ Visa   _____ MasterCard

Credit card # _____   Exp. Date _____   Signature _____

Ship to: Name _____

Street Address* _____

City _____ State _____ Zip _____ Telephone _____

* UPS cannot deliver to P.O. boxes. Please allow 2-3 weeks for processing and delivery.
Please mail your order to: John T. Reed, P.O. Box 27311, Concord, CA 94527
These prices are effective December 1990 and are subject to change.
Source Code: 03

For faster service, ☎ phone toll-free:
800-635-5425

John T. Reed's Order Form

		Unit Price	Total

Newsletter

		Unit Price	Total
_____ one-year subscriptions to *John T. Reed's Real Estate Investor's Monthly* (12 monthly issues)		$ 96.00	$_____
_____ two-year subscriptions to *John T. Reed's Real Estate Investor's Monthly* (24 monthly issues)		$186.00	$_____
_____ binders for newsletters (holds 24 issues)		$ 7.00	$_____
_____ back issues (Please see catalog for list. <u>Minimum order is 3.</u>)	1 to 11 back issues	$ 7.00 ea.	$_____
	12 or more back issues	$ 6.50 ea.	$_____
	All back issues starting Feb. '86	$ 6.25 ea.	$_____

Seminars

Current seminars will be listed in our catalog which we will send you upon request.

Books

	Unit Price	Total
_____ copies of *Aggressive Tax Avoidance for Real Estate Investors*	$23.95	$_____
_____ copies of *How to Increase the Value of Real Estate*	$19.95	$_____
_____ copies of *How to Manage Residential Property for Maximum Cash Flow and Resale Value*	$21.95	$_____
_____ copies of *Office Building Acquisition Handbook* (loose leaf)	$39.95	$_____
_____ copies of *Real Estate Investor's Monthly on Real Estate Investment Strategy*	$39.95	$_____
_____ copies of *Residential Property Acquisition Handbook*	$19.95	$_____

Cassettes   (Two 60-minute cassettes in a binder)

	Unit Price	Total
_____ copies of *High Leverage Real Estate Financing*	$29.95	$_____
_____ copies of *How to Buy Real Estate for at Least 20% Below MarketValue*	$29.95	$_____
_____ copies of *How to Find Deals That Make Sense in Today's Market*	$29.95	$_____
_____ copies of *How to Manage Residential Property for Maximum Cash Flow and Resale Value*	$29.95	$_____
_____ copies of *How to Save Tens of Thousands of Tax Dollars by Exchanging*	$29.95	$_____

Software

_____ copies of *Landlording*™ *On Disk* software by Leigh Robinson

IMPORTANT: <u>Circle one</u>: Macintosh **OR** IBM 5 1/4" **OR** IBM 3 1/2" $39.95 $_____

		Total
	Subtotal	$_____
Discount 5% for orders over $100		$_____
California residents: add your area's **sales tax** (except on newsletter subscription)		$_____
Shipping: $3 per item (If you need a **Rush Order,** add $5 to the total.)		$_____
(Including shipping, a subscription is $99 for one year and $189 for two years		
and there is one $3.00 charge for any number of back issues.)	**Total**	$_____

─────── **Satisfaction guaranteed** ───────
or your money back

Method of Payment: _____ Check enclosed payable to John T. Reed   _____ Visa   _____ MasterCard

Credit card # _____ Exp. Date _____ Signature _____

Ship to: Name _____

Street Address* _____

City _____ State _____ Zip _____ Telephone _____

* UPS cannot deliver to P.O. boxes. Please allow 2-3 weeks for processing and delivery.
Please mail your order to: John T. Reed, P.O. Box 27311, Concord, CA 94527
These prices are effective December 1990 and are subject to change.
Source Code: 03

For faster service, phone toll-free:
800-635-5425